The German Urban Experience 1900–1945

D0219981

By the 1930s over two-thirds of Germans lived in towns and cities, and those who did not found themselves inexorably affected by the ever-growing urban vortex. *The German Urban Experience, 1900–1945* surveys the social and cultural history of Germany in this crucial period through written, visual and oral sources. Focusing on urbanism as one of the major forces of change, this book presents a wide range of archive sources, many available for the first time, as well as screen shots from films, literature and art.

Exploring the German experience of 'urbanism as a way of life' in cities from Berlin and Dresden to Hamburg and Leipzig, this book discusses:

- the concept of the urban experience
- the built environment and traffic tempo
- the nature of the urban slum and its cultural reception
- health and the effects of the city on the body
- consumption and leisure in the city
- the city as a challenge to traditional gender hierarchies

Anthony McElligott is Lecturer in Modern History at the University of St Andrews and author of *Contested City: Municipal Politics and the Rise of Nazism in Altona 1917–1937* (University of Michigan Press, 1998).

The German Urban Experience 1900–1945

Modernity and Crisis

Anthony McElligott

London and New York

First published 2001
by Routledge
11 New Fetter Lane, London EC4P 4EE

Simultaneously published in the USA and Canada
by Routledge
29 West 35th Street, New York, NY 10001

Routledge is an imprint of the Taylor & Francis Group

Typeset in Galliard and Gill by Keystroke, Jacaranda Lodge, Wolverhampton

British Library Cataloguing in Publication Data
A catalogue record for this book is available from the British Library

Library of Congress Cataloging in Publication Data
McElligott, Anthony, 1955–
    The German urban experience, 1900–1945 : modernity and crisis / Anthony McElligott.
    p. cm. — (Routledge sources in history)
    Includes bibliographical references and index.
    1. City and town life—Germany—History—Sources. 2. Cities and towns—
Germany—History—Sources. 3. Sociology, Urban—Germany—
History—Sources. I. Title. II. Series.

HT384.G3 M39 2001
307.76′0943′09041—dc21   00–068035

ISBN 0–415–12114–0 (hbk)
ISBN 0–415–12115–9 (pbk)

Henning Matthiesen, 1949–1998

Contents

Series editor's preface

Sources in History is a new series responding to the continued shift of emphasis in the teaching of history in schools and universities towards the use of primary sources and the testing of historical skills. By using documentary evidence, the series is intended to reflect the skills historians have to master when challenged by problems of evidence, interpretation and presentation.

A distinctive feature of *Sources in History* will be the manner in which the content, style and significance of documents is analysed. The commentary and the sources are not discrete, but rather merge to become part of a continuous and integrated narrative. After reading each volume a student should be well versed in the historiographical problems which sources present. In short, the series aims to provide texts which will allow students to achieve facility in 'thinking historically' and place them in a stronger position to test their historical skills. Wherever possible the intention has been to retain the integrity of a document and not simply to present a 'gobbet', which can be misleading. Documentary evidence thus forces the student to confront a series of questions with which professional historians also have to grapple. Such questions can be summarised as follows:

1 *What* type of source is the document?
* Is it a written source or an oral or visual source?
* What, in your estimation, is its importance?
* Did it, for example, have an effect on events or the decision-making process?
2 *Who* wrote the document?
* A person, a group, or a government?
* If it was a person, what was their position?
* What basic attitudes might have affected the nature of the information and language used?
3 *When* was the document written?
* The date, and even the time, might be significant.
* You may need to understand when the document was written in order to understand its context.
* Are there any special problems in understanding the document as contemporaries would have understood it?
4 *Why* was the document written?
* For what purpose(s) did the document come into existence, and for *whom* was it intended?

- Was the document 'author-initiated' or was it commissioned for somebody? If the document was ordered by someone, the author could possibly have 'tailored' his piece.
5 *What* was written?
- This is the obvious question, but never be afraid to state the obvious.
- Remember, it may prove more revealing to ask the question: what was *not* written?
- That is, read between the lines. In order to do this you will need to ask what other references (to persons, events, other documents, etc.) need to be explained before the document can be fully understood.

Sources in History is intended to reflect the individual voice of the volume author(s) with the aim of bringing the central themes of specific topics into sharper focus. Each volume will consist of an authoritative introduction to the topic and chapters will discuss the historical significance of the sources. Authors will also provide an annotated bibliography and suggestions for further reading. These books will become contributions to the historical debate in their own right.

Anthony McElligott's *Modernity and Crisis* provides a fascinating exploration of the German experience of urban life in the first half of the twentieth century. Taking the urban experience as a paradigm for modernity this volume sets out, by means of a rich array of sources, to explore the wider social history of its everyday reception in the German context. The author contends that the German urban experience serves also as a paradigm for the European experience.

The development of the modern city transformed the old structures and hierarchies that once governed society and stimulated an international debate on the nature of the urban experience. For its many critics, modernity was an experience characterised by a crisis of control, a crisis of identity and a crisis of spirit. However, for all its uncertainties the massing of European populations into the cities also represented exhilarating challenges.

Using a wide variety of historical sources, McElligott examines critically the manner in which Germans responded to urbanism as a way of life. *Modernity and Crisis* represents an important work of extraordinary scope and perception. Anthony McElligott's text will become an indispensable aid to all students who wish to a possess a deeper understanding of the nature of the urban experience in the twentieth century.

David Welch
Canterbury, 2001

Acknowledgements

The origins of this book go back to a course I taught to postgraduates in the Graduate School at the University of Michigan in 1992; I owe much to the very talented students who took part, some of whom have since gone on to make their own individual mark as historians. It has changed much since then, and successive generations of St Andrews students have been my guinea pigs as I formulated and reformulated sometimes rather wild ideas. The development from taught course into a book was encouraged by the series editor, David Welch, and supported by Lynn Abrams. At Routledge, Heather McCallum was the original commissioning editor and showed incredible patience and faith in the project, even if she was somewhat bemused by 'the fingerprint' (Doc. 9.7). Vicky Peters saw the book through to publication.

My thanks also go to the archivists and librarians in Germany and Britain without whose friendly cooperation this project would not have been completed. In Berlin, I particularly want to thank Frau Hartmann at the Bauhaus-Archiv, Frau Anke Matelowski and Frau Antje Keller at the Akademie der Künste, and Herr Andreas Matschenz at the Landesarchiv for their vital interest; their cooperation helped me to put the 'final touches' to the sources. In St Andrews, Margaret Grundy and her colleagues at Interlibrary Loans have patiently and efficiently dealt with my sometimes hurried and erratic orders. Similarly Jim Allan and Sean Earnshaw in the University's photographic and reprographic department have kindly persevered with my last-minute requests over the past years. I am grateful to them all. The Research Committee of the School of History at St Andrews granted indispensable financial aid enabling me to work in Germany for extended periods. Many friends and colleagues in Germany made my research trips more than bearable. Professors Ahrens, Goertz, Hilger, and Troitzsch at the Institut für Sozial- und Wirtschaftsgeschichte, University of Hamburg, kindly put the facilities of their institute at my disposal, inviting me to spend a very enjoyable semester during the winter of 1995/6 teaching some of the ideas and material in this book. Once again, Frau Irmingard Lamersdorf provided good food and a congenial shelter during the final phase of writing.

The book would probably not have been completed had it not been for three people close to me who provided support and encouragement. My 'last but not least' acknowledgements, therefore, go to them. I wish to thank my good friends Barry Doyle and Tim Kirk. In spite of their own heavy commitments, they read drafts of the book in its various stages, provided invaluable criticism, made helpful suggestions (and corrections), but, of course, they are in no way responsible for any remaining idiosyncrasies. I am truly indebted to them. As I am to Wiltrud Lamersdorf, who had to live with the continual pressures and absences I inflicted upon her in the course of researching and writing this book. When illness almost put an end to the project she provided TLC, and the much-needed help in translating some last-minute additions to the sources.

Every effort has been made to ensure that copyright of any secondary material used in this book has not been breached. But if I have overlooked permission for copyright in any way, authors and publishers are invited to inform Routledge.

Finally, this book is dedicated to the memory of a close friend, Henning Matthiesen, whose sharp eye caught every detail, and whose acerbic tongue caricatured everyday life in the city, even if only a provincial one. He is sorely missed.

The author and publishers wish to thank the following for their permission to reproduce copyright material:

Extracts from *The Temple* by Stephen Spender (Faber and Faber and Grove/Atlantic Inc., 1988). Reproduced by permission of the Publishers; 'The Slums of Victorian London' pp. 130–2 in *Exploring the Urban Past: Essays in Urban History* by H J Dyos by David Cannadine and David Reeder (Cambridge University Press, 1982). Reproduced by permission of the Publisher; Extracts from *Cities and Economic Development* by Paul Bairoch (University of Chicago Press, 1988). Reproduced by permission of the Publisher; Reprinted by permission of the publisher from *The Mass Ornament: Weimar Essays* by Siegfried Kracauer, translated, edited and with an introduction by Thomas Y. Levin, Cambridge, Mass.: Harvard University Press, (English Translation) Copyright © 1995 by the President and Fellows of Harvard College; Extracts from *An Introduction to Civic Design* by S.D. Adshead, TPR Vol. 1, No. 1, April 1910, and *Ideology, Planning Theory and the German City in the Interwar Years, part 1* by John Mullin, TPR Vol. 53, No. 2, April 1982 both published by Liverpool University Press; *Südwestkorso Berlin, 5 am* © by Ludwig Meidner – Archiv, Jüdisches Museum der Stadt Frankfurt am Main; *Berlin Friedrichstrasse vor 1933* © Erich Comeriner Archiv / Galerie David, (D) Bielefeld; *Die Neue Auslage 1929–30* by Kurt Weinhold, by permission of Städtische Galerie Böblingen; *Der Traum der Tietzmaedchen, 1921* by Karl Hubbuch, reproduced by permission of Myriam Hubbuch; *Licht-Luft-Sportbad am Kurfürstendam, 1902* by Franz Stoedtner, reproduced by permission of Berlinische Galerie, Landesmuseum für Moderne Kunst, Photographie und Architektur; *Healthy Body, Small Intellect* and *The Shop Man* both by Herbert Marxen reproduced by permission of Museumsberg Flensburg; *New Architecture and New Man* by Molnar Farkas and *New Couple and Home* by Molnar Farkas by permission of Bauhaus-Archiv Berlin and *Luckhardt Brothers Competition Entry 1928: Alexanderplatz shaped by Commerce* courtesy of Bauhaus-Archiv Berlin / Köster; *Gerhart Bettermann, Orientalische Hafengasse* published in *Wohnsitz Nirgendwo* (1982) by permission of Künstlerhaus Bethanien, Berlin; *Lonely Metropolitan* by Herbert Bayer © DACS 2001, *Old and New Germany, 1926* in the *Dessau Brochure* by Herbert Bayer © DACS 2001, *Laerm der Strasse, 1921* by Otto Dix © DACS 2001, *Portrait of Sylvia von Harden* by

Otto Dix © DACS 2001, *The Sex Murderer* by Otto Dix © DACS 2001, *The Cathedral of Socialism, 1919* by Lyonel Feininger © DACS 2001, *Berlin Friedrichstrasse, 1918* by George Grosz © DACS 2001, *Die Rationalisierung Marschiert! 1927* by John Heartfield © DACS 2001; *Kuhle Wampe oder Wem gehört die Welt?* © Nachlass Lilly Schoenborn-Anspach, donated by Bernd Kummer; photographs in Document 9.6 © Ullstein Bilderdienst.

Abbreviations

AfA	Allgemeine Freie Angestelltenbund
BAK	Bundesarchiv Koblenz
BZR	British Zone Review
FZ	Frankfurter Zeitung
HSTAW	Hauptstaatsarchiv Wiesbaden
IfZ	Institut für Zeitgeschichte
ILO	International Labour Office
LAB	Landesarchiv Berlin
LAS	Landesarchiv Schleswig-Holstein
MNN	Münchenner Neuesten Nachrichten
STAD	Staatsarchiv Dresden
STAM	Staatsarchiv Munich
StAH	Staatsarchiv Hamburg
StDR	Statistik des Deutschen Reichs
StHDR	Statistisches Handbuch des Deutschen Reichs
StJBDR	Statistisches Jahrbuch für das Deutsche Reich
StJBDS	Statistisches Jahrbuch Deutscher Städte
StJB	Altona Statistisches Jahrbuch der Stadt Altona
StJB	Berlin Statistisches Jahrbuch der Stadt Berlin
VStDR	Vierteljahreschrift für das Deutsche Reich

Introduction: 'Urbanism as a way of life'

This book is not a history of German urbanization, as it is usually conceived (Lee 1978; Bosl 1983; Kenny and Kertzer 1983; Matzerath 1981; *idem* 1985; Reulecke 1985; de Vries 1984). Nor is it a 'city history' (Lenger 1986; Benevolo 1993). Rather, its aim is to explore the German experience of 'urbanism as a way of life', to borrow Louis Wirth's memorable phrase (Wirth 1938). Writing in the late 1930s, Wirth developed three criteria which he thought analytically useful for the study of urbanism.

Document 1.1 Urbanism as a Characteristic Mode of Life

Urbanism as a characteristic mode of life may be approached empirically from three interrelated perspectives: (1) as a physical structure comprising a population base, a technology, and an ecological order; (2) as a system of social organization involving a characteristic social structure, a series of social institutions, and a typical pattern of social relationships; and (3) as a set of attitudes and ideas, and a constellation of personalities engaging in typical forms of collective behavior and subject to characteristic mechanisms of social control.

Source: Louis Wirth, 'Urbanism as a way of life', American Journal of Sociology, Vol. 44 (1938), 18–19.

By the third decade of the twentieth century over two-thirds of Germans lived in towns and cities, and those who did not, found themselves inexorably sucked into an ever-widening urban vortex. For Wirth noted an *intensification* of urban life as a social and cultural phenomenon from the end of the nineteenth century to the beginning of the twentieth century that inaugurated a 'modern age' of the city lasting, perhaps, until the 1960s (Wirth 1938: 2, 5, 7; Hall 1998; Gee *et al.* 1999). Taking the urban experience as a paradigm for modernity (Harvey 1985; *idem* 1989; Katznelson 1991; Lees 1991; Hays 1993), this book sets out to explore the wider social history of its everyday reception in the German context.

If, as I argue, the urban experience is a paradigm for German society, can the German urban experience serve as a paradigm for the European experience? I believe it can. The urban population of Europe had grown sixfold between 1800 and 1910, with the period of greatest *concentration* occurring roughly between 1900 and 1913, before tailing off into the early 1920s. The process was most marked in north-western and central Europe, with the rest of Europe only 'catching up' from the 1950s (Lampard 1973: 7; Bairoch 1988: 217). On the eve of the First World War, just over 43 per cent of all Europeans (including those living in the British Isles) were living in a town or city. An urban map of Europe would show Britain as the most heavily urbanized country: by 1936, 79 per cent of its population lived in towns and cities; closely followed by the small nations of the Netherlands and Belgium; by Germany with an urban population of 67 per cent; by Italy and then France with 51.2 per cent (Denby 1938: 21–9; Hohenberg and Lees 1985: 215–29; Pounds 1990: 443–6). To the north, south and east of this band (excluding the USSR), the levels of urbanization dropped off dramatically to around 33 per cent and less.

A similar urban geography of a mainly urbanized west and rural east existed in Germany (Bairoch 1977: 217–19; Lichtenberger 1984: 6–10). The most heavily urbanized areas were also the most industrially developed, with sophisticated commercial economies. They were to be found west of the river Elbe. By contrast, to the east of the Elbe in East Prussia, the few urban centres of importance, apart from Berlin, such as Breslau or Königsberg, remained embedded in largely agrarian landscapes (Pollock 1940: 205–337; Bessel 1978: 199–218). Horst Matzerath has shown that by 1910 more than 50 per cent of the population of the industrialized western provinces of Prussia was urbanized, compared with just a third in the eastern provinces (Matzerath 1985: 88–93). Germany, from its geographically centred position in Europe, straddled the urban/rural axis and as such, displayed fully the varied and often contradictory experiences of European urbanization.

From the 1890s, cities and towns become larger, a growth that continued into the 1920s and even into the 1930s in some parts of Europe. By 1910 there were at least 150 large cities with populations over 100,000 (Pounds 1990: 443), the numerical point defining a 'big city', with more than half of these in north-west and central Europe (see Chapter 2). Their number grew over the next two decades. In fact, at the turn of the century, there were 96 big cities in north-west and central Europe. The metropolises – or world cities – with populations over 1 million, however, numbered only seven at this date, with a further eight 'big cities' of between a half and 1 million (Lawton 1989: 4). At the beginning of the twentieth century in an area of continental Europe designated by the Germans as 'Mitteleuropa', there were only two cities that met this criterion for metropolis.

Document 1.2 Metropolis and 'Big City' in 'Mitteleuropa', *c.*1917

[See illustration opposite]

Source: Emil Stutzer, Die Deutschen Großstädte, Einst und Jetzt *(Berlin, Braunschweig and Hamburg, 1917), front map.*

Published at the height of the First World War, Stutzer portrayed a central region of continental Europe dominated by the urban axis of Berlin–Vienna. The national

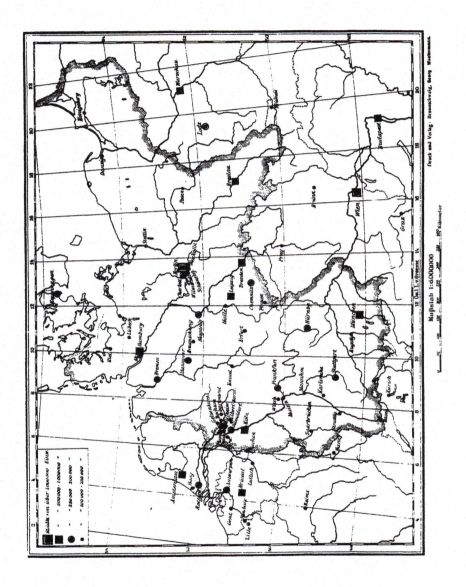

metropoles of Warsaw, Budapest, Amsterdam and Brussels, in the geopolitical terms of his urban map, have been relegated to 'regional' capitals, acquiring a similar rank to Hamburg, Breslau, Leipzig, Dresden or Munich. Because Vienna, like Budapest, was a metropolis that had reached its 'high noon' before the war (Schorske 1980; Lukacs 1988), whereas Berlin was the acknowledged newcomer, Stutzer's map also underscores Berlin's paradigmatic position as the centre of a European urban modernity (Hall 1998: 239–43). For Thomas Mann, writing more than a decade later at a point of crisis, this shift in Europe's civic gravity brought with it a heavy and necessary burden of responsibility (Kaes *et al.* 1994: 150–9).

The terms modernity and modernism are often employed interchangeably, as evidenced in the writings of those cultural critics engaged in recent debates over modernity and postmodernity (Turner 1990; Boyne and Rattansi 1990; Docherty 1993). Historians of early twentieth-century Germany, and notably those discussing the urban context during the Weimar period, also tend to use the terms interchangeably, adding modernization to the list (Feldman 1986; Peukert 1987; Lees 1991; Buse 1993: 521; Hall 1998: 937). This can be confusing to the student of urban Germany. In this section, therefore, I will try to define these terms more closely as they are understood in this book.

The German philosopher Jürgen Habermas locates the onset of our modern period in Europe in the second half of the nineteenth century (Habermas 1993: 98–9), reaching its climax around 1930. Its distinguishing feature was its rupturing of time and spatial consciousness, and its anticipation of the future. In order to distinguish it from previous 'modern' epochs, this period of innovation and change is referred to as 'classical modernity', denoting its authenticity and formative role in what was to become familiar to the late twentieth century (Habermas 1993: 99; Harvey 1989: 23). Because of the close alignment to the 'cultural explosion' of the Weimar years, the foreclosure of 'classical modernity' coincides with the epochal rupture represented by the Nazi takeover of power in 1933 (Peukert 1991: 3–18, 275–81). Yet some of the documents included in the present volume might suggest that there is a good case to extend the periodization to include the decade after 1930 (Hein 1992: 10, 14; Nerdinger 1993: 9–23; Gassert 1997: 151–8).

Although Habermas was concerned more with the shift in artistic engagement with the 'modern', the cultural break from mid-century was only made possible because of the rapid and thoroughgoing transformations taking place in European society. The primary change was that of industrialization and urbanization, which appeared to go hand-in-hand, heralding a process of societal modernization. The European big city became emblematic in this process (Bosl 1983: 7–16; Lichtenberger 1987: 4). And increasingly, contemporaries turned to Germany where they believed the process was paradigmatic, though not unique. It was here that modernization in its guise of technological advancement was most visible and actively promoted (Hietala 1987). The Dresden City Exhibition in 1903, for instance, celebrated the urban sphere as a site of progress in the sense not only of machine technology, but also of technical processes of bureaucratic organization, data intelligence, and so on (Wuttke 1904); it is understood in this way in the present volume. As well as being the product of cultural processes, technological modernization also influenced cultural change. It is interesting to note that the relationship between culture and technology was the keynote subject of the first conference of German sociologists in Frankfurt am Main in 1910, and it appeared with some regularity thereafter in the pages of their learned journals (Sombart 1911; Schulze-Gävernitz 1930).

Perhaps the most important outcome of the dialectics of culture and technological modernization of 'classical modernity' was the altered consciousness of time, which shifted from a static experience to a 'transitory', 'elusive', 'ephemeral' and 'dynamic' one, whose very celebration, according to Habermas, also 'discloses a longing for an undefiled, immaculate and stable present', but one which was also always on the point of vanishing into the future (Habermas 1993: 99; Frisby 1985: 4, 141; Kern 1983: 31, 81–104). That is to say, the *quintessence* of 'classical modernity' lay in the reception of its own crisis-ridden ambiguity (Peukert 1988: 133–44). 'Modernity' is thus understood as a *consciousness* that was spatially rooted in the city (Frisby 1985: 71), and that, as Andrew Lees has shown, worked itself out in a vehement discursive battle between supporters and opponents of the urban experience (Lees 1985).

Through his writings at the turn of the century, Georg Simmel, increasingly recognized as Germany's first great cultural sociologist of modernity (Sennett 1969: 8–10; Frisby 1985: 70; Weinstein and Weinstein 1990: 75–7), subjected the experience of this shift in consciousness to sociological interrogation in his study of the inner life of the modern city (Doc. 2.12). Simmel's approach to the modernity of the city was developed in numerous writings by his former student, the cultural critic Siegfried Kracauer, during the 1920s (Levin 1995: 1–30). Kracauer's work deals with the perceived impermanence and impersonal nature of the urban experience. Consonant with contemporary thinking, his early work portrays a city socially constituted by multitudes of transitory and fleeting liaisons that intersected randomly within the spatial confines of the 'lonely city' (Kracauer 1995: 42–3, 129; Frisby 1985: 105, 111–17, 147ff.; Mumford 1938: 266). By the later 1920s, Kracauer's most incisive essay on the modern experience, *The Mass Ornament*, suggested a more controlled environment linked to the invisible unifying force of production and markets.

Document 1.3 The Mass Ornament

The ornament, detached from its bearers, must be understood *rationally*. It consists of lines and circles like those found in textbooks on Euclidean geometry, and also incorporates the elementary components of physics, such as waves and spirals. Both the proliferations of organic forms and the emanations of spiritual life remain excluded. [. . .]

The structure of the mass ornament reflects that of the entire contemporary situation. Since the principle of the *capitalist production process* does not arise purely out of nature, it must destroy the natural organisms that it regards either as means or as resistance. Community and personality perish when what is demanded is calculability; it is only as a tiny piece of the mass that the individual can clamber up charts and service machines without any friction. A system oblivious to differences in form leads on its own to the blurring of national characteristics and to the production of worker masses that can be employed equally well at any point on the globe. – Like the mass ornament, the capitalist production process is an end in itself.

Source: Siegfried Kracauer, The Mass Ornament. Weimar essays, *translated, edited, and with an introduction by Thomas Y. Levin (Cambridge, Mass., and London, 1995), 77–8.*

Simmel and Kracauer were not only dispassionate observers chronicling and dissecting change, they were themselves also grappling with the transformed conditions of the big city. And in doing so, they textualized their own experiences of urban modernity, giving it an aesthetic form. For the purposes of this book, I implicitly allude to this 'aesthetic modernity' as 'modernism', referring to the particular style of the cultural artefact (i.e. as written text, architecture, and in works of art and film). Many of the sources in this book are modernist in this sense: from the sometimes dissonant images of the expressionist artists, depicting what Kracauer in 1918 termed the 'unbound arbitrary individualism' of mass society, to the cool and totalizing New Objectivity from the mid-1920s that corralled these earlier wild energies (Gay 1969: 125–8). These forms not only stylized modernity, they filtered it too (Smart 1990; Hughes 1980). Thus, like sociological texts, statistical compilations, and official reports, these representations were both *articulations* and *constitutive* of the urban experience.

As we have noted, urban modernity was an *experiential* and *existential* phenomenon, but one which was not haphazard, not least because of the role of institutions in attempting to shape lives into what we might call an architectural edifice of collective cultural experience. Indeed, in order to combat the putative chaos inherent in the transitory nature of the urban experience, enlightenment science sought to organize everyday life into a cogent 'whole' (Foucault 1972: 178–95; Hein 1992: 13), according to the principles of what Habermas terms 'cultural rationalization'.

Document 1.4 The Project of Modernity

The idea of modernity is intimately tied to the development of European art, but what I call 'the project of modernity' comes into focus only when we dispense with the usual concentration upon art. Let me start a different analysis by recalling an idea from Max Weber. He characterized cultural modernity as the separation of the substantive reason expressed in religion and metaphysics into three autonomous spheres. They are: science, morality and art. These came to be differentiated because the unified world-views of religion and metaphysics fell apart. Since the eighteenth century, the problems inherited from these older world-views could be arranged so as to fall under specific aspects of validity: truth, normative rightness, authenticity and beauty. They could then be handled as questions of knowledge, or of justice and morality, or of taste. Scientific discourse, theories of morality, jurisprudence, and the production and criticism of art could in turn be institutionalized. Each domain of culture could be made to correspond to cultural professions in which problems could be dealt with as the concern of special experts. This professionalized treatment of the cultural tradition brings to the fore the intrinsic structures of each of the three dimensions of culture. There appear the structures of cognitive–instrumental, of moral–practical and of aesthetic–expressive rationality, each of these under the control of specialists who seem more adept at being logical in these particular ways than other people are. [. . .]

Source: Jürgen Habermas, 'Modernity: An incomplete project', in New German Critique, *22 (Winter 1981), 3–15, reprinted in Thomas Docherty (ed.),* Postmodernism: A reader *(New York, London, Toronto, Sydney, Tokyo and Singapore, 1993), 103.*

This 'cultural rationalization' was predicated on pathologizing what were perceived as the negative experiences of urban modernity (Kaes 1998: 184). For the period of 'classical modernity' was one when the *potential* for disorder appeared at its greatest, and the means to control that disorder were in their infancy. The transformation from intimate to mass society since the 1890s, the political upheavals during and after the war, the economic anarchy of the postwar years, all solidified into a paradigm of urban chaos (Leinert 1925: 241ff.). Clearly, in the modern city old structures and hierarchies that had once governed society appeared to dissolve, precipitating a climate that was at once exhilarating but full of uncertainty.

There was thus no single character to Weimar's urban modernity. Left to itself, it threatened fragmentation and chaos; regulated by urban institutions in the search for a new cartesian 'organic wholeness' it heralded the disciplining of society on a hitherto unprecedented scale; subordinated to the invisible hand of the production process, it produced the 'despiritualized mass' (Kracauer) of 'geometric inanimate' objects captured in the ethos of the 'machine'. For its many critics, modernity was an experience characterized by a crisis of control, a crisis of identity, and a crisis of spirit (Kaes et al. 1994: 373). The documents in this book exemplify some of the textual proofs that 'speak' to us (Evans 1997: 126) of the way Germany's early twentieth-century moderns encountered this crisis of 'urbanism as a way of life'.

2 | Defining and deciphering the urban experience

The massing of European populations into existing cities, as well as the creation of new industrial towns from the 1860s onwards, stimulated an international debate on the urban experience. At first, attention was paid to the expansion and demographic transformation of towns and only later did contemporaries begin to probe the sociological and cultural impact of urbanization with regard to the well-being of the nation. A statistical study by the American Adna Ferrin Weber at the turn of the century and concentrating on the demographic aspects of urbanization, exemplifies the first approach to defining the urban experience (Weber 1899, repr. 1963). The importance of Weber's study, in which he grappled with the widespread view that cities were responsible for a quantitative and qualitative decline in population, lay in the collection and deployment of comparative data in order to identify national patterns (Hietala 1987: 207). Weber's approach had its roots in the mid-nineteenth century when British statisticians, as later their German counterparts, introduced a quantitative-based definition in order to distinguish between an 'urban settlement' and a 'town', the latter being a legal definition usually deriving from its incorporated status based on [royal] charter (Waller 1983: 8; Krabbe 1989: 27–31; Matzerath 1985: 241–8). Weber's approach partly reflected the contemporary obsession with the size and racial quality of the nation (Theilhaber 1913; Hellpach 1939; de Rudder 1940); in methodological terms, his study has exerted an influence on a later generation of comparative urban historians (Stoob 1978: 316–41; Diederiks 1981; Lampard 1983: 3–53; Wischermann 1996), and particularly on those working specifically on Germany (Köllmann 1969; Poor 1974: 111–27; Schäfers 1977: 243–68; Matzerath 1981: 145–79; Hietala 1987: 108–16).

Almost contemporaneous with Adna Ferrin Weber, a burgeoning corpus of urban sociological and cultural anthropological studies began to explore the ecology and the socio-cultural experiences of the city. This approach became more widely adopted in the interwar years, and is exemplified in the work of Robert Ezra Park and the Chicago school of [urban] sociology in the 1920s (Park et al. 1925; Lindner 1990: 50–150). This method of deciphering the urban experience, however, has only recently been fully acknowledged by scholars as significant, and is yet to be fully 'discovered' by historians of the German experience of 'urbanism as a way of life' (Hays 1993: 3–4; Korff 1985; Lindner 1999: 289–94; Hengartner 1999: 16, 69–112). Traditionally, historians have been content to rely on the German sociologist Max Weber's account of the development and functions of the city, originally published in 1921, and reproduced many times since. Its key passage is on 'concepts and categories', and is probably the best known work on the city to which urban geographers, urban sociologists and urban historians, repeatedly turn. It is, therefore, the classic starting point for any discussion of the subject.

Document 2.1 Max Weber, The City: Concepts and Categories

The many definitions of the city have only one element in common: namely that the city consists simply of a collection of one or more separate dwellings but is a relatively closed settlement. Customarily, though not exclusively, in cities the houses are built closely [sic] to each other, often, today, wall to wall. This massing of elements interpenetrates the everyday concept of the 'city' which is thought of quantitatively as a large locality. In itself this is not imprecise for the city often represents a locality and dense settlement of dwellings forming a colony so extensive that personal reciprocal acquaintance of the inhabitants is lacking. However, if interpreted in this way only very large localities could qualify as cities; moreover it would be ambiguous, for various cultural factors determine the size at which 'impersonality' tends to appear. Precisely this impersonality was absent in many historical localities possessing the legal character of cities. Even in contemporary Russia there are villages comprising many thousands of inhabitants which are, thus, larger than many old 'cities' (for example, in the Polish colonial area of the German East) which had only a few hundred inhabitants. Both in terms of what it would include and what it would exclude size alone can hardly be sufficient to define the city.

Source: Max Weber, The City, *translated by Don Martindale and Gertrud Neuwirth (London, Melbourne and Toronto, 1958), 65–6; orig. Max Weber, 'Die Stadt' in* Archiv für Sozialwissenschaft und Sozialpolitik, *47 (Tübingen, 1921), 621–772.*

Writing alongside Weber were a sizable number of statisticians, economists, sociologists, and geographers (but as yet, barely a handful of historians), pursuing one or other aspect of the German urban experience. Indeed, by the mid-1920s, there were at least 112 German-language studies considered influential enough to be included in an extensive compendium of international titles on the city (Park et al. 1925: 161–228).

In spite of the developing corpus of scholarly work, there was not a clear consensus on how to define a city. Thus academics from those disciplines most concerned with the urban experience, namely, economics, statistics, sociology, cultural anthropology and geography, tackled the subject employing terms of reference that differed accordingly (Matzerath 1985: 245; Lawton 1989: 13–15). Indeed, the distinguished German sociologist Werner Sombart had already tackled this question of defining and deciphering the city in a short essay in 1907 (Sombart 1907: 1–9). He returned to it in a longer article published in 1931, but overlooked by scholars of the urban experience. The excerpted passages are interesting for a number of reasons, not least for highlighting the various, and perhaps conflicting, definitions current at the time. Eventually, in the third volume of his magnum opus, *Modern Capitalism*, Sombart developed more fully what he refers to here as the 'economic definition' of the city, to include a fully fledged commerce and consumerism as defining traits of the city (cf., Doc. 6.3). According to Matzerath, and one might legitimately take issue with his view, such a definition could apply to only a handful of cities at the beginning of the twentieth century, notably, Berlin, Munich, Cologne, Dresden, Leipzig and Hamburg (Matzerath 1985: 246).

Document 2.2 Defining the 'City'

I Concepts: [. . .]
2. Urban community: synthetic town concept. We can define an urban settlement as a collectively defined group of people who settle according to urban principles. The meaning of urban settlement is the same as the cultural concept: town. A town in this sense is formed by the inhabitants of a tenement in an open field; formed by a castle or an abbey with their occupants.

I name such a concept: synthetic. It is formed by the drawing together of characteristics that prescribe for whatever reason of recognition an important significance and receive an arbitrarily chosen label: in our case that of town.

There are several such synthetic urban concepts. For instance, the geographical. 'For geographers', writes Ratzel, 'a town is a continuous concentration of people and human habitation, which cover a sizable area and which lies at the centre of important lines of communication.'

Or [there is] the economic urban concept: I call a town according to economic terms a community of people who are dependent for their nourishment on the products of others' agricultural labours.

There is even a 'sociological' urban conception which is derived according to the rule: *lucus a non lucendo*. According to this a town is a settlement in which the inhabitants are alienated from one another.

These synthetic concepts are held by a few professors or similar academics; they are independent of 'linguistic usage' [*Sprachgebrauche*], they are also mostly not recognized by 'scholarship'. I don't know whether or not geographers are in agreement with Ratzel's urban definition. Aside from my use of it, the economic definition, which I consider especially important, has been used only by Max Weber, and he uses it differently. One finds the sociological concept only among [sociologists]. The cultural notion of the town is used only by a few cultural philosophers such as Spengler, Barrès *et al.*, whose understanding of it differs from mine. Otherwise no one would arrive at the idea to construct the concept of town in the way shown above and so, for instance, call a settlement of Roman centurians or an Italian village or an abbey or an African artisanal village a town. One would at least combine a few of the named features: such as residence and size; or size and economic situation of the inhabitants etc. With this, however, 'one' already leaves the point of view of synthetic conceptualization and shifts to the territory of 'linguistics' where concepts of an entirely different type are customary: the analytical. I call them analytical because we find and determine them through an 'analysis' of linguistic usage. This task is made difficult by the variety of languages.

3. Interpretational–analytical urban concept: urban types. We can determine without doubt a definition of 'town' corresponding to language usage for the German-speaking area. For we do not know which expression in a foreign language corresponds to the German term for town: polis or ästou, urbs, oppidum or civitas; city or town etc. With each translation, which we have already found, we must doubt if it is 'right'. [. . .]

III Urban Statistics. However one approaches the various 'sciences' of the town and especially a 'sociology' of urban communities, it is, nonetheless, interesting to know about the spread and breadth of 'towns' in a statistical sense. [. . .]

[. . .] It is pointed out correctly that statistics, which show the size of towns as political units, do not give a proper picture of the scale of towns as economic units. For included in these are also those populations which live in surrounding non-incorporated suburbs of cities, whose economic or social centre, however, is nonetheless in these same cities. 'Greater Berlin' or 'Greater London' [or] 'Greater Paris' etc., are substantially larger population complexes than they appear in the statistics as Berlin, London, Paris etc. and these 'greater cities' have been developing only recently.

Source: Werner Sombart, 'Städtische Siedlung, Stadt', in Handwörterbuch der Soziologie, *edited by Alfred Vierkandt (Stuttgart, 1931), 527–8, 531–2.*

Sombart's intellectual cynicism displayed in parts of this article, and his partial turn to linguistics, place him alongside those 'reactionary modernists' such as Oswald Spengler and Ernst Jünger, who embraced modernity, and in Sombart's case, urban modernity, but who at the same time rejected its democratizing implications in favour of an authoritarian model of state and society (Herf 1984; Sieferle 1995: 74). Nevertheless, his observation concerning the narrowness of purely statistical interpretations of cities is an important one. For the influence of the city on its hinterland must also be understood in cultural and mental terms as well as in terms of its economic influence (Hohenberg and Lees 1985: 232; Lee 1978: 279–93; Hietala 1987: 92, 96–103).

As we can see from the foregoing, defining 'urban' or 'city' is not straightforward once we start to consider the different criteria. And even though today the emphasis has shifted towards the social and cultural dimensions of the urban experience, most studies will begin with some sort of statistical criterion. But there is still little agreement among urban historians as to where to set the statistical definition of 'urban'.

The lowest acceptable criterion is the figure of 2,000, first adopted by the German Imperial Statistical Office from 1871, which remained in use throughout the interwar period, and was also used in the British censuses of the nineteenth century (Matzerath 1984: 86; *idem* 1985: 243; Reulecke 1985: 70; Hohenberg and Lees 1985: 226; Waller 1983: 1–23). While this is true to the historical methodology of the time, some historians find this criterion too low. Erich Lampard goes to the other extreme and takes 20,000 as his statistical base-line for defining an urban place. The British urban historian Philip Waller places the threshold between the two at 10,000, arguing that only when a place has achieved a population level of between 10,000 and 50,000 can it be designated a proper town; a population level of over 50,000 but under 100,000 signifies a large town; a population of between 100,000 and 200,000 makes it a city; and 200,000 to 1 million transforms it into a 'great city', that is, it earns the status of a 'metropolis' (Waller 1983: 6). Although contemporaries may not have used this latter term, keeping to the more usual *Großstadt* (Zahlen 1995: 30), using Waller's criterion, Germany in 1910 had 48 cities and 15 'metropolises', two of which, Charlottenburg and Rixdorf, were part of the Berlin conurbation until their incorporation into Greater Berlin in 1920 (when Rixdorf was renamed Neukölln). Yet according to this statistical criterion Germany would not have reached full urbanization until 1939, an experience not dissimilar to that of the United States, but one which would seem to belie its experience. Thus the Swiss economic historian Paul Bairoch argues the case for using a population level of 5,000 as the most reliable threshold for defining 'urban'.

Document 2.3 Bairoch's Criteria Defining an Urban Population

[Earlier] I discussed the general problems of the criteria used to define urban population. At that point, I justified the compromise I had to make in a case like this where the analysis not only covers a very long time span and very different societies but must also often rely on fairly dubious data. Under these circumstances the only workable criterion proved to be the size of urban agglomerations. And given the wide margin of error surrounding the figures available for smaller cities and towns, I adopted a population of 5,000 as the limit starting from which an agglomeration would qualify as urban. As I stressed at that time, this limit is certainly a little high for traditional European societies; a limit of 2,000 would unquestionably have been more suitable, and I have in fact occasionally made use of it. The time has come, however, to justify this limit of 5,000 more thoroughly. [. . .]

The first and most important justification is the fact that in those instances where use is made of the criterion of size (that is, in most censuses), the limit of 5,000 most nearly approximates the average of the various limits employed. Thus in the censuses taken at the beginning and during the latter half of the nineteenth century, for example, for the fourteen countries for which information of this kind is available, five chose the limit of 2,000, two the limit of 5,000, one 6,000, one 8,000, four 10,000, and one 20,000, making an average of 6,700 if I include this last case and 5,700 if I do not. In censuses taken in the twentieth century, the limit of 5,000 predominates even more clearly. [. . .]

The evidence presented above, and also the comparisons that can be made for nations in which for recent censuses urban population has been determined using many different complex criteria, prove that the limit of 5,000 provides a very good approximation, though there is probably a slight bias tending to underestimate urban population. And while a limit of 3,000 or 4,000 would provide an even closer approximation, neither has shown itself to be practicable. Also, even if one adopted a limit of 2,000, this would make only a fairly small difference to my measures of the levels of urbanization in developed countries. For once the levels of urbanization in the developed countries of the nineteenth century have been reached, most of the urban population has already been concentrated in larger cities.

Source: Paul Bairoch, Cities and Economic Development: From the dawn of history to the present *(Chicago and London, 1988), 217–18.*

By taking Bairoch's statistical criterion of 5,000 as our working baseline, just under 60 per cent of the population lived in towns and cities (with fully fledged urban infrastructures and cultures by the end of our period). Indeed, Germany between 1910 and 1945 was statistically in the first rank of urban societies in Europe – behind England, the Netherlands and Belgium, but ahead of the rest of the continent, including France in the west and Russia in the east (Bairoch 1988: 221).

Bairoch nevertheless cautions his readers against the face-value acceptance of statistical data (as a consequence of their reification as 'hard fact'), reminding us of: (i) the incompleteness of data, thus limiting the value of spatial and chronological comparisons, and (ii) the irregular and sometimes poor quality of data, calling into question their reliability as a historical source. This latter point is apposite in the German case. For in spite of the creation of a Reich Statistical Office in 1871, statistical methodology in Germany was still developing as late as the early part of the twentieth century. The collection and collation of data also remained complicated by the fact that practices varied betweeen Reich, Länder and the municipal statistical offices established since the 1860s and which had the ultimate responsibility in this process. As a consequence, practices in collecting and collating data on urbanization, and on the conditions of urban life, continued to vary in spite of attempts since the 1890s to systematize practices (Morgenroth 1936: 105–24; Hietala 1987: 78–83).

The Reich Statistical Office noted five categories of settlement: the rural community with a population of less than 2,000; the rural town with a population exceeding 2,000 but less than 5,000; the small town, which had a population greater than 5,000 but less than 20,000; the medium-sized town that was greater than 20,000 inhabitants but less than 100,000; and the big city (*Großstadt*) with a population in excess of 100,000 (Matzerath 1985: 246; Hietala 1987: 91). Meanwhile, the Deutsche Städtetag

Defining and deciphering the urban experience

(Association of German Cities), the official body representing Germany's municipal authorities since 1905, differentiated between seven main categories of settlement. Thus we can allow ourselves to construct a statistical framework of urbanization in Germany before going on to examine it as a social and cultural process.

Document 2.4 Distribution of Population by Size of Settlement,[1] 1900–39

	Population '000s	Percentage						
		A	B	C	D	E	F	G
1900	56,367	45.6	12.1	13.4		12.6		16.2
1910[2]	64,926	40.0	11.2	7.6	6.5	7.9	5.4	21.3
1925	62,411	35.6	10.8	6.9	6.2	8.0	5.7	26.8
1933	65,218	32.9	10.6	7.1	6.2	7.7	5.2	30.4
1939[2]	69,314	30.1	10.8	7.4	6.4	8.4	5.3	31.6

[1] A:<2,000; B:2,000–<5,000; C:5,000 <10,000; D:10,000–<20,000; E:20,000<50,000; F:50,000<100,000; G100,000>; [2] excludes incorporated Austria.

Source: Adapted from: Statistisches Jahrbuch des Deutschen Reichs, *Vol. 28 (Berlin, 1907),* 5; Statistisches Jahrbuch für das Deutsche Reich *(Leipzig/Berlin, 1938), 19; Dietmar Petzina, Werner Abelshauser, Anselm Faust (eds.),* Sozialgeschichtliches Arbeitsbuch II: Materialien zur Statistik des Deutsche Reiches 1870–1914 *(Munich, 1978), 42–3.*

From the 1890s Germany's towns and cities not only became larger, some of them growing at striking rates, but their overall number increased too. National and regional capitals grew in terms of population, as did industrial and port towns and cities. As already noted, by 1910 there were 48 *Großstädte*, many more than elsewhere in Europe, including Britain where there were just 42 in 1911 (Morris and Rodger 1993: 2). By the mid-1920s, Britain briefly overtook Germany, when it boasted 54 big cities to Germany's 48; by comparison Italy had only 22, and France, with a population commensurate with that of Germany, had just 17.

Historians assessing the pace of German urban growth usually do so in a linear fashion. Broadly speaking, they believe urbanization in Germany occurred in three phases: a first period of initial change in mid-century; then a period of rapid change and high rates coinciding with industrialization between 1875/1910; followed by a period of slower growth between 1910/1939, when a process of *suburbanization* set in (Leinert 1925: 177–8; Köllmann 1969: 59–65; Lee 1978: 279; Bollerey and Hartmann 1980: 135–64; Reulecke 1985: 149; Stoob 1978: 338). This approach is typical of quantitative-based studies up to the mid-1980s. While it perhaps offers a convenient way of getting

Document 2.5 Distribution of Settlements by Size,[1] 1900–39

Total no. settlements		Distributed between different size of urban settlement						
		A	B	C	D	E	F	G
1900	76,959	73,599	2,269	864		194		33
1910[2]	75,939	72,199	2,441	702	326	172	51	48
1925	63,556	60,126	2,249	637	283	166	50	45[3]
1933	50,881	47,362	2,290	682	284	164	47	52
1939	48,595	44,772	2,456	750	318	188	52	59

[1] A:<2,000; B:2,000–<5,000; C:5,000 <10,000; D:10,000–<20,000; E:20,000<50,000; F:50,000<100,000; G100,000>; [2] 1 December 1910; the other census dates are 16 May 1925; 16 June 1933; 17 May 1939.
[3] Slight variation due to different method of calculation by the Bundesamt für Wirtschaft, Wiesbaden.

Source: Adapted from: Statistisches Jahrbuch des deutschen Reichs, *Vol. 28 (Berlin, 1907), 5; Statistisches Bundesamt Wiesbaden,* Bevölkerung und Wirtschaft 1872–1972 *(Stuttgart and Mainz, 1972), 94.*

to grips with urbanization over the long term, it empties urbanization of its historical specificity. For the process in Germany, as elsewhere in central Europe, was a markedly uneven one. Rather than providing an inevitably uniform and linear pattern of development, urbanization as a *quantitative* phenomenon proceeded more patchily, consolidating regional disparities, which, arguably, have persisted until very recent times (Matzerath 1985: 248; Hohenberg and Lees 1985: 222–3; Bairoch 1988: 217).

In a similar vein, the process of urbanization was experienced neither as a static nor as a universal process. It did not involve simply the transformation of the physical landscape, but that of the mental landscape too. For urbanization embraced much more than territorial expansion, or population transfers from country to city, as mere statistics might suggest (Wirth 1938: 5). Experiences were formed by a number of factors: encounters with new worlds; the stimuli of new places, relationships, the sights, smells, noise of large population numbers compressed within a small space; collective experiences both at the workplace and in the physical confines of the neighbourhood; finally, both class and urban consciousness crystallized as towns and cities grew and their physical shape altered, administrations developed, and as civic groups and political parties emerged (Hohenberg and Lees 1985: 248–89). Moreover, the individual and collective experience of living in an urban environment changed over time. Perhaps the most important factor shaping the urban experience was the population itself, not only in terms of its overall numbers but also in terms of its age and gender structure, what its own experiences and mental worlds were, and how these impinged upon the city.

Germany's urban population at the turn of the century, was still a relatively recent one. Nearly 57 per cent of the inhabitants of 33 big cities were first-generation migrants (Leinert 1925: 54ff.; Lee 1978: 286–7; Stoob 1978: 319; Kampfhoefner 1983: 114; Laux 1984: 104–9). In Berlin only 40 per cent of the 1.5 million population in 1890 had been born there (Korff 1985: 349). A census taken on 1 December 1905 of 28 large manufacturing and commercial towns revealed that in 22 towns over 50 per cent of the population present on that day had been born elsewhere. In some of the towns of the Ruhr region, the hothouse of industrialization in the second half of the nineteenth century, recent arrivals might account for as much as 60 per cent of the local population, as in Bochum or the textile town of Barmen. A study in 1938 of schoolchildren in Gelsenkirchen showed that more than 50 per cent had grandparents who had migrated there before the First World War (Bredpohl 1948: 76, 108; Köllmann 1965: 589, 598; *idem* 1969: 66ff.; Crew 1979: 60–1).

Document 2.6 Migrants

Migration is predominantly a short-distance movement, but the centers of attraction are the great cities, toward which currents of migration set in from the remotest counties. The larger the city, the greater its power of attraction (*i.e.*, the larger its proportion of outsiders, and the more distant the counties or districts which contribute to it).

[. . .]

Women are greater migrants than men, but move only short distances; marriage and domestic service being the levers of their action.

Most migrants are young people, so that about 80 per cent of the adult population of great cities is of outside birth.

Two-thirds of the immigrants have lived in the great city less than 15 years.

Source: A.F. Weber, The Growth of Cities in the Nineteenth Century: A study in statistics *(1899, reprint Ithaca 1963), 283–4.*

While their demographic contribution to urbanization has recently been challenged (Matzerath 1985: 305), the economic, social and cultural influence of the migrant to the city must be assumed. For instance, migrants were young, and their preponderance among the urban population rejuvenated towns and cities: 60 per cent of Prussia's urban population was under the age of 30 (Matzerath 1985: 323; Tenfelde 1982: 197ff., 203; Kamphoefner 1983: 99). Until the final decade of the nineteenth century, migrants had tended to come from within a medium to short radius of the town. But with improved and cheaper transport, migrants now travelled from further afield, from the agrarian and poverty-stricken eastern regions of the empire (Langewiesche 1977; *idem* 1979: 70–93; Kamphoefner 1983: 96–7). Towns and cities thus harboured large migrant populations who spoke in different dialects (indeed, in the Ruhr many migrants spoke a different language, usually Polish, often wore differing styles of clothing, and practised different customs (Kleßmann 1984: 486–505)). There has been little ethnographic study to date of such migrant urban communities, though

Hsi-Huey Liang's sketch of migrant populations in imperial Berlin, Allen Newman's work on migrants' kin and friendship networks, and James Jackson's study of migration to Duisburg provide a point of departure for future work (Liang 1970; Newman 1979; Jackson 1981; *idem* 1982).

The spread of railways from the mid-nineteenth century not only shortened the distance between country and city, it also blurred mental boundaries between the two as populations were ferried between country and town. But it was not just a matter of rural migrants having to adapt to an urban environment that was already *in situ* (Kaes 1998: 184–92). The migrant at the turn of the century would have found much that was familiar as well as strange in the city. In fact, migrants transformed the urban strangeness into something more familiar by 'ruralizing' the city, as they brought with them habits of the countryside. Richard Evans's remarkably graphic study of Germany's second largest city, Hamburg, at the end of the nineteenth century, reveals the extent to which rural traits, especially those of animal husbandry, still persisted in this great city of three-quarters of a million inhabitants.

Document 2.7 Animals in the City

The first, and to the casual observer of the everyday street scene, the most obvious problem caused by rapid urban growth was the tremendous increase it brought in the number of animals inhabiting or moving through the city. To an extent that would be inconceivable in a great urban centre today, the citizens of nineteenth-century Hamburg lived in close proximity to a large variety of animals, big and small. This was, of course, a horse-drawn society: not only omnibuses, but also hansom cabs, trams, carriages, carts, and wagons of all kinds were pulled by horses well after the turn of the century, [. . .]

Not only horses but also many other kinds of animals shared the streets and courtyards of Hamburg with the human population. The animal census [*Viehzählung*] of 1873 revealed that the Altstadt and Neustadt housed between them a total of 2,171 chickens, 77 ducks, 43 goats, 32 head of cattle, 17 pigs, 7 sheep, 6 geese, one donkey, and a turkey. Some of these animals were of course counted at the slaughterhouse, caught by the census-taker at the arbitrary moment of the last day of their existence. On the other hand, the thousands of cattle and pigs regularly driven through the streets to the slaughterhouse, like the horses and other animals sold on the markets, were not included in this enumeration.

Source: R. J. Evans, Death in Hamburg: Society and politics in the cholera years, 1830–1910 *(Oxford, New York, 1987), 111–12.*

As newcomers to the city settled, married and adapted to evolving structures of urban life (Reulecke 1985: 91–109), rural patterns of behaviour did eventually alter, but they did not necessarily disappear. Animals were still part of the urban experience during the 1920s, as some of the street scenes from Walter Ruttmann's celebrated cross-section film *Berlin: Symphony of a city* (1927) testify. The habits, and even some of the physiognomy, of the country still pervaded Berlin a decade later, as Douglas Chandler found on his visit to the world's fourth largest city in 1936.

Document 2.8 The Country in the City

Behold the anomaly of an urban agglomeration with a total population of some 4,220,000, a city which can boast one of the most highly perfected transportation systems in the world, with every convenience contributed by science – and yet which contains within its limits the following:

Twenty thousand cows (providing a third of the milk supply), 30,000 pigs, 10,000 goats, 700,000 chickens, 180,000 rabbits, 5,800 people keeping bees, only three or four buildings that I could find as much as ten stories high, twelve windmills still functioning, and more than 100,000 little gardens, the harvests of which include such imposing yearly figures as 46,000 tons of potatoes and proportionate quantities of other vegetables and grains.

Such items would appear fantastic to the dweller on narrow, rock-ribbed Manhattan.

These little 'Schreber Gartens' [sic] afford city workers easily accessible contact with the land which is so dear to the German heart; they promote bodily fitness through exercise, and minimize food cost.

Beside each garden is a neat little house for storing equipment. Here centers the odd-hour and week-end life of a substantial number of families. During times of crisis, these wee shelters have even housed many who would otherwise have been roofless.

[. . .]

Trees and rivers . . . more rivers and more trees. Therein lies Berlin's greatest hold on the hearts of its dwellers.

The two rivers, Havel and Spree (pronounced 'Shpray'), with their eccentric twistings and turnings, form a network of waterways which makes it possible to reach many parts of the city by water.

[. . .]

Through the watery lanes, under gracefully arched bridges – of which Berlin has 1,006, even more than Venice itself! – glide long wooden barges, heavy-laden carriers of coal, building materials, petroleum, and an infinite variety of other products.

Large numbers of fruit barges come in from the provinces, bringing apples, pears, and peaches in their holds. In some cases these loads are marketed directly from the barges, which find moorings at advantageous points within the town.

The banks of the rivers are planted densely with trees. Rows of lindens or plane trees line the majority of the streets. The public parks are standing armies of trees in close formation, through which cut beguiling avenues and paths.

The most numerous member of the tree family is the linden. Also in large numbers are found most of our familiar American trees, such as maple, elm, horse chestnut (much beloved by the Germans), oak, acacia, poplar, and birch.

A census of trees standing in streets and squares alone – entirely exclusive of the parks – totals a half million.

The Berliner's love of trees is so deep that in many cases, where city appropriations have not provided the necessary funds, private citizens have paid for the planting of their own streets.

Source: Douglas Chandler, 'Changing Berlin', in The National Geographic Magazine, *Vol. LXXI, No. 2 (Feb. 1937), p. 134.*

Given the emphasis these authors place on the extent to which the 'rural' could be found in the big city, it may seem pertinent to ask the question: How different was living in the big city to living in the small provincial town where 45 per cent of the German population still lived by the mid-1920s? The following article by Valentin Lupescu suggests that the difference may not be as great as was sometimes assumed.

Document 2.9 Sociology of a German Small Town

Whereas in the city the complexity of social and economic relationships [*Wechselbeziehungen*] between individuals is already so confusing that it now appears almost impossible 'to see behind things', the small town still allows the limited possibility, especially for the outsider, the city person, to understand its social structure.

The town X shows all the characteristics of a typical German small town. It is situated at roughly equal train distance from all relevant cities; therefore it is almost completely outside their individual sphere of influence. It is surrounded from all sides by an agrarian hinterland populated by a homogeneous wealthy farming population with which the town is inextricably connected economically. The town's population has remained constant for decades; industrialization was artifically kept at bay. Because X is a distinctly mercantile town, neither civil servants nor workers, but rather manufacturers, merchants and craftsmen, play a significant role among the 15,000 inhabitants.

[. . .]

The Problematic of Small Town Life

Life in a German small town does not stand still, it is 'not so separate from this world', as many outsiders believe. And yet it is in danger of fossilizing in a social sense, and in terms of social consciousness, as a consequence of the narrow sociological space. To call this 'reactionary' is to simplify the problem. The inhabitant of X is essentially no different from a typical Berliner of 1930. The small town citizen also no longer possesses the ideology of the prewar era. He too has become uncertain in his thinking as he is insecure in his basic economic position. Traditions do not hold any more, but the social upheavals were not incisive enough to create something new. So one stands there 'inbetween'. One no longer thinks beyond the narrowest radius of life. And that is the danger!

Source: Valentin Lupescu: 'Sociology of the German small town', Die Gesellschaft, VIII (1931), 464, 471.

In spite of these apparently similar conditions, there was still a huge difference between living in a small, or even medium-sized town, and in a city (Latten 1929: 314, 322, 324; Reulecke 1985: 73). Especially for the migrant to the city, the change in scale of the built environment, the apparently anonymous and fleeting human relationships, in contrast to the perceived stable networks of the small community, were important factors shaping the urban sensory experience, and distinguished it from the sanctity of the rural world.

Document 2.10 Small Town and City

Habit deceived you there; the quiet worry
be dead and buried behind timbered-frame
and green ivy and mossy shingle;
and never would a foreign eye spy from dead alleys
through the trellis-work gloatingly
upon the modesty and regret of your trembling soul.

And yearning showed you the golden tableaux
of grandeur and power, thousand-fold wills
at lofty heights, the glow of blissful creation;
and left you tranquil in befitting times
according to your heart's rhythm speeding on
until the eye of the world discovered you at your goal.

There, suddenly, leaning on marble palaces
in the bright market and shameless, that which frightens you
and names you its own! And reveals how you shudder too
at your own fate and displays it to the crowd;
harries you with blood, the mighty drinks the roots,
and your beautiful crowns the gutter wears.

Damn the turmoil which makes you weak and small.
Damn yourself and seize as in a dream with feverish hands the foreign wills,
which merciless and restless pass over you.
Here loneliness chokes you. Now listen in the roar
and feel: In meditation your will succumbs!
What accustomed you longingly to overhear,
screams out of the chaos of this big city.

Source: Hermann Strauß-Olsen, 'Kleinstadt und Großstadt', Die Zukunft, XXXIII Jg., Nr. 2 (10 Oct. 1914), 42.

Strauß-Ohlen, a writer from Schwerin, near the Baltic coastline, here juxtaposes the tranquillity of the small town in the province with the hustle and bustle of the big city, and its impact on the inner experience of the individual. Was there, then, as the anthropologist Gottfried Korff recently asserted, an 'inner urbanization' that belied the appearance of a leftover rural past? (Korff 1985: 346, 355).

Document 2.11 The City Is Man: Inner Urbanization

Different to the period of the monarchy, Berlin's importance in the 1920s was no longer seen as the consequence of Prussian statecraft and the will of the Hohenzollerns, but as a result of the endeavours of a new human species which had crystallized in the course of Berlin's intense urbanization. In this connection, Heinrich Mann spoke in 1921 of 'the people workshop [*Menschenwerkstatt*] of Berlin'. Thus a concept was found with which Berlin's successful urbanization was accurately characterized. Berlin had become the synonym for an urbanity in a mature sense, it had become the definition of urbane pure and simple [. . .] with all its contradictions and paradoxes from boulevard to allotments, Romanische Café to slums, tenements to forest breezes, cosmopolitanism and intolerance. [. . .]

From the mid-nineteenth century Berlin was not only a place of new factories where progress was manufactured, but also a place of new mentalities whose trademark was to be found in the general observable and comprehensible model experiences and experience models. In Berlin the era of steam and innovative technical power was not only a thing of the 'Physics Society . . . ', but also of everyday experiences which were dictated by the rhythm of new work and transport conditions, new forms of movement and awareness. The optimism which Berlin already emitted in the 1840s, profited not only from the elan of the Borsig, Egell or Schwarzkopf factory workers, who saw in engine building a service for progress, but also from the perspective of migrants which was focused on the future. [. . .] The euphoria for railways buttressed itself in a subtle way with the expectations and plans of migrants: movement was not only in the city, movement was also in the heads of the new city inhabitants. [. . .]

Unlike any other city in Germany, Berlin appeared as a metaphor for an automatically developing progress, which the individual in moments of encounter and awareness experienced as a new metropolitan reality, and a sensation, in the original meaning of the word, was experienced, and so impinged on the Berlin consciousness. [. . .]

Contradictions, paradoxes and dysynchronies [*Ungleichzeitigkeiten*] belong to the essence of the big city which is characterized by the jumble of multifarious social groups, by the combination of the most different life styles, and which offers cultural stimuli in full. The city as a kaleidoscopic system of stimulation and challenges, living forms and orientation patterns, impressions and suggestions, was the theme of a study by the Berlin philosopher and sociologist, Georg Simmel in 1903.

Source: Gottfried Korff, 'Die Stadt aber ist der Mensch', in Gottfried Korff and Reinhard Rürup, eds., Berlin, Berlin. Die Ausstellung zur Geschichte der Stadt (Berlin, 1987), 645–7, 656.

Korff's work is representative of a recent shift from a positivist approach based on quantitative methodology, and exemplified in the work of Wolfgang Köllmann and Horst Matzerath, towards a cultural anthropology of the 'urban experience', which has yet to be incorporated into the mainstream of German urban and social history (Korff 1985: 343–61). But Korff, and others who adopt a similar approach, are returning to one that was already heralded in Germany at the turn of the century in the work of Georg Simmel, long ignored by scholars, but now increasingly acknowledged as the 'father' of German cultural (urban) sociology (Frisby 1992; Frisby and Featherstone 1997).

Simmel, focusing on Berlin, deciphered the urban experience in terms of a social and cultural learning process in the context of a heightened interaction and increasing nervous stimulation of city life. In his seminal essay, 'Metropolis and mental life', first published in 1903, and heralded by Louis Wirth as 'the most important single article on the city from the sociological standpoint' (Park et al. 1925: 219; Frisby 1985: 75–83), Simmel, like C.F.G. Masterman in Britain three years before (Masterman 1901: 27–9), posits the idea of a 'metropolitan type'.

Document 2.12 The Metropolis and Mental Life

The psychological basis of the metropolitan type of individuality consists in the *intensification of nervous stimulation* which results from the swift and uninterrupted change of outer and inner stimuli. Man is a differentiating creature. His mind is stimulated by the difference between a momentary impression and the one which preceded it. Lasting impressions, impressions which differ only slightly from one another, impressions which take a regular and habitual course and show regular and habitual contrasts – all these use up, so to speak, less consciousness than does the rapid crowding of changing images, the sharp discontinuity in the grasp of a single glance, and the unexpectedness of onrushing impressions. These are the psychological conditions which the metropolis creates. With each crossing of the street, with the tempo and multiplicity of economic, occupational and social life, the city sets up a deep contrast with small town and rural life with reference to the sensory foundations of psychic life. The metropolis exacts from man as a discriminating creature a different amount of consciousness than does rural life. Here the rhythm of life and sensory mental imagery flows more slowly, more habitually, and more evenly. Precisely in this connection the sophisticated character of metropolitan psychic life becomes understandable – as over against small town life which rests more upon deeply felt and emotional relationships. These latter are rooted in the more unconscious layers of the psyche and grow most readily in the steady rhythm of uninterrupted habituations. The intellect, however, has its locus in the transparent, conscious, higher layers of the psyche; it is the most adaptable of our inner forces. In order to accommodate to change and to the contrast of phenomena, the intellect does not require any shocks and inner upheavals; it is only through such upheavals that the more conservative mind could accommodate to the metropolitan rhythm of events. Thus the metropolitan type of man – which, of course, exists in a thousand individual variants – develops an organ protecting him against the threatening currents and discrepancies of his external environment which would uproot him. He reacts with his head instead of his heart. In this an increased awareness assumes the psychic prerogative. Metropolitan life, thus, underlies a heightened awareness and a predominance of intelligence in metropolitan man. The reaction to metropolitan phenomena is shifted to that organ which is least sensitive and quite remote from the depth of the personality. Intellectuality is thus seen to preserve subjective life against the overwhelming power of metropolitan life, and intellectuality branches out in many directions and is integrated with numerous discrete phenomena.

Source: Georg Simmel, 'Metropolis and mental life', translated and reprinted in Karl Wolff (ed.), The Sociology of Georg Simmel *(Chicago, 1950), 410–11.*

Many of the texts on the urban experience in Germany, as elsewhere, were mostly concerned with the city's 'strangeness' (see Chapter 4), or with its demographic aspects and how these related to the nation at large (Weisstein 1905; Theilhaber 1913; Burgdörfer 1934: 32–44; cf. Lees 1975: 31–47). But much of this writing was carried on by publicists frequently hostile to the city, who failed to offer a rigorous and systematic intellectual critique of the urban experience. Even Hans Ostwald's 50-volume series of social reportage, the *Großstadt Dokumente* published between 1904 and 1908, and acclaimed by Peter Fritzsche as having 'unfurled new maps' of Berlin, contented itself with simply chronicling the phenomenology of city life rather than offering a rigorous analysis (Fritzsche 1994: 387, 389, 391–5; Lees and Hollen Lees 1976; Lees 1979: 61–83; Sofsky 1986). As we have noted, the latter came only in the final decade of the nineteenth century with the emergent 'urban sociology' of Adolf Weber, Max Weber and Georg Simmel, all of whom were sons of Berlin. Yet, in a strange way, much of their work was trapped in the anti-urban paradigm, in the sense that it too was guided by what were understood to be the negative influences and conditions of the city.

The early sociologists increasingly focused their work on the psychological impact of the modern city, its nervous tempo, noise, alienating monumentalism and apparently ruptured social cohesion, that frightened and reviled a large number of observers (Weber 1918; Radkau 1994: 211–41). This was nowhere more in evidence than in the scholarly and popular focus on suicide as a condition of the urban experience (Durkheim 1888; Weber 1899, repr. 1963: 403). Karl Henning, a social statistician from Cologne, noted that the number of suicides rose continuously in that city from the beginning of the century, before falling in 1915 to their 1907 level.

Congruent with Durkheim's theory of anomie (alienation), Henning also found that urban rates generally tended to be higher in towns than in the countryside (Henning 1920/1: 325–33; Matzarath 1985: 332–4). This sort of scholarly enquiry, underpinned by copious statistical data, gave credence to Louis Wirth's later remark concerning alienation and loneliness in the city that 'typically, our physical contacts are close but our social contacts are distant' (Wirth 1938: 14). Alienation and the impotence of the individual in a mass society where human relations were fluid and superficial became a leitmotif of publicist and literary works spanning the 1920s that took the modern urban experience as their subject (Kracauer 1995; Döblin 1932; Wirth 1938: 16–17, 22). Kurt Tucholsky, a left-liberal lawyer and social critic made alienation the subject of his poem, 'Eyes in the City' (1929).

Document 2.13 Kurt Tucholsky, Eyes in the City

When you go to work
in the early morning
when you stand at the station
with your worries:
    there the city reveals
    to you asphalt clear
    in a human crater
    millions of faces:
two foreign eyes, a quick glance,
the brows, pupils, eyelids –
What was that? perhaps your life joy . . .
over, dead end, never again.

You go your whole life
along a thousand streets;
you see along your way
those who forgot you.
    An eye winks,
    the soul rings,
    you have found,
    only for seconds . . .
two foreign eyes, a quick glance,
the brows, pupils, eyelids;
What was that? no one turns back the time . . .
over, dead end, never again.

On your way you must
wander through cities;
see for a pulsation long
other strangers.

One might be an enemy,
one might be a friend,
one might in struggle be your comrade
one looks across and passes by . . .
Two foreign eyes, a quick glance,
brows, pupils, eyelids.
Of the great humanity a piece!
Over, dead end, never again.

Source: Kurt Tucholsky, Gesammelte Werke, 3: 1929–32 (Reinbeck, 1960), 379–80.

Eyes in Tucholsky's poem symbolize the possibility of bridging the loneliness of the city, but they can also represent an element of social control, of the type Strauß-Ohlen alludes to in his poem, and from which the anonymity of the city provided a welcome release (Kamphoefner 1983: 97). The collage by Bauhaus photographer Herbert Bayer is ambivalent in this respect, in spite of its title.

Document 2.14 Herbert Bayer: Lonely Metropolitan, 1932

[see illustration on page 26]

Source: Courtesy of the Bauhaus-Archiv Berlin.

For although the windows of the court tenement are void, suggesting the emptiness of the city experience, the eyes remind the viewer of its inhabitants, who are hidden from immediate view but see all that passes below.

Negative images of the city were not confined to conservative discourse. As Andrew Lees has pointed out, the left critique, while wary of the city, was one aimed ultimately at the dominant social relations that governed city experiences, rather than the city per se, notably during the 1920s (Lees 1985: 273–5). The drawing of the city in 1918 by George Grosz combines the epigrams of urban commercial and consumer culture (the west end of cinemas, hotels and department stores), with symbols of social and sexual corruption (alcohol and prostitution), and figurative representations of the economic and social inequality that had widened by the end of the First World War (war-cripples, officers, speculators and capitalists), that turns the German city into a chaotic and divided experience.

Document 2.15: City as Chaos: Grosz's Metropolis, 1918

[see illustration on page 27]

Source: Courtesy of Die Akademie der Künste, Berlin.

Nevertheless, the most sustained and pervasive critique of the city came from the right. In arguably the most powerful and influential critique of urban modernity, the

second volume of *Decline of the West*, published in 1923, Oswald Spengler presented a culturally pessimistic assessment of decline coming about as a result of the creation of 'soulless megalopolis' where man, transplanted onto the barren terrain of the city, lived, estranged from nature and the cosmos, a sterile existence. Like his American contemporary Lewis Mumford, Spengler, a retired schoolteacher turned cultural philosopher (Hughes 1992), saw this coming about through the development of great metropolises, world cities alienated from the soil, rootless, capable of alteration but not of evolution, and therefore dammed to die (Mumford 1938: 289). The excerpts taken from the chapter 'The soul of the city' provide the kernel of Spengler's thinking with regard to the cultural crisis of urban modernity.

Document 2.16 Spengler, The Soul of the City

The town, too, is a plantlike being, as far removed as a peasantry is from nomadism and the purely microcosmic. Hence the development of a high form-language is linked always to a landscape. Neither an art nor a religion can alter the site of its growth; only in the Civilization with its giant cities do we come again to despise and disengage ourselves from these roots. Man is civilized, as *intellectual nomad*, is again wholly microcosmic, wholly homeless, as free *intellectually* as hunter and herdsman were free sensually. [. . .]

It goes without saying that what distinguishes a town from a village is not size, but the presence of a soul. Not only in primitive conditions, such as those of central Africa, but in Late conditions too – China, India, and industrialized Europe and America – we find very large settlements that are nevertheless not to be called cities. They are centres of landscape; they do not inwardly form worlds in themselves. They have no soul. Every primitive population lives wholly as peasant and son of the soil – the being 'City' does not exist for it. That which in externals develops from the village is not the city, but the market, a mere meeting-point of rural life-interest. Here there can be no question of a separate existence. The inhabitant of a market may be a craftsman or a tradesman, but he lives and thinks as a peasant. We have to go back and sense accurately what it means when out of a primitive Egyptian or Chinese or Germanic – a little spot in a wide land – a city comes into being. It is quite possibly not differentiated in any outward feature, but spiritually it is *a place from which the countryside is henceforth regarded, felt, and experienced as 'environs'*, as something different and subordinate. From now on there are two lives, that of the inside and that of the outside, and the peasant understands this just as clearly as the townsman. The village smith and the smith in the city, the village headman and the burgomaster, live in two different worlds. The man of the land and the man of the city are different essences. First of all they feel the difference, then they are dominated by it, and at last they cease to understand each other at all. To-day a Brandenburg peasant is closer to a Sicilian peasant than he is to a Berliner. From the moment of this specific attunement, the City comes into being, and it is this attunement which underlies, as something that goes without saying, the entire waking-consciousness of every Culture.

[. . .]

Presently there arrived an epoch when the development of the city had reached such a point of power that it had no longer to defend itself against country and chivalry, but on the contrary had become a despotism against which the land and its basic orders of society were fighting a hopeless defensive battle – in the spiritual domain against nationalism, in the political against democracy, in the economic against money. [. . .] And with this there arose the profound distinction – which was above all a spiritual distinction – between the great city and the little city or town. The latter, very significantly called the country-town, was a part of the no longer co-efficient countryside. It was not that the difference between townsman and rustic had become lessened in such towns, but that this difference had become negligible as compared with the new difference between them and the great city. The sly-shrewdness of the country and the intelligence of the megalopolis are two forms of waking-consciousness between which reciprocal understanding is scarcely possible. Here again it is evident that what counts is not the number of inhabitants, but the spirit. [. . .]

Finally, there arises the monstrous symbol and vessel of the completely emancipated intellect, the world-city, the centre in which the course of a world-history ends by winding itself up. A handful of gigantic places in each Civilization disfranchises and disvalues the entire motherland of its own Culture under the contemptuous name of 'the provinces'. The 'provinces' are now everything whatsoever – land, town, *and* city – except these two or three points. There are no longer noblesse and bourgeoisie, freemen and slaves, Hellenes and Barbarians, believers and unbelievers, *but only cosmopolitans and provincials*. All other contrasts pale before this one, which dominates all events, all habits of life, all views of the world.

[. . .]

The stone Colossus 'Cosmopolis' stands at the end of the life's course of every great Culture. The Culture-man whom the land has spiritually formed is seized and possessed by his own creation, the City, and is made into its creature, its executive organ, and finally its victim. This stony mass is the *absolute* city. Its image, as it appears with all its grandiose beauty in the light-world of the human eye, contains the whole noble death-symbolism of the definitive thing-become. The spirit-pervaded stone of Gothic buildings, after a millennium of the style-evolution, has become the soulless material of this daemonic stone-desert.

[. . .]

Now the old mature cities with their Gothic nucleus of cathedral, town-halls, and high-gabled streets, with their old walls, towers, and gates, ringed about by the Baroque growth of brighter and more elegant patricians' houses, palaces, and hall-churches, begin to overflow in all directions in formless tenements and utility buildings, and to destroy the noble aspect of the old time by clearances and rebuildings. Looking down from one of the old towers upon the sea of houses, we perceive in this petrification of a historic being the exact epoch that marks the end of organic growth and the beginning of an inorganic and therefore unrestrained process of massing without limit. And now, too, appears that artificial, mathematical, utterly land-alien product of a pure intellectual satisfaction in the appropriate, the city of the city-architect. In all Civilizations alike, these cities aim at the chessboard form, which is the symbol of soullessness. [. . .]

If the Early period is characterized by the birth of the City out of the country, and the Late by the battle between city and country, the period of Civilization is that of the victory of city over country, whereby it frees itself from the grip of the ground, but to its own ultimate ruin. Rootless, dead to the cosmic, irrevocably committed to stone and to intellectualism, it develops a form-language that reproduces every trait of its essence – not the language of a becoming and growth, but that of a becomeness and completion, capable of alteration certainly, but not of evolution.

Source: Oswald Spengler, Der Untergang des Abendlandes: Umrisse einer Morphologie der Weltgeschichte. Zweiter Band: Welthistorische Perspektiven *(Munich, 1923), from the translation with notes by Charles Francis Atkinson,* The Decline of the West: Perspectives of world-history, *Vol. 2 (London, n.d., c.1928), 90, 91, 97–100, 107.*

There is much that can be elicited from these passages by the historian, not least the allegation of a dislocated Germandom (*Deutschtum*) resulting from urban rootlessness, a common indictment against the metropolis in the antiurbanist armoury of this period (Poor 1976: 177–92). Spengler's book had a powerful influence on critiques of urban modernity, especially on those of the extreme right. In an important study of the city-form published at the end of the 1930s by the Nazi ideologue Gottfried Feder, a combination of Spenglerian thinking with a more universal and mundane anti-urbanism is in evidence. Indeed, in his advocacy of more 'organic' settlements 'rooted in the soil', Feder was as much in tune with Ebenezer Howard's model of the Garden City and the more extreme determinist biological-organicism of Patrick Geddes in Britain (Meller 1980: 199–223; *idem* 1997: 53–4), as he was with the Nazi mantra of 'Blood and soil'.

Document 2.17 Gottfried Feder: Drawbacks of the City

Drawbacks of the city.
1. Child poverty (illus. 2.17.i) resulting from:
a) unhealthy and small apartments in tenements
b) increased cost of living
c) excessive dependence on leisure and thirst for pleasure
d) moral and health risks
e) alienation from nature and lack of union with the soil:

'Only when city people return again to nature can one hope that the dangers of urbanization be overcome and with the love of the soil of the Heimat will the will for the child also return again.'
2. Lack of settledness. Berlin is the largest 'nomad city' (immigration, changes of address, migration, see illus. 2.17.iii 21). Thorough investigations and the resulting knowledge are put down in volume 3 'Workplaces and Residence' in the series by the Reich Working Group for Spatial Research at the Technical University Berlin, edited by state secretary Prof. Gottfried Feder.

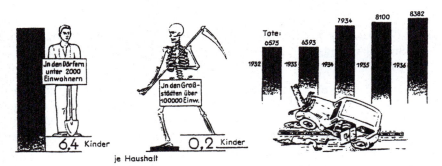

Illustration 2.17.i: The City, the Biological Death of the People!

Illustration 2.17.ii: Deaths in the Reich due to Traffic Accidents

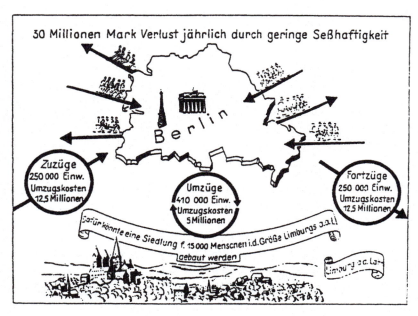

Illustration 2.17.iii: Migration in Berlin

3. Victims of Traffic. The massive volume of traffic demands victims and costs nervous energy and time. Too much traffic is not the sign of a pulsating blossoming life, but the expression of a poor coordination of city institutions to one another (see illus. 2.17.ii).

Source: Gottfried Feder, Die Neue Stadt. Versuch der Begründung einer neuen Stadtplannungskunst aus der sozialen Struktur der Bevölkerung *(Berlin, 1939), 24.*

As we saw in the case of Grosz and Tucholsky, critics of the urban experience were not confined to those on the right. The conclusions of Jürgen Kuczynski, a leading economic and social historian of the former German Democratic Republic, in Volume 4 of his magisterial five-volume *History of Everyday Life of the German People*, equally demonstrate hostility to what was perceived as the darker side of the modern urban experience.

Document 2.18 Jürgen Kuczynski

When one speaks of 'big city people', one must think also of their anonymity, the opposite of which is the village and small town where one can do little without the neighbour knowing. But this anonymity is at the same time the basis for the atomization and anomie of people in the city and also the root of a greater criminality.

The modern city, that is, the city that is not an agglomeration of villages as were Paris and London beyond their city centres in the eighteenth century and well into the nineteenth century, is the modern city, which through transport means has been welded into a sort of unity, has brought great progress for society at the cost of people exactly as Capital has done. The workers were condemned to a terrible material and spiritual poverty, and the rich, the capitalists, were, finally, also no credit to humanity. And the cities had a similar effect: they were places of social progress where the majority of people were devoid of humane lives.

The relations of production can change many important things. But also in real-existing socialism the machine has generally not had a stimulating effect, and for this reason, as Marx predicted, the individual would exit at some time from the production process. Also in real-existing socialism the many ravages of the city cannot be overcome and for this reason, as Engels demanded, the modern city must disappear in the course of time.

Source: Jürgen Kuczynski, Geschichte des Alltags des Deutschen Volkes, *5 Vols., Vol. 4: 1871–1918 (Cologne, 1982), pp. 221–2.*

Kuczynski was assessing the modern urban experience since the late nineteenth century from both a qualitative and a cultural perspective. In the final extract, the liberal American historian Harold Poor seeks to counter such anti-urban arguments with a call to arms to investigate the 'myths and realities of the German Großstadt'.

Document 2.19 Harold Poor, City versus Country

The history of the development of the German Großstadt is clouded by the myths and distortions of the antiurban mentality. Probably in no other country has there been such a powerful combination of agrarian romanticism and hatred of the large city as in Germany. It is a process which reached i[t]s culmination in the blood and soil fantasies of the Nazis and in a sense brought about the virtual destruction of the German cities between 1941 and 1945. [. . .] the cities which developed in the nineteenth century were accused of fostering diseases, lowering life expectancy, destroying the family, impairing fertility and weakening national and community loyalties. Above all, the city destroyed the supposed natural harmony between man and nature by "atomizing" the individual and shutting him up in highrise tenaments [sic] far above the ground and far away from fields and lakes. Antiurban attitudes were ubiquitous, creeping into the writings and utterances of even those who considered themselves friends of the city. [. . .]

The great period of urban growth, of course, occurred in the nineteenth century, but the Weimar Republican [sic] period witnessed the most vociferous articulation of the antiurban bias and the blood and soil philosophy. For this reason Weimar provides a good starting place for investigating the myths and realities of the German Großstadt. [. . .]

Source: Harold Poor, 'City versus country: Urban change and development in the Weimar Republic', in Hans Mommsen et al. (eds.), Industrielles System und Politische Entwicklung in der Weimarer Republik, *2 vols. (Düsseldorf, 1974), Vol. 1, 111–27.*

In the following chapters we will attempt to take up Poor's challenge.

3 | *Metropolis*: From imagining to planning the city

The vast strides of progress in science and technology undertaken since the 1860s had opened a new world of innovation to Germans by the turn of the century, and at the centre of that world stood the city (Hietala 1987: 185–6, 195, 356). The electrification of the city in the last decade of the nineteenth century, the spread of surface and underground transport, and the further development of the urban infrastructure not only transformed the face of the city, but also altered the people's relationship to it (König 1990: 303–13; Reulecke 1985: 57; Hietala 1987: 195; Krabbe 1989: 99–128). However, the greatest impact upon the urban imagination was a development taking place across the Atlantic in the 'new world' of America, to which many Germans had migrated. The introduction of new building technologies making use of steel girders and concrete, coupled with rising premiums for inner-city land, allowed for high-rise buildings, so-called skyscrapers, to shift the urban landscape from a horizontal to a vertical view. The sum effect of this urban modernization was a 'shock of the new' among Germans that cannot be underestimated. Machines, transport, and electricity altered the ecological organization of the urban environment and shifted the mental parameters of the city's population (Park et al. 1925: 2, 23).

Such developments had a marked influence upon the popular imagination, and not just in Germany, producing utopian and dystopian visions of the urban future. In no small way also influenced by a *fin-de-siècle* mood, contemporaries merged their daily experiences of change into futuristic worlds of a markedly *linear* design. That is, they took contemporary experience and imagined their own modernity. In Britain, for example, H.G. Wells's *The Time Machine* of 1895 was just one such expression of a dystopian future city based on the contemporary, troubled reception of urban modernity (Kern 1983: 95, 104ff.; Doyle 1998: 74). In Germany, the ambivalent fascination with a vertical urban modernity based on subterranean and upper worlds could be found in the works of a number of writers, such as Oscar Justinius (also known as Oscar Cohn) and Theodor Hertzka, and notably in Bernhard Kellermann's *Der Tunnel* (1913). As Hildegard Glass notes, *Der Tunnel* 'celebrates the role of technological advancement as a vehicle of progress, but it also presents discordant, ominous images of a powerful, ubiquitous machinery and of the modern industrialized urban environment' (Glass 1992: 201). The fascination with technological utopias remained embedded in the interwar discourse on urban modernity, surfacing occasionally in its scientific literature.

Document 3.1 German Technological Utopias

Along the ground waved the fields of grain wherever light and air permitted growth; above this, on firm and lofty pillars, stood the buildings of men; industry carried on its busy life in the lower floors; above this were the private dwellings, and the crown of the whole was formed by pleasant gardens, whose open healthy atmosphere made them the favourite resorts.

Source: Kurd Lasswitz, Bilder aus der Zukunft (Breslau, 1878), 2, cited in Edwin M.J. Kretzmann, 'German technological utopias of the pre-war period', Annals of Science, 3 (1938), 417–30. Illustration 1929, Courtesy Landesarchiv, Berlin.

As we can already see from this brief extract, the linearity of the vertical urban world was not seamless, but predicated upon a physical division between upper and lower worlds, mirroring the contemporary social division between bourgeoisie and proletarians. Perhaps the most powerful and enduring of these visions of the technologized vertical city with its discordant social relations is that of Thea von Harbou and Fritz Lang's *Metropolis* (1926). This film contained a combination of historical, contemporary and futuristic visions of urban social organization. Lang took the horizontal spatial arrangements of the late nineteenth- and early twentieth-century German city and transposed them to vertical space (in many ways reminiscent of H.G. Wells's *Time Machine*). As such, he presented an ambiguous statement on urban modernity as it was being experienced and imagined, and sometimes denied, at the time (Weber 1908: 77; Kaes *et al.* 1994: 623–5).

In the film the workers' tenement quarters of the inner-city (*Altstadt*), which had grown up since the mid-nineteenth century, are displaced to beneath the earth, while the middle-class world found in the city's commerical centre and suburbs form the upper world. Thus the contemporary *experience* of a capitalist world of leisured consumerism and a wretched world of regimented production and reproduction were figuratively projected into a future world upon the screen.

Document 3.2 Fritz Lang, Metropolis, 1926

[see illustrations opposite]

Source: Courtesy of Stiftung Deutsche Kinemathek, Berlin.

The vision of the dystopian vertical city was, however, countered by an alternative utopian vision of the vertical city where a democratic civitas would prevail as a new social religion. The artist Lyon Feininger, born in New York at the beginning of the 1870s, had moved to Berlin in 1887 in order to study at the academy. Here he experienced the rapid changes in the city, the creation of an architecturally represen-tative centre ringed by tenements, embodying the crass social divisions of Wilhelmine society. In Feininger's woodcut, *Die Kathedrale des Sozialismus*, which appeared as the frontispiece of the *Bauhaus* manifesto in 1919, the linear city of urban modernity is devoid of the dissonant notes of social and class conflict, but instead symbolizes a modern urban utopia in which social relations would be organically harmonious (a goal that is alluded to in the final scene of *Metropolis*).

Document 3.3 Lyon Feininger, The Cathedral of Socialism, 1919

[see illustration on page 38]

Source: Courtesy of the Bauhaus-Archiv, Berlin.

In the 1920s, leading architects, designers and artists, especially those associated with the Bauhaus under Marin Gropius, and later under Mies van der Rohe, sought to adapt this positive vision of 'Chicago' to German conditions. Gropius, the founding director of the Bauhaus in Weimar, told his students at their first exhibition in June 1919 that 'we find ourselves in a terrible catastrophe of world history, in an upheaval of entire life and of the entire spiritual being', and that therefore, as society's future architects, it would be their task to create a world of harmony (Hüter 1976: 210).

While some were imagining the city of the future, urban planners were grappling with the city of the present. On the eve of the First World War, the British civil servant and expert on German municipal life, William Harbutt Dawson, observed how 'the German regards his town as a living organism, whose development both deserves and needs to be controlled with the utmost thought and care' (Dawson 1914: 142). As in much of Europe at that time, there was little *centrally* directed town and regional planning in Germany before the end of the nineteenth century (Tarn 1980: 84;

[Document 3.2 Fritz Lang, Metropolis, 1926]

[Document 3.3
Lyon Feininger,
*The Cathedral of
Socialism*, 1919]

Bollerey and Hartmann 1980: 140ff.; Sutcliffe 1983: 469). But considered from the local perspective, the period between 1890 and 1910 was nevertheless a prolific one, even if planning was sometimes limited to the curbing of building excesses, the alteration of the medieval street plan in order to facilitate the efficient flow of traffic, or the acquisition of cheap building land at the urban periphery (Horsfall 1904: 145–7; Sutcliffe 1980: 6; *idem* 1981: 27ff.; Ladd 1990: 77–110).

The emphasis upon the regulation of the built environment reflected the increasing recognition in Germany, as elsewhere, of the importance of the juxtaposition between the exterior world shared by the mass and that of the inner, spiritual world of the individual (Sutcliffe 1981: 9–46; Ladd 1990: 227–35). The relationship between the two was set out in general terms by S.D. Adshead, Britain's first professor of civic design at Liverpool University, who had witnessed first-hand developments in Germany and elsewhere in Europe before the First World War.

Document 3.4 The Influence of the City on City Life

That the planning of the city will influence physical growth is too well known to need comment here. That it can have a moral influence (using the word moral in its strictest sense, meaning regulation of conduct) is an idea which has had less consideration; but it is very obvious that in the planning of the streets and in the grouping of buildings, where these are regular, ample in width, and suited in every way to the purpose for which they are designed there is not only a saving in actual time in moving from place to place, but also a freedom from that mental worry and anxiety which accompanies all movement amidst irregularity and complication. [. . .]

But proceeding to its intellectual influence, this we may aptly dwell upon at greater length. It is expressed in its character and its style, and it is here that the modern city when compared with cities of the past is at so deplorable a discount. We of this generation are too apt to associate civic existence with gaunt and ugly buildings, flaring advertisements, entanglements of electrified wires, collections of chimney pots, crowded slums, jostling and noisy traffic, squalor and dirt. Let us think of a city rather as a chosen place wherein to dwell, as a rendezvous of daily entertainment, as a vast expression of the sympathies of the human race, as the greatest and noblest of works of art; elevating to the imagination, and inspiring to the enthusiasm. All this and more is what a city ought to be.

The city is, in the first place, the envelope of its inhabitants; its buildings are their constant horizon, and its streets have their daily regard. As such it should exist primarily for their edification, their pleasure, and their well-being. To talk of a city as existing solely for purposes of trade is to talk of mankind as existing for meat alone. In the city of the future mining, manufacturing, and other necessary but mechanical occupations which are under existing conditions smoke producing, accompanied by excessive noise or in which are emitted pungent smells, need not be identified with city life. [. . .]

Great is the city whose architecture is passed unnoticed by the crowd, but not unfelt. Great is its presentment when its more important buildings alone demand conscious attention, leaving the rest but subconsciously felt. Convincing is its merit when the persistent formality of its street is conducive to a sense of respect, and arouses in the heart of the citizen that pride of citizenship alone engendered by civic art. [. . .]

In its essential requirements it calls not only for more highly-organised buildings but for entirely new types. We have wonderful machinery for construction, erection, and rapid completion. We have skilled mechanics standing each by his perfected tools. We have splendid trains, smooth-running trams, and rapid cars. We have city life with a modern character entirely its own. The city itself must express all this. Relegated to the good old days is the city which slumbers 'neath its cosy old roofs, whose windows all mullioned delighted in tiny panes, and whose walls were supported on rough-hewn beams. Such cities were full of charm, but they have passed away, their day has gone never to return.

True, our outlying suburbs, our country villages, our places of relaxation and retreat, may still partake of the character of these old-world towns; but in the city proper, where throbs the pulse of modern life, new conditions must prevail. Here, where complexity of existence is intensified by the rapid movement of modern life, greatness of conception must have stringent control. We must have a character about the buildings of our streets which suggests strength held in reserve, and abundance of force most subtly controlled. [. . .]

A great city has continuity in its character, and a oneness in its many phases of expression. It is here that it exemplifies the strength of its organisation. It is in its tone and colour that this is most clearly shown. The city which is white has the greatest refinement and charm. Paris, of modern cities the most beautiful in the world, is a city of ivory studded with pearly grey in a setting of green. [. . .]

The character of a city is most evident when seen through the medium of its colour, but it is also seen through its texture and its form.

The buildings and the outline of the streets, to be a fit complement to modern city life should be regarded in the first place as a background and as a foil. In their form and outline they should be simple and strongly composed. Their surface should be hard and their enrichments delicate to a degree. . . .

The characteristics of a city expressed in its colour, its texture, and its form, reflect on the citizen himself. Its design, the grouping of its buildings, and its outward expression are matters of vital importance to his well-being; and that these should have been left to blind chance to develop in the past shows a lack of appreciation amongst those responsible for city building difficult to comprehend.

Source: S.D. Adshead, 'An introduction to civic design', The Town Planning Review, *Vol. 1, No. 1 (April 1910), 14–17.*

Apart from the fact that Adshead celebrates precisely that which Spengler laments, his general observations can be followed in the German context in a report by a fact-finding mission from Rochdale before the war.

Document 3.5 Frankfurt am Main

Between English and German towns there is a vast difference. Our first impressions were of Frankfort [*sic*]. The magnificent public buildings, wide tree-lined streets and boulevards, and the town gardens and parks showed us what a town might be made by careful forethought. Frankfort [*sic*] has developed amazingly during the last thirty years. Thirty years ago it was not much larger than Rochdale, now it is a city of about 300,000 inhabitants. Its streets, buildings, shops, and general aspect would make Manchester look squalid by comparison. The new part, built during this period of rapid expansion, was deliberately planned, and built to last. There are twenty miles of tree-lined streets, with open spaces at intervals, beautifully ornamented with plants, flowers, and occasionally a fountain or monument to add to the beauty of the scene. It would, of course, be unsafe to generalise from one particular town, but at Cologne, and again at Düsseldorf and Mannheim we saw how beautiful the towns are being made. The old part of Cologne is not handsome, but one soon comes to the circle outside which all the streets are planned and tree-lined. While we in England allow our towns to grow haphazardly so long as certain elementary regulations are complied with, the Germans insist upon wide tree-lined and open spaces being provided. In the matter of town planning we have a great deal to learn from Germany. Having unrestricted power to own land, and encouraged by town planning legislation, the German municipalities can combine in the laying out of their towns, the beautiful, the healthful, and the useful. Instead of the planless growth which has been characteristic of English towns and cities during the last century, where factory and railway, slum and suburb, are separated only by mere accidents of personal ownership, or crushed together in confusion, the German towns are growing according to a carefully made plan, handsome and clean, with trees in the main thoroughfares, and present the appearance of Garden Cities.

Source: Rochdale Education Guild, Report of a visit to Germany made by members of the Guild, May 28th – June 12th, 1909 *(Rochdale, 1909), 13–14.*

It was not only social reformers who travelled to Germany before 1914 in search of an urban ideal of harmony and order. Municipal experts from Britain, the United States and Sweden also conducted many tours, remarking favourably upon what they considered to be its model town planning, especially the new garden settlements (but had they cared to look closer, they would undoubtedly have found conditions approximating the Victorian industrial slum, as documents in Chapter 4 demonstrate) (Shaw 1895; Horsfall 1904; Dawson 1914; Lees 1985: 239–47; Hietala 1987: 361ff.).

Only partly influenced by the ideas of Ebenezer Howard in Britain, but notably by the Austrian architect Camillo Sitte and by Theodor Goecke in Germany, the movement for garden settlements caught the imagination of progressive town architects and benevolent employers, such as the iron magnate Alfred Krupp in Essen, who built the showpiece Margaretenhof estate for his workers (Abercrombie 1910: 246–50; Sutcliffe 1980: 8; Bollerey and Hartmann 1980: 143–51). Germany's first garden settlement was at Hellerau, founded on the outskirts of Dresden in 1907. Although originally conceived as a settlement for craft workers, it did little to redress the problems of the crowded mass of the city. Indeed, like its Berlin counterpart, Falkenberg (1910), or even Letchworth and Hampstead Garden Suburb in England, this garden settlement soon developed into a utopian colony seeking an experimental 'new spirit of living' (Hartmann 1976: 46ff.; *idem* 1985: 106–7; Bollerey and Hartmann 1980: 151–8; Marsh 1982: 185).

Meanwhile, a number of municipal authorities initiated garden exhibitions which featured cottage-style housing in a ruralized setting. They hoped that the garden settlements, as part of a new, enlightened town planning, would act as vehicles for a new social harmony under open skies, thus overcoming the decay and conflict of the tenement city (Bullock and Read 1985: 137–47). Ultimately, in an effort at social engineering, the purpose of these garden estates was to condition the individual household to a 'better way of life' (Docs. 5.10, 5.13). Such ideas were also tinged with a strong dose of social Darwinism (Bollerey and Hartmann 1980: 146–7), that not only predates its later espousal by Nazi hygienicists and planners, but was widespread throughout Europe and in North America at the time Document 3.6 was written.

Document 3.6 Garden Estate in Altona

A serious question of far-reaching importance for our national development constitutes the accommodation of the masses streaming into the cities. Perhaps a time will come when one will hardly comprehend how it was possible that people lived in dark, airless and sunless rear-tenements and courts many floors over one another, deprived of nature and mother earth. From the future looking back to the present one will be better able to gain an overview of the awesome damage and deprivation of our present day housing than we can. Although the modern city can be named almost as a child of our present day, the early statistics already convey a serious message to the economist that he must be worried about the future of our German people. The terrible losses which the world war exacts, almost pall – in purely statistical terms – compared to the fact that year in and year out in our Fatherland around 300,000 infants die. And it is known that this terrible mortality is greatest in the apartments where the possibility of airing is lacking. We already know today that every third city generation which does not get fresh blood from the country expires. The fertility decline makes great strides nowhere as in the city. Many degenerative signs, which today can be traced historically in the decayed nations, are appearing among our people. Even if we also get the upper hand in the terrible struggle of nations, the danger that with the peak of development of a nation the decline begins, will also face the German people. History teaches that the decline of nations stands in close relation to the relinquishing of rootedness in the soil. History as teacher shows the path to follow in order to protect our nation from regression and to lead it to further heights: namely the greatest numbers must be kept close to the soil; city housing must be so organized that the dangers to human development are excluded as far as possible. It would be utopian simply to demand the dissolution of the cities and to resettle the people once again in the country. Our economic body would not be able to sustain such a violent cure, and each development must have its time. Migration to the city will not stop, even after the end of the war. Ways and means must be found, therefore, through the making available of good housing conditions to minimize the dangers of city life. With the improvement of transport, even more people will have the possibility to live even further from the city centre. Tenements are not to be the lifestyle of the future but instead the small house in a spacious style surrounded by gardens in which our growing population has the necessary freedom, air, and sun for its development. [. . .]

Altona's crest shows an open gate through which the current of time can flow unhindered. The current today goes out beyond the gates of the cities; the city population wish to rehabilitate themselves out there.

Source: H. Frank, 'Charakteristisches von der Emmichstraße', in Altonaer Stadtkalendar, *5 (1916), 105–7.*

The garden suburb was typical of the prewar effort to turn the 'city inside out' by emptying the overfilled inner-city. The idea spread rapidly throughout Germany, reflecting the desire of city fathers to harness positively and give shape to social forces through the immediate habitat. Their efforts were interrupted by the war, but after the collapse of imperial authority and the founding of the republic, postwar municipal authorities renewed this tradition, combining it with more exciting perspectives of modernism. An opportunity thus presented itself in 1918 to draw a line under a dismal past and the terrible present, and to start afresh. As Gropius told the Thuringian parliament in July 1920, the times had changed, irrevocably it seemed, and the new era called for a new architecture.

Document 3.7 Reconstruction and Experimentation, 1920

First I have to elaborate further to make myself understood. Because the adaptation to the different situation demands great flexibility from the public, because the old preconditions are simply not valid any more, because people have changed mainly through the war, today reconstruction means experimentation everywhere in the well-known sense. You can see it even in politics. So many pillars of the material and intellectual world have collapsed, that a politician, irrespective of his party, has to regard his government today as only an experiment. There is hardly anything left that is secure and upon which we can rely completely. Compared with before when we lived in simple clear-cut and secure conditions, intellectual matters especially can no longer be considered from a comfortably partial view. Today they necessitate getting to grips with the totality of life. [. . .] The new ideological outlook is still an uncertain foundation for everyone, and no one can say with conviction what will come of it for we are placed between two epochs.

Source: From 'Minutes of 83rd sitting of the Thuringian Parliament, 9 July 1920, Point 1, First reading of the budget for the State Bauhaus in Weimar', reproduced in Hans M. Wingler, Das Bauhaus 1919–1933: Weimar Dessau Berlin und die Nachfolge in Chicago seit 1937 *(Bramsche, 1968 edn), 52.*

By placing the emphasis upon spaces and vistas rather than stressing the particularities of individual buildings, interwar planners, according to the historian of German town planning Hans Albers, discovered an urban aesthetic as a totality which was socially grounded and organically defined (Albers 1986). Or, in Adshead's apposite observation: 'in the well-organised city individual expression is subordinate to the civic expression of the city as a whole' (Adshead 1910: 3). The contemporary definitions of this totality were left to individual city planners. In the mid-1920s modernist architects interpreted the new totality according to the sober technology of the 'city as machine' where 'measure will reign, chaos will resolve itself – logic, clarity, mathematics, order' (Ludwig Hilbersheimer); at the same time mobilizing the 'dynamic forces of business and industry' (Martin Wagner); they sought to recast the nation by reshaping the urban landscape. To quote Berlin's chief planner Martin Wagner: 'Our new era must create new forms for both its inner and its outer life [. . .] and this new style must find its first concrete expression in city planning and in housing' (Miller Lane 1985: 90; *idem* 1986: 284; Lees 1985: 181–6).

In spite of being confronted by an ongoing housing shortage, and dogged by budgetary realities, the republic's new city planners set about their task with gusto. Among the larger cities in 1929, responsible for a quarter of the 312,270 dwellings built in that peak year for housing construction, private investment stood at around 37 per cent, housing cooperatives accounted for nearly 48 per cent, and the local authority, with public utilities, for 15 per cent (McElligott 1992: 102–5; Silverman 1970: 123). As Document 3.8 shows, however, there was clearly a good deal of variation between cities.

As in Britain, the distribution between the private and public sectors was not necessarily dependent on the political hue of city government (McElligott 1992: 104; Daunton 1987). Typically, direct responsibility for house construction in the 1920s was left to semi-public bodies, such as housing cooperatives and occupational trade unions, with municipal bodies accounting for only a small share of construction. In Berlin, for instance, 64 per cent of housing construction between 1924 and 1932 was undertaken by cooperatives and housing associations (Rexroth and Wolter 1987: 48). Of this proportion, 70 per cent was constructed by the socialist trade union housing association *Gehag* (Gemeinnutzige Heimstatten-Aktiengesellschaft), which was also responsible for the monumental Bauhaus 'Horse Shoe Estate' (*Hufeisensiedlung*) in Britz, and the 'Forest Estate' (*Waldsiedlung*) in Zehlendorf, both on the outskirts of Berlin (Miller Lane 1985: 104).

The internationalist style employed on estates such as the Weissenhofsiedlung in Stuttgart, the Britzsiedlung in Berlin, or the Praunheim estate in Frankfurt, emphasized, as the name suggests, a style that could be found equally at home in any country. The absence of any decoration, the use of light-coloured materials, or concrete and glass wrapped around steel and iron skeletal frames, created the impression of 'buildings consisting of skin and bones' (Mies von der Rohe). But the geometric forms and the discarding of the traditional pitched roof in favour of the flat sun-terrace drew vitriolic

Document 3.8 New Housing Construction in Selected Cities, 1928/9 (Populations over 50,000), by Contractor

City category ( )	Local authority	Public housing utility	Public corpn	Private	Others
Groups					
000s	(percentages of annual total of each place)				
200+ (A)	5.3	9.4	0.5	37.1	47.7
100–200 (B)	11.1	6.8	2.0	43.2	36.8
50–100 (C)	12.8	0.9	0.9	41.3	44.1
Individual Cities					
Category A					
Altona	27.8	–	–	45.2	27.0
Berlin	–	13.4	0.6	21.9	64.0
Bremen	–	–	0.3	80.2	9.5
Düsseldorf	4.6	–	–	55.7	39.7
Frankfurt/M	23.5	30.5	0.1	11.6	34.3
Hamburg	0.2	–	–	48.2	51.6
Nuremberg	38.8	–	0.6	16.4	44.2
Category B					
Aachen	53.3	–	–	40.5	6.2
Augsburg	2.6	38.5	–	22.0	36.9
Barmen	19.1	–	0.4	57.1	23.4
Krefeld	29.3	–	–	60.4	10.3
Category C					
Elbing	59.0	–	–	17.2	23.8
Koblenz	46.0	–	–	31.0	23.0
Liegnitz	25.1	–	–	38.7	36.2
Recklinghausen	6.1	–	–	43.0	50.9
Trier	51.2	–	2.6	17.4	28.8

Source: Statistisches Jahrbuch Deutscher Städte, *25 (1930), 211–16.*

criticism from conservatives who labelled these as 'asiatic'. They accused modernist architects of 'foreignizing' (*Entfremdung*) the German urban landscape, and described the architecture as 'un-German' and unorganic (Timm 1984: 156–7; Miller Lane 1986: 290), as the illustration distorting the original photograph of the Weissenhofsiedlung in Stuttgart shows.

Document 3.9 Weissenhofsiedlung, *(a) c.1927 and (b) as 'Arab village' (c.1934/1940).*

Source: Orig. (a) Stuttgart Landesbildstelle reprinted in Richard Pommer and Christian F. Otto, Weissenhof 1927 and the Modern Movement in Architecture *(Chicago, 1991), plates 3, 85 and (b) Courtesy of Bauhaus-Archiv Berlin.*

While it is a fact that the new estates both attracted and repelled contemporaries, and have since remained a central focus of attention among architectural and social historians, they were not commonplace in interwar Germany. Less than half of the new construction since 1919, 46.9 per cent to be exact, took place in medium-to-large towns and cities; by far the greater part was carried out in smaller towns, and notably in rural communities. Moreover, housing developments were on a more modest scale compared with the modernist projects, and built by private corporations usually in a more traditionalist and vernacular style (StHDR 1933: 143; McElligott 1992: 105).

The extent to which the modern estates during the Weimar Republic really expressed a revolutionary departure from traditional modes can be questioned (Meller 1980: 202). In a seminal manifesto published in 1919, Bruno Taut, like fellow utopians Gustav Landauer and Heinrich Tessenow, propagated the reconciliation of the industrial city (modernity) with nature (tradition) through its 'dissolution' by creating smaller *Trabantenstädte* or satellite towns, joined to a metropolitan crown (Docs. 3.16, 3.17). Their inhabitants would carry out different activities in specifically designated areas, harmonized through greenbelts, and organically linked to the centre (to the Volkshaus) by modern transport networks (Timm 1984: 104; *idem* 1985: 100; Willett 1978: 118–32; Miller Lane 1985: Chs. 2 and 4). Similar to an earlier manifesto that sought to rehabilitate and unify the energies of the nation (Kaes *et al.* 1994: 432–4; Hilpert 1978: 160–1), Taut's manifesto rehumanized the 'soul of the city' by placing the 'people' at the heart of an organically constructed wholeness.

Document 3.10 House of the People

[see illustration on page 48]

Source: Bruno Taut, Die Auflösung der Städte (Hagen i. Westfalen 1920), 12. Courtesy Bauhaus – Archiv Berlin.

In Taut's diagram humanity has spread beyond the cities to fill the globe; states and cities have been superseded by the *Heimat*; the old division between town and country has disappeared, as too has war and peace; all life is now located in an elysian community of common interest and honest toil. Such sentiments later surfaced in the Nazi idea of 'blood and soil'. But while Taut's model is clearly anti-metropolitan, it can be understood as a reaction to the social and political upheavals of war and revolution in the city. The decentred form of living envisaged by Taut and his contemporaries surfaced in the idea of the cellular city, also common in American discussions on planning (Fischler 1998: 708; see Chapter 5). In a quite different publication of 1939, Gottfried Feder proposed that the medium-sized town of 20,000 provided a compromise between the city with its strong centralization, sense of participation in public life, work and consumption, and the needs of an urban population for recreation in the open nature. However, the centrality of political ideology in the Third Reich meant that the Party, and not the people, would be the fulcrum and embodiment of urban life.

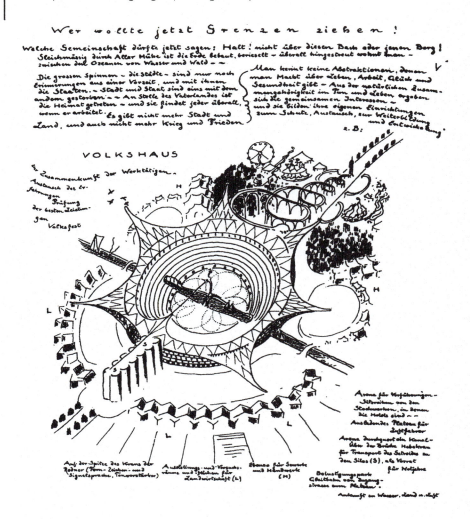

Document 3.11 House of the NSDAP

In order that it can be equally easily reached from all districts, it will be built to best advantage in the inner part of the city, without having to be – like the town hall – in the main market place, namely at the centre of commerce. Since the House of the NSDAP belongs to the most important institutions of the future town, its importance should also be emphasized outwardly. One achieves this most simply by surrounding it with a modest border of green and open space. At least the choice of location should be one of the smaller squares so that for the viewer the building stands dignified apart from its environs of terraced houses.

Source: Gottfried Feder, Die Neue Stadt: Versuch der Begründung einer neuen Stadtplannungskunst aus der sozialen Struktur der Bevölkerung *(Berlin, 1939), 110.*

This privileging of the party office over the *Volkshaus* reflected the political shift from parliamentary politics to party direction (*Lenkung*), that characterized the organization of life in the Third Reich. But the superficial similarities between Taut's ideas and those of Feder, for example, have led some urban and architectural historians to question the earlier republican phase of modernity and instead to make links to the apparent anti-urbanism of the later Nazi period.

Document 3.12 Ideology and Planning

In ideological terms, can these town planners be considered pro-urban? Like the escapists of the pre-war period, these planners seemed to desire an alternative to the city. Yet, also wished to maintain a tie to the central city while not being an integral part of it. They saw their *Siedlungen* [housing estates] as capturing the best of nature and the best of technique and, for this reason, felt that their ideas were unique. These *Siedlungen* were conceptualised as 'daughter towns' attached to the 'mother' city by mass transit umbilical cords. In each settlement there were to be such facilities as schools, laundries, local shops and even local work places. Housing was often designed in standardised and prefabricated forms for the minimum existence and at the price level of the common worker. The structures lacked ornamentation, but were painted with vivid colours. From their designs, it seems that the members of the avant garde were endeavouring to develop a sense of separation from the old cities without losing the economic symbiosis necessary for survival. They felt that the new locations were critical for the creation of a new *Wohnkultur* (literally, living style). They also perceived that the sense of a new cultural standard could not be developed in the old city because the cultural social system, with its traditional values, precluded the opportunity to attempt change in a comprehensive framework. In the new settlements, the *Wohnkultur* could be attempted because the separateness enabled the designers to create a new, manufactured sense of communitarian morality without the intervention of the older, more traditional values.

In a sense the Weimar era theorists were anti-urban. Most members of the avant garde maintained a fundamental view of the city as inherently negative. The large city, they felt, displayed all the attributes of Toennies' *Gesellschaft* while the new *Siedlungen* – designed to overcome the negative aspects of the metropolis – seemed a part of the *Gemeinschaft*. . . . In essence, man, to be fulfilled, must come to grips with both nature and technology. Neither the rootless urbanite nor the 'tied to the soil' peasant fit. Modern man with a sense of the land and the skill of the factory would emerge as the product of the new culture. . . .

Some social critics view the Weimar Era as being 'urban' oriented. The modern designers of the Bauhaus, the art of Klee, Gross [*sic.*] and Kandinsky, the music of Hindemith, the plays of Brecht and the acting of Dietrich have all been labelled as citified. Can it be said that the planners of the Weimar Era were pro-urban? There is little evidence to support such a position. It is clear that none of the Weimar town planning theorists focussed upon the city as an ideal form. Rather, they emphasised escapist, small scale, limited size, balanced communities placed within green belts. In essence these theorists saw the city as too complex, disorderly, traditional and unchangeable. For these reasons they advocated a new form of community. This new form, in theory, would simplify the complexity of the community experience, bring order to community form and reflect a new *Gesamtkultur* or *Wohnkultur*.

Source: John Mullin, 'Ideology, planning theory and the German city in the interwar years', Part 1, Town Planning Review, *Vol. 53, No. 2 (April 1982), 125, 127.*

As we have noted, war and revolution created the desire in Germany for a thorough-going reconstruction. Henceforth, urban planning became more comprehensive and state-led. Two key laws allowed for the recasting of the urban landscape. The first was the Prussian Expropriation Law of 1918, which explicitly aimed at urban zoning. As its name suggests, this law allowed cities to expropriate land and property deemed to have fallen within their urban plan. It was followed by a Reich law in 1920, and this allowed for expropriation of unused land for building purposes. Larger cities in particular made use of these laws to consolidate their influence over the urban landscape (ILO 1924: 333ff.; Hegemann 1930: 375; 455–7), that perforce extended beyond their formal boundaries.

Document 3.13 The City and Its Hinterland

Cities are never in themselves rounded-off and complete. They will always somehow have neighbouring areas bordering them which in reality lie within their sphere of influence. The larger a city is, the more important its centre of gravity, all the more its influence. Exact statistics for such zones of influence cannot be marshalled here. [But] the urban statistician Schott in his book on agglomeration which appeared before the war, worked in general on the basis of a ten kilometre boundary. Practice shows that larger cities and towns exceed this and must, and smaller ones – or under certain conditions – can manage with a much smaller radius. Comparisons are difficult, almost impossible. [. . .]

One can set a city's wider zone of influence at 40, 50 and more kilometres without any problem. [. . .] To be sure, this is only possible where within such a zone there is no other city of the same or higher rank. [. . .]

Source: LAB 142/I StB 500, Erich Feldhaus, Mitteldeutschland, Die Mitteldeutsche Frage: Gedanken über Verwaltungsreform und Verwaltungssitz *(Magdeburg Verlag der Faber'schen Buchdruckerei, c.1928), 27–8.*

Indeed, after the First World War the boundary between town and country became increasingly an artifical one. It existed only for statistical and legal purposes, or as an imaginary construct in the town–country discourse.

Document 3.14 Boundaries

As soon as we near the city boundaries, we pass through a singular zone where town and rural culture struggle for supremacy. With extensive factory and transport installations, gas and electricity works, trams and abattoirs, the city pushes itself further outward from year to year, and in the wreckage dumps of former quarries, sewage plants, knacker's yards, in the warehouses of raw and waste materials, are gathered the detritus of city life. With them, albeit without organic cohesion, are linked the outposts of rural life. The urban estates expand with dilating groundplans between the suburban roads; on extensively parcelled allotments of vegetables and potatoes, the 'common man' carries on a hard but not futile struggle with the rubble and stones which bedeck the ground here. Further out, the influence of the land begins gradually to tip the balance, we sigh with relief, we have escaped the spell of the city.

Source: Dr. Gustav Schulze, 'Die Heimat als Jungbrunnen für Körper und Geist', in Gewerkschaftsbund der Angestellten Jugendbund, Führerschriften, 1 (Berlin, 1921), 2–6.

The extension of the urban influence over its hinterland, thus blurring the boundaries between town and country, had begun before the First World War as a consequence of over 100 town amalgamations and incorporations between 1881 and 1910, a process continued at a slower pace until 1918 (Matzerath 1978: 78–9; Reulecke 1985: 148–9). The pace picked up again after the war. Using data from the statistical year-books of German cities, it can be estimated that between 1925 and 1933, there were around 133 incorporations affecting medium-sized towns and cities, a trend that was in marked contrast to Britain where there was a decrease in the number of interwar incorporations (StJbDS 24 1929: 233–4; StJbDS 25 1930: 239; Hall 1988: Ch. 2). This era of incorporations was inaugurated with the creation of Greater Berlin in 1920, but there were other, no less spectacular, city expansions, such as that of Düsseldorf.

Document 3.15 Düsseldorf Incorporations, 1909–29

[see illustration on page 52]

Source: Peter Hüttenberger, Düsseldorf Geschichte von den Ursprüngen bis ins 20.Jahrhundert, vol. 3: Die Industrie- und Verwaltungsstadt 20.Jahrhundert (Düsseldorf, 1989), 401.

There were cases where expansion through incorporation was much more spectacular, such as Altona (1927) or Breslau (1929), and notably, Berlin itself, which, after the territorial adjustment of 1920, grew to 883.57 square kilometres, while its population eventually rose to 4.3 million by 1939 (Petzina et al. 1978: 38; Engeli 1983: 57; Ladd 1990: 210–27).

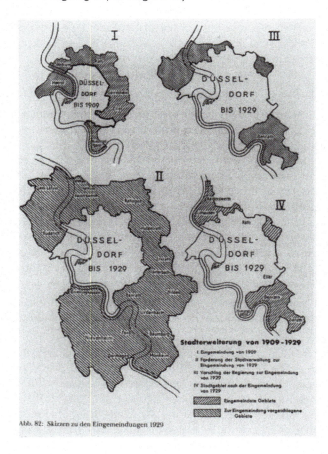

Abb. 82: Skizzen zu den Eingemeindungen 1929

The widespread territorial adjustments of the 1920s signified a pattern of ration-alization of urban administration and resources that extended the city's influence over entire regions (Hohenberg and Lees 1985: 238–44). The arguments for and against the creation of metropolitan sites almost echo those of the nineteenth century for German unification, and anticipate Hitler's later intention to rid Europe of the 'rag-bag' of splintered nation states.

Document 3.16 German Particularism

People, places and states which through the power-political wills and power-political boundaries, have been until now unnaturally and violently hindered in their natural-inclined communal life, have been finally brought closer together again by the technology of our day in a matchessly modern conquest of space and time. Thus a spatial reconfiguration of the greatest scale has been unleashed over the whole of Germany. This spatial reconfiguration here in

south-west Germany, the Rhine–Franconian region, stretches over an area of more than 40,000 square kilometres with a population of about 6–7 million.
[. . .]

A south-west German regional organization with enhanced self-government developing itself in the context of the German unitary state, will make unnecessary not only the five state governments but also their parliaments and ambassadorial and consular activities. Instead of the existing 13 provincial or county authorities, about six–eight county administrations would suffice – in addition to the city crowns (*Stadtkröne*) as interest associations – as far as these will be still considered at all necessary in the administrative and institutional reform. [. . .]

The new regional division of the Rhine–Main crown will be joined organically to the core area of Greater Frankfurt am Main – the largest incorporated area. [. . .]

Here in this area of around 2,800 square kilometres with approximately 1.6 million inhabitants, the vision of those farsighted municipal and economic planners has long asserted itself, [so] that the creation of a commual-economic interest organization [*Zweckverband*] has become the most pressing need. . . .

Here also, it is the people with their technology who constitute a viable unit and in memory of their cultural similarity are bringing about this spatial reconfiguration, while the different state administrations which overlap each other here, have become more or less estranged from one another, and believe they must persevere in the maintenance of only a formal autonomy contrary to the demands of a dynamic present.

The Kurhessen, Upper Hessen, Naussau, Rhine–Hesse, Starkenburg and Lower Franconia regions, which over the course of the most recent historical periods have been already subjected to so many political transformations to their detriment, are finally coming together with the former Free Imperial and Confederation capital of Frankfurt am Main in the era of communications and technology to form a closely connected economic and communication–technical whole so as to face a new era of growth with united strength.

Thus in the long run the forging of unitary procedures is inevitable for regions criss-crossed by all too many administrative borders, and cut up by a confusion of particularist competences. [. . .]

Source: Landesarchiv Berlin 142/I StB 498, 'Zur Deutschen Klein- und Vielstaaterei. Die raumverschiebende Auswirkung der Neugliederung in Südwestdeutschland, dem rheinfränkischen Wirtschaftsgebiet' (1927), 1–4.

As the document states, a Greater Frankfurt would form the hub of this new 'megalopolis' (Barker and Sutcliffe 1993). The city had already incorporated 16 outlying communities between 1877 and 1910, increasing its population more than fourfold to 414,576. A further incorporation in 1928 meant not only further population growth, but almost a doubling of its physical size from 7,005 hectares to 13,477 hectares. Overall its population grew by 34 per cent and its physical size expanded by 45 per cent between 1910 and 1939.

Document 3.17 The Rhine-Main Cities Crown, 1927

With a description of what is happening in the illustration

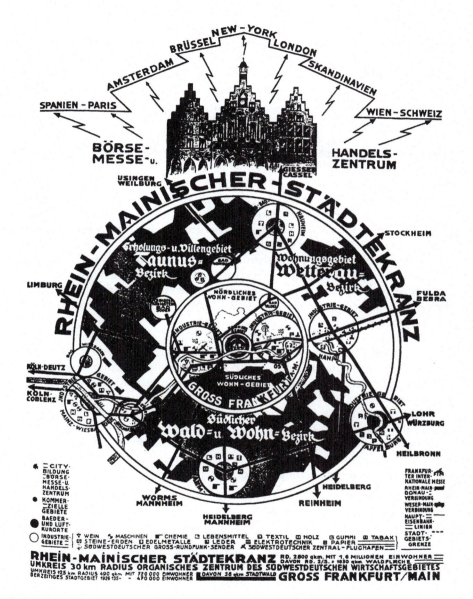

Source: Landesarchiv Berlin 142/I StB9 3170d.

The perceived 'metropolitanization' of whole regions, as evidenced in Document 3.17 showing the Rhine–Main region with Frankfurt at its core, precipitated a considerable social crisis as small communities resisted vehemently what they took to be the extinction of home towns in which resided a traditional German *Kultur* by the 'soulless city' of modern *Zivilisation* (Krabbe 1980: 368–87; McElligott 1998: 95–123). Thus according to Dr Schlenker, a businessman from Düsseldorf, 'Just as it cannot be the aim of a healthy industrial economy to create only a few giant corporations, so it is not desirable to create a few giant cities [*Riesenstädte*]. [. . .] Nowhere is civic sense more alive to the needs of the commonweal than in the smaller and middling communities' (Telegraphen-Union, Internationaler Nachrichtendienst GmbH, Kommunalpolitische Beiträge: Regionale Verwaltungsreform, 16 May 1928). The logic was clear: if cities continued to grow by feasting upon smaller communities, then the basis for a civic nation would disappear with them (Doc. 10.2).

Document 3.18 Boa Constrictor Ruhrensis 'Bracht-Schmidt'?

[see illustration on page 56]

Source: Mühlheimer Zeitung *39 (8 Feb. 1928).*

By the beginning of the 1930s, the argument for a return to smaller forms invoking the cherished ideas of *Gemeinschaft* over *Gesellschaft*, *Kultur* over *Zivilisation*, were growing stronger. During the Third Reich such ideas took on the force of official policy, and a number of smaller settlements 'rooted in the soil', were, indeed, established.

Document 3.19 Organic Urban Order

The juxtaposition and entanglement of the individual parts of our towns and settlements must give way to a planned, clear order so that the individual parts, though in themselves closed structures [*Glieder*], are brought together in strong harmony into a viable total organism. What we are searching for, and must find, is a communal form in which, so to speak, each lives through and for the other.

Source: Gottfried Feder, Die Neue Stadt: Versuch der Begründung einer neuen Stadtplannungskunst aus der sozialen Struktur der Bevölkerung *(Berlin, 1939), 19, 24.*

In spite of the cant that small is beautiful, the Nazi regime also continued the process of creating vast metropolitan centres that would express the power of the state. At the beginning of October 1937, the regime passed the Law for the Reorganization of German Cities (*Gesetz für die Neugestaltung Deutscher Städte*) (Dülffer et al. 1978). Through this law, the regime sanctified the very same megalopolises that Spengler

Ein confruirtes Ruhrreich „Bracht-Schmidt"?

Das Regierungsschema, an dem nur kleine Aenderungen möglich sind **Effens sehr bewegliche Gliederungs-Politik** **Kleine Aenderungen am Regierungsschema, wie Effen sie sich etwas ve...**

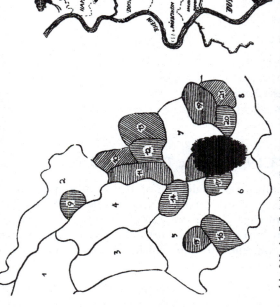

had warned against. Speer's plan for Berlin is often cited as the most spectacular example of urban modernity under the Nazis (Miller Lane 1986: 296–308; Nerdinger 1993), and has been subjected to a critical appraisal by Stephen Helmer that places it within a longer-term development.

Document 3.20 Speer's Berlin

Like the 19th-century garden cities from which they drew so much [sic] of their ideas, the National Socialist New Towns were oriented to the countryside, while the Speer Plan remained focused on the city. Not that the Party's New Towns looked to the country simply as an escape to fresh air, sunlight and decent housing. To the rabid 'blood and soil' philosophers behind so many of these plans it was closeness to the sacred German earth that the new settlements offered, and an environment conducive to the establishment of a community life like that of the Middle Ages, the period from which these thinkers felt the German race could trace its greatest achievements.

By comparison, the Speer Plan seemed to embrace the modern metropolis enthusiastically. Certainly its central portion exalted those complex governmental, military, business and cultural institutions so peculiarly a product of the big city. Monumental in scale, cosmopolitan in architectural approach, the heart of the Speer Plan was an obsessively man-made and man-dominated environment running almost continuously for five miles, the only real break being the large section of wooded Tiergarten that intervened just south of the Koenigsplatz. [. . .]

This aggressive assertion of urban values is not set down in so many words, but it can be detected between the lines of the texts as well as in the plans themselves. A recognition of it sets the stage for what actually is said. These discussions tend to focus quite specifically on planning, rather than urbanism in general.

We might begin by noting the seeming commitment to 'planning', as opposed to either urban design or the view of the city as simply architecture. There appears to be a general acceptance of the quite recently evolved approach to city building which we think of today as 'rational' or 'scientific' planning, a systematic ordering of urban functions within a spacial [sic] context. The publications coming out of Speer's office at the time demonstrate a clear intent to combat what Rudolf Wolters [one of Speer's associates in the Planning Office] terms the 'planless expansion' of the city. This is not surprising coming from the experienced planners on the staff, though those who were also trained architects belonged to a profession which was still vigorously reacting to earlier preoccupations with traffic, other technical concerns, and generally a two-dimensional concept of the city, [. . .]

Judging from his memoirs, there is no doubt that Speer himself is also a champion of rational efficiency in planning. However, there is a serious question as to how well he grasped specific applications of it at the time he worked on the Plan. His memoirs were written long after the fact, and of the several articles attributed to him from the 1930's, all but one is of questionable authorship.

Source: Stephen Dean Helmer, 'Hitler's Berlin: Plans for Reshaping the Central City Developed by Albert Speer' (Cornell University, Ph.D. thesis, 1980), 94–7.

Speer's plans for rebuilding Berlin remained on the drawing board; as too did those for other cities, including Hamburg, Munich and Hitler's own 'home town', Linz (Arndt 1984: 163–4; von Dücker 1985: 105; Garlay 1984: 167; Klotz 1984: 209; Schäche 1991; Reichhardt and Schäche 1998). Within a few years Speer's would-be 'Germania' (the name Berlin was to be given once it had become the capital of a Nazi-unified Europe), like its sister cities, lay in ruins. James Pollock, an American political scientist and specialist on Germany, travelled extensively throughout the country as a civilian observer with the American occupying forces from July 1945 until the following summer. During this period he kept a diary, recording his experience. Pollock, who had visited Germany during the early 1930s, was deeply shocked at what he saw. On 23 July he travelled through Wiesbaden and Mannheim, which he found in a poor state, but not totally destroyed, unlike Darmstadt which 'was scarcely recognisable to me – only the big monument in the centre of the town providing me with a landmark I recalled'. He finally arrived in Berlin on 25 July.

Document 3.21 Journey through Destroyed Cities

25 July: [. . .] Through Neukölln and Schöneberg our bus took us to the permanent headquarters of the American Group of the Control Council – the former Luftgauamt in Dahlem. The condition of Berlin beggars description – some walls standing but street after street a perfect shambles. And yet people moved about in the street – a few shops were open but the traffic was mostly army vehicles. [. . .] Got my things and drove around Berlin from Wannsee down to the Linden. Scarcely a house or building intact. The Tiergarten blown to pieces – trees blown off – wreckage lying around – stark destruction in every direction. The Reichstag portal and walls still standing but utterly useless. The Brandenburg gate [sic] by strange coincidence still standing but the Pausen Platz with the Blücher Palais which we bought for an Embassy, the French Embassy, the Adlon, the British Embassy – everything along the Linden and the Wilhelmstraße – a complete wreck. What a lesson to 'the master race'. The Schloss, the Dom, the University – alles kaput [sic].

I walked throught the Reichskanzlei – that huge, ornate nerve center of the Nazi system. Everything wrecked. I picked up a card in Hitler's room to remind me of the visit. Outside Russian soldiers were trading German medals out of the building.

[12 August] I hunted for the Römer [Frankfurt], the Goethe house and other spots of historical interest I had previously visited in years gone by. Crawling over and through piles of rubble I finally found the old 16th Century edifices pretty much in ruins.

Source: Institut für Zeitgeschichte Munich, ED122/1–3 Pollock Papers, Book 1, 'Occupation Diary'.

Over 1 million tons of bombs were dropped on Germany. From 1943, the allies targeted Germany's 61 large cities (*Großstädte*), with a total of 25 million inhabitants. During 1943 and 1944, firestorms raged over Hamburg, Cologne, Kassel, Frankfurt am Main, Frankfurt an der Oder, Munich and Dresden, as half a million tons of high explosive and incendiaries were dropped on these cities. Berlin was covered in 55 million cubic metres of rubble when Pollock arrived there; Frankfurt am Main had 12.7 million cubic metres of rubble. Hamburg was still clearing away 35.8 million cubic metres of rubble (*Trümmer*) as late as 1948 (Rumpf 1961: 195).

Document 3.22 Hamburg in Rubble

[see illustration on page 60]

Source: Courtesy Westermann Verlag Hamburg

As after the First World War, the extensive physical and spiritual damage of the Nazi years offered architects and planners new opportunities for reconstructing the postwar city (Diefendorf 1993). Similarly, old debates were reopened. On the one hand, conservatives argued a case for a specifically untainted German city. Philipp Rappaport, a civil engineer from Essen, demanded that the reconstruction of urban Germany should not be the result of decisions taken by a central bureau under Allied control producing 'colonial cities' that had few, if any, local German features.

Document 3.23 German Cities or Colonial Cities?

The city must regenerate from within itself, from the wishes and demands of its population, from the prevailing economic possibilities, from the aims and thoughts of German town planning. One can never build a city with legal imperatives alone, especially not with laws foreign to us imposed from outside. With such conscious negation of the extant [structures] generous new cities might be built with broad avenues, mighty tower blocks, regular housing, in short, colonial cities, as they are everywhere ordained by a conquering colonial power, where the indigenous will of the population is lacking; but not cities which preserve traditional character and the traditional style, as far as they are healthy and have potential for the future (viable). Should such cities really come into being in Germany? Are we really not capable of creating from ourselves, from our own ability, from our opportunities, of reconstructing the shape of the German city in the way we think right and necessary? A jump into politics is needed here, albeit a cautious one and not tied to any particular political party. Who is it that is rebuilding Germany? It is the worker who works in the mines, the worker who runs the railways, the worker who is involved in

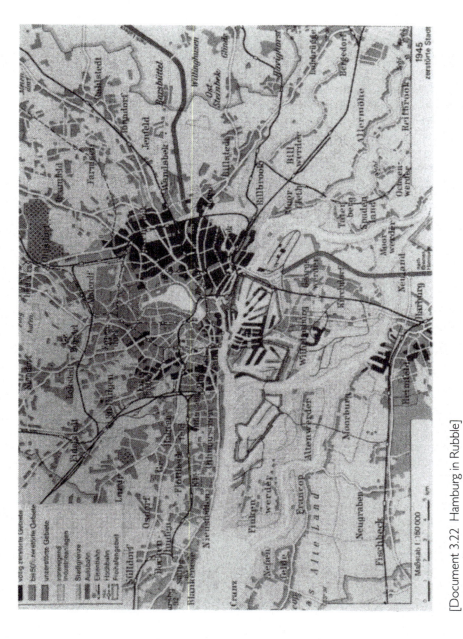

[Document 3.22 Hamburg in Rubble]

Note: Darkest shaded areas were completely destroyed; grey areas were up to 50 per cent destroyed

all the thousands of industries and crafts, and the worker who carries out the actual reconstruction technically; moreover it is the worker involved in trade and industry as well as the intellectual worker. They are the constituent elements of reconstruction.

The wishes of these workers determine reconstruction to the highest degree. It is the duty of the town-planner to understand the mentality and thinking of the working population and to incorporate this into his overall planning. It can be stated without exaggeration that this working population does not desire the expanse of symmetrical colonial cities, instead it desires the healthy and homegrown development of German cities.

Source: Philipp Rappaport, 'Deutsche Städte oder Kolonialstädte', in Deutsche Städtetag in der britischen Zone, Wiederaufbau-Mitteilungen (Essen, 31 March 1947), 1-2.

On the other hand, progressive architects and planners, some of whom, like Hans Sharoun, had designed and built under the Weimar Republic (he had participated in the creation of the Weissenhof Estate), envisioned a future plan for the city that clearly challenged the conservative model that Rappaport favoured. Sharoun's model for postwar Berlin was clearly based on interwar avant garde visions of the city as *metropolis*. Indeed, his plan for Berlin's reconstruction recalls the designs of Ludwig Hilberseimer and is also reminiscent of the futuristic images conjured up in Fritz Lang's *Metropolis*.

Document 3.24 Envisioning Berlin

Recently, too, the imagination of the Berliner has been stimulated by the much-publicised dream city, planned for the future by Professor Hans Sharoun, head of the Building and Housing Department of the Berlin Magistrat. Theoretically, he considers, his plan could be carried out in thirty years.

Professor Sharoun envisages a city intersected by a network of autobahnen [sic] with clover-leaf flyovers at their crossing points. Within the city the main administrative, commercial and cultural functions are contained in a long rectangle, having an east–west axis and approximately following the line of the River Spree. All the offices of a particular function – for example, banking – are grouped together in one of the many streets which cut the rectangle from north to south. Both north and south of the rectangle are situated the residential areas, permitting the employees to live adjacent to their place of work. Planned as large, interrelated units, these areas contain an appropriate balance of ten-storey flats, three-storey flats and individual houses, sufficient both to accommodate the population and yet permit the provision of parks, recreational activities and communal buildings. Industry remains in its proper position with relation to the natural communications of the area but is developed on the rectangle principle with adjacent residential groups.

The fulfilment of this Utopian vision is fraught with imponderables and beset with practical difficulties. At the highest level must be placed the decisions of the Peace Conference with regard to Germany's future and the part Berlin will play in that future.

Source: T.J.T., 'Replanning for the future', British Zone Review (28 Sept. 1946), 17.

Thus the postwar period saw the return of earlier tensions between a German vernacular form and a modernist international style, that some commentators sought to defuse by offering what they saw as a compromise solution: embracing the modern but also incorporating particularist (i.e. German) traditions.

Document 3.25 The Dissolution of Workplace and Residence, 1947

Our old inner-cities are for the most part a heap of rubble, and offer a once in a lifetime opportunity to restructure them socially and for the remaining historical buildings to be rebuilt as living areas for independent people. This will be the most exciting project for architects, those responsible who influence the face of the city [. . .], to construct moderate buildings with roofgardens, blossoming courts, individual houses with workshops, studios, studyrooms, and apartments as well; with particularly specialized shops for jewellery, books, art objects, delicatessen, haute couture, cosy taverns, apartments for workers, clerks and civil servants, who know how to carry their poverty with noble dignity. But also the most distant task which stands at the end of reconstruction. The area which the actual 'city' [commercial centre], the department stores, offices, hotels etc., needs, is very small. For a city of ½ million, we have calculated 500×500 [square metres]; it can lie at the edge of the highrise estate [Hochstadt].

I believe we must free ourselves from false ideas and concepts. Decentralization does not mean a city of out-of-town housing estates linked by rail. The modern city does not necessarily mean skyscrapers, fast trains, extreme mechanization. We must free ourselves from Americanism, which we probably falsely understand as well.

Dispersal – indeed the whole thing – means the recreation of the village which will increasingly have a non-agricultural character; more circumspect expansion of the small town and break-up of the teeming cities into easily comprehended, clearly delimited independent districts, grouped according to the actual realities of each town round about the highrise estate, which in its turn, is the most beautiful expression of a new national order.

Thus we get the most modern cities, which in their material form, mirror the social form of the twentieth century, and a regional plan which involves the entire countryside, including the village, in a real shaping also in terms of construction.

Source: Ludwig Neundörfer, Auflockerung von Arbeits- und Wohnstätten (Frankfurt am Main, 1947), 22–3.

The importance of the *form* of the built environment that was to rise again from the rubble of the Third Reich, in terms of what it expressed about society, or indeed the revival of a German nation, is evident from these documents. It also underpins the observations of a British visitor to Cologne in 1946.

Document 3.26 'I Came to a City'

Ten years ago, almost to the day, I was in Cologne. Now I am here again and my mind almost refuses to accept what my eyes see. Then it was a city of broad, sweeping streets and tall buildings, a city of lights, hotels, restaurants, theatres, cinemas, and surging crowds of people – all intent and purpose. Life was full and pleasant.

Now, we have Hitler's legacy, his gift to his master race, his reward for years of suppression and hardship, and, too, the world's answer to any such dreams of conquest.

It is not just the destruction of what was once one of the loveliest cities of Europe. One expects material destruction in any war, but here in Cologne it is as if the soul of a people had been destroyed, something more than bricks and mortar.

Instead of the once gay crowds, one meets few people, who look at you, dull-eyed, with cheeks that tell of hunger and cold, apathetic men and women, children with spindle legs and thin little bodies – the price of a nation's lust to conquer.

Over all there is a strange quiet, a stillness that chills the heart, while the mind is exercised with the question that arises: how could any people possibly survive after this cataclysm that tore down their proud buildings reducing them to dust and rubble?

One moralises. Why should this have to happen? Cologne was a city with years of tradition and story – and all the rich heritage of the ages disappeared in a night or two under the destructive forces of modern warfare.

But what was destroyed must be built up again. Is it too much to hope that in the rebuilding of Cologne and the shattered cities of Germany something more than the re-erection of houses, of bricks and mortar may be achieved, so that the future citizens of Cologne, as in every other city shattered by war, may never experience what their forbears did because of one man's monomania and a nation's megalomania?

I look at the ruined bridges lying in the Rhine, the river they once so nobly spanned. The cathedral towers stand out in silhouette against the September evening sky.

The calm of evening is descending, but it is shaken by the silence of destruction.

Source: N.L., 'I came to a city', British Zone Review (28 Sept. 1946), 9.

By emphasizing the centrality of the individual in the city, this anonymous contributor to the *BZR* unconsciously connected to Simmel's sociology of the city, recognizing that the daily interface between *people* and their immediate habitat, however envisioned, constituted the urban *experience*. But there could not be a *single* urban experience, because the city was in fact made up of a multitude of habitats, not least that of the 'slum'.

'Slum': Encounters with the urban 'other'

From around the mid-nineteenth century, social investigators from Charles Dickens to Henry Mayhew and John Hollingshead in London, from M.A. Frégier to Balzac and Zola in France, began exploring and writing about the social conditions of the urban poor in Europe's cities. In addition to their accounts, church organizations, government commissions, medical men, and local public agencies first investigated the housing conditions of 'the people', and then pronounced on the morality of their collective lifestyle (as it appeared to these observers). What they encountered frequently seemed both strange and somehow threatening, but at the same time, exciting. Writing in the 1830s, Frégier coined the term 'dangerous classes' for the urban poor of Paris who, he asserted, constituted a 'fourth estate', living in idleness and misery from gaming, vagabondage and prostitution, 'whom the police watch, and for whom justice waits. They live in their own particular districts; they have a language, habits, disorderliness, a life which is their own' (Chevalier 1973; Lees 1985: 15–90, 142–8; Emsley 1987: 31ff., 59ff., 78ff., 133; Schlör 1998: 197–201).

There was no shortage of similar accounts in Germany (Südekum 1905; Bergmann 1984). Together with official inquiries and reports of the medical fraternity and the police, these accounts, described by Bass Warner as 'colonial anthropology' (Warner 1983: 388), increasingly pathologized urban poverty in a discourse that had shifted from descriptions of general conditions to accounts of life-style peculiar to the dark side of the modern urban experience. Some, like the conservative German historian Treitschke, drily observed that poverty was the consequence of fecklessness and the generally uncivilized nature of the people concerned (Hegemann 1930: 19–20; Emsley 1987: 50, 58, 63). For others, such as Hans Ostwald and the various authors of the *Großstadt Dokumente*, the sights, sounds and smells of the 'great unwashed' in their particular districts presented a veritable *tableau vivant* that beckoned and fascinated (Fritzsche 1994: 393), but that also repelled, as the following account by the medical doctor Franz Oppenheimer shows.

Document 4.1 Encounters with the Urban Slum, *c.*1890

Eichendorffstraße, close to the north end of the north–south arterial road of Berlin, the Friedrichstraße, and situated near the Stettin station, at that time belonged to the 'Latin quarter' which appears to me to have shifted gradually towards the area of the Zoological Gardens and Sauvigny Square ever since public transport has improved. This means that there were a lot of petit bourgeoisie, namely old people, who were making a living from renting rooms to students, and a massive scale of prostitution. There were also very many workers, albeit not from the lowest class of the lumpenproletariat, more skilled than unskilled.

Here I was looking for the first time with growing awareness and ever-increasing horror into the Medusa's face of the social question. The surgery was a practice for the common people [*Kleineleutepraxis*], often even for the poor; it happened more and more often that whole families turned to me instead of the official 'poor doctor'; the whole misery of the city unfolded itself in front of my eyes and the social causes for so many diseases became very evident. As a doctor for the first aid station, I frequently had to deal with the consequences of serious fights. Once I was called out to the most horrible milieu I had ever come across: an old prostitute had been injured by her pimp, allegedly with a broken plate, but probably with a more dangerous instrument; the edge of her shoulder blade lay exposed in the gaping wound in her back. Every four weeks I was called to one of those dingy dosshouses in the area to issue a death certificate for a suicide couple; and I had a regular income from the attestation of bruises and other small injuries, documents which were supposed to serve a successful court case. What an appalling coarseness, shameful grotesqueness, horrible ignorance!

Source Franz Oppenheimer, Erlebtes, Erstrebtes *(1931), pp. 100–2, excerpted and reprinted in Walter Steitz,* Quellen zur deutschen Wirtschafts- und Sozialgeschichte von der Reichsgründung bis zum ersten Weltkrieg *(Darmstadt, 1985), 472.*

Oppenheimer's testimony captures in a few ambivalent yet racy observations the nub of bourgeois *angst*: the shared space of the mass; the proximity of poverty and sickness; raw violence and excessive drinking; untrammelled sexuality; all of which stood in crass antithesis to 'polite' society in the modern period. The encounters of the bourgeoisie – either directly or through official agencies – with the urban poor consciously or not typologized them and their habitat in terms of a 'slum' discourse (Chevalier 1973: 210; Warner 1983: 385–91; Evans 1989: 13ff., 21ff.; Ladd 1990: 140; Mayne 1993).

Document 4.2 What Is a Slum?

What is a slum? According to J.H. Vaux's *Flash Dictionary* (1812), 'slum' was little more than a name for a room, though by the 1820s the word had three distinct meanings as a slang expression for various kinds of tavern and eating house, for loose talk and gipsy language, and, more vaguely, for a room in which low goings-on occurred. It was this last root from which the modern meaning of the word has developed to include whole houses and districts in town and country. [. . .]

As a straightforward term for bad housing, its form had evidently soon started to change simply to 'slums', as it appeared in a letter to *The Times* in January 1845, and from this time it passed into very general use as a semi-slang expression, a synonym for 'rookeries', 'fever-dens', 'little hells', 'devil's acres', 'dark purlieus', until eventually the iverted commas disappeared. This took a surprisingly long time to happen and some writers in the 1880s were still using the term in this tentative way. [. . .]

These semantic adjustments may be significant, for the lack of a word for such a common phenomenon does not necessarily correspond with an experience too esoteric for ordinary speech, but with one too readily accepted to require a perjorative term. Did those living in the slums ever use the term as readily as those that did not? What was being overlooked, I think, before 'slum' was properly coined was the existence of a housing problem – itself not normally referred to as such until nearly the end of the century – as distinct from one of sanitation or public health. The changing meaning of this term seems to reveal a changing public attitude to the phenomenon itself.

[. . .]

The implication of this is that, like poverty itself, slums have always been, as they now are, relative things, both in terms of neighbouring affluence and in terms of what is intolerable or accepted by those living in or near them. Such a term has no fixity. The study of it requires a sociology of language, for it was being applied with varying force over the period and with different emphasis at any one time by different social classes; it was being used in effect for a whole range of social and political purposes; and the very districts which were liable to be labelled with it were approaching that condition at different speeds and for various reasons. [. . .]

Source: H.J. Dyos, 'The slums of Victorian London', in David Cannadine and David Reeder (eds.), Exploring the Urban Past: Essays in urban history by H.J. Dyos *(Cambridge, 1982), 130–2.*

These comments by Dyos were first written in the 1960s and focus on the British experience of the 'slum' for which there has been a tradition of scholarly interest (Roberts 1973; White 1979; Davies 1992). Apart from a few exceptions (Rosenhaft 1981; *idem* 1982; Bajohr 1982; Grüttner 1983: 350–72; *idem* 1984: 107–13; McElligott 1983; *idem* 1998: 56–86; Evans 1987: 78–108; Bleek 1991; Schlör 1998: 119–44), the 'slum' as a specific focus of inquiry continues to be overlooked by German urban historians (Wischermann 1996). Instead, discussion has been limited to the development of social welfare policy in Germany, in which contemporary accounts of the 'slum' are treated at face value, and, with only rare exceptions (Reulecke and zu Castell Rudenhausen 1991), simply reproduce the contemporary discourse (Sachße 1986; *idem* and Tennstedt 1988; Ritter 1986; vom Bruch 1985). Although this approach was challenged in the 1980s by a generation of critical historians who saw in the nineteenth-century debates on poverty a new paradigm of 'social control' (Doc. 4.26; cf., Bajohr 1982; Grüttner 1983; Brüggemeier 1983), they still took as their point of departure the original paradigm of the 'slum'. Yet as Alan Mayne in his critical study *The Imagined Slum*, has argued, 'To discuss slums is to deal with words, with discourse, with signs, and with the concepts they communicated, rather than with the social geography of inner cities' (Mayne 1993: 1ff., 128). Mayne's argument notwithstanding, we need not entirely discard contemporary accounts, statistics and social surveys, whatever their perceived ballast. Treated with critical caution, they will help us to understand the nature of the 'other urban experience' that was being discovered in our period.

As we noted in Chapter 2, migrants flocked to the cities during the last quarter of the nineteenth century. It did not take long for particular districts to 'fill up', resulting in severe overcrowding (Weber 1899, repr. 1963: 377; Cahn 1902: 440–72; Hall 1988: 43; Wischermann 1983: 343).

Between 1871 and 1910 average population density in Germany rose from around 77 persons per square kilometre to 120 persons, and continued to rise until the early 1930s. By 1933 it stood at 140 persons per square kilometre (StDR 451:1 1933: 54). Nearly 9 per cent of the population of the 48 *Großstädte* lived in overcrowded conditions in 1927, a lesser share than in medium-sized towns where the proportion was 14.3 per cent. Nevertheless, when measured in relation to residents per building, conditions had deteriorated in some German cities between 1905 and 1920, placing them among the worst culprits for overcrowding in Europe.

Document 4.3 Density per Building in Germany, *c.*1920

[see illustration opposite]

Source: Werner Hegemann, Steinerne Berlin *(Berlin, 1930), 468.*

Hegemann's data represent aggregate figures. Local conditions were often much worse as migrants headed for those districts where contacts existed, work could be obtained relatively easily, and accommodation was cheap (Newman 1979: 61–134). At the turn of the century, residential density in parts of the Altona-Altstadt stood at nearly 1,000 persons per built hectare, almost three times the figures Reulecke has calculated, and remained little changed for much of the interwar period (Reulecke 1985: 218).

Document 4.4 Population Density in 20 Sub-districts, Altona-Altstadt, 1895

[see illustration on page 70]

Source Bericht über die Gemeinde-Verwaltung Altona in den Jahren 1863 bis 1888, 1863 bis 1900, *3 vols. (Altona, 1889–1906): II, Karte No. 24 zu Seite 154.*

This spatial distribution of overcrowding could be found in many major cities and industrial towns throughout the Reich at the turn of the century. Moreover, the

City	Population	%
BRADFORD	288505	4,08
LEEDS	445568	4,37
NOTTINGHAM	259942	4,38
SHEFFIELD	454653	4,63
BIRMINGHAM	525960	4,79
MANCHESTER	714427	4,86
CROYDON	169559	4,93
BRISTOL	357059	5,30
HORNSEY	84602	5,48
EAST HAM	133504	5,50
LIVERPOOL	746566	5,57
LONDON	4522961	7,89
NEWCASTLE	266671	8,13
ENGLD.KGREICH	(520	5,05
städt.Bez	540	5,23
Ländl.Bez	(460	4,51
GENT	162477	4,48
LÜTTICH	170346	6,74
ANTWERPEN	312884	8,11
BRÜSSEL	177078	8,53
BELGIEN KGR	7423784	4,83
ALKMAAR	20467	4,28
LEEUWARDEN	3031	4,76
UTRECHT	115382	5,56
GRONINGEN	68591	5,65
HAAG	265900	6,52
ARNHEIM	61330	6,69
ROTTERDAM	408907	1090
AMSTERDAM	550547	1344
HOLLAND KGRO	5667088	558
PHILADELPHIA	1293697	5,4
BALTIMORE	508957	5,7
CLEVELAND	381768	6,0
MILWAUKEE	285315	6,2
BUFFALO	352387	7,1
CINNCINNATI	325902	8,0
BOSTON	560892	8,4
CHICAGO	1698575	8,8
NEW- MANHATTAN	2050600	20,4
YORK BROOKLYN	1166582	10,2
SCHAFFHAUSEN	18101	11,19
BASEL	132276	1292
BERN	85651	14,63
ST.GALLEN	123153	1518
CHAUX DE FONDS	37751	1624

City	Population	%
ZÜRICH	190733	1726
GENF	58337	2343
PARIS	2659128	3800
KOPENHAGEN	403472	2660
JÖNKÖPING	25141	900
NORRKÖPPING	42781	1400
GOETEBORG	162776	2300
MALMÖ	90771	2900
STOCKHOLM	331272	3200
BERGEN	75888	1597
CHRISTIANIA	242850	2921
BREMEN	247437	7,83
CREFELD	129406	1269
FRANKFURT	414576	1709
ESSEN	294653	1761
ELBEREELD	170195	1802
CÖLN	516527	1805
STRASSBURG	178891	1825
STUTTGART	286218	1861
DÜSSELDORF	358728	1911
HANNOVER	302375	2004
NÜRNBERG	333142	2048
MANNHEIM	193902	2227
LEIPZIG	589850	2739
CHEMNITZ	287807	3035
MAGDEBURG	279629	3108
DRESDEN	548308	3456
MÜNCHEN	596467	3659
HAMBURG	931035	3866
BRESLAU	512105	5197
POSEN	156691	5180
CHARLOTTENB	305978	6613
BERLIN	2071257	7590
KRONSTADT	41050	847
HERMANNSTADT	33489	1058
REICHENBERG	34790	1649
TRIEST	226458	1989
SALZBURG	34176	1996
LINZ	61197	2500
GRAZ	145338	2559
INNSBRUCK	50389	2624
BRÜNN	122114	3558
PRAG	218573	4092
BUDAPEST	880371	4128
WIEN	2004939	5074

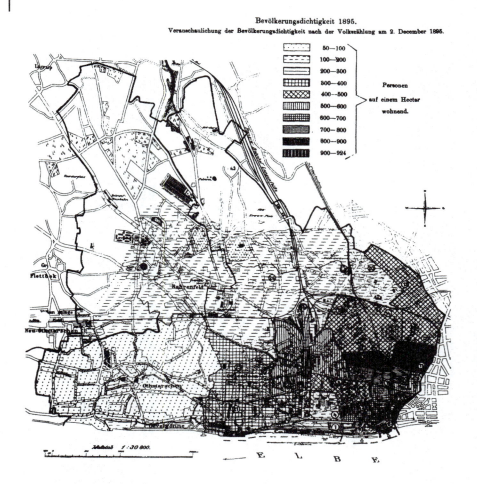

Bevölkerungsdichtigkeit 1895.
Veranschaulichung der Bevölkerungsdichtigkeit nach der Volkszählung am 2. December 1895.

problem was exacerbated by the inadequacy of the housing available. In Berlin in 1900, 43 per cent of households lived in dwellings consisting of a single room, and 28 per cent in two-room dwellings; in 1925, over 70,000 Berliners lived in dilapidated cellar dwellings (Hegemann 1930: 337, 463). In prewar Hamburg, terrace dwellings, mostly concentrated in the inner-city districts, comprised about a sixth of the city's housing. Four per cent of the city's 1 million inhabitants lived in cellars in these areas. In neighbouring Altona, the figure for cellar and attic dwellers was 6 per cent in the 1920s (Wischermann 1983: 140–3; McElligott 1998: 60). Furthermore, the occupants of this housing lived in appalling conditions, since many buildings were without basic internal sanitary amenities. In 1918, for instance, the Reich Statistical Office found that nearly a third of small dwellings (1–3 rooms; these made up half the nation's total housing stock) lacked a kitchen and toilet (StDR 287 1919: 5, 96; Teuteberg and Wischermann 1985: 220–42).

Document 4.5 Poor Housing in Altona-Altstadt, *c.*1932

Source: Landesarchiv Schleswig-Holstein 352/1250.

Newcomers to the city sought flexible arrangements for accommodation that would suit their situation. Given that most migrants had little in the way of personal property or capital, and that work was often casual and for a fixed period, the best solution was to lodge. This flexible demand was supplied by a bare necessity. Rents were usually high in relation to low and insecure wages, and therefore many households had to resort to taking in strangers: either as subtenants of rooms (*Zimmervermieter*), or as temporary lodgers paying only for a place to sleep (*Schlafgänger*), or those who also took meals with the family (*Kostgänger*) (Teuteberg and Wischermann 1985: 317–18).

By the turn of the century in large cities such as Berlin, Breslau, Dortmund, Frankfurt am Main, and Cologne, between a fifth and a quarter of households took in temporary lodgers (Niethammer and Brüggemeier 1976: 116; Reulecke 1985: 105), compared with about 12 per cent in smaller provincial towns such as Bayreuth (Cahn 1902: 469). Sub-letting, or family-sharing in poorer districts of a town or city, was a common phenomenon. In Hamburg about a fifth of households had lodgers, with the proportion rising in the older alley quarters (Wischermann 1983: 352; Grüttner 1984: 104; Evans 1987: 69). Similarly, in Munich, lodgers made up three-quarters of subtenants in the overcrowded housing of the west end district (Bauer *et al.* 1989: 27–8). In the Ruhr where demand for labour was strong, almost one family in two took in *Kostgänger* (Brüggemeier 1983: 52ff.; Friedberger 1923: 39).

Document 4.6 Lodgers in Berlin, *c.*1880

Of the 253,365 households counted in 1880, 18,318 or 7.1 per cent had tenants and 39,298 or 15.3 per cent had lodgers. [. . .]

These 39,298 households with lodgers throw a dark shadow across Berlin's living conditions, which darkens even more when one goes into details. [. . .] There was a person (male or female) in each of 16,192, or 9,165 households respectively, 2 male lodgers in each of 6,284 households, 1 male and 1 female lodgers in each of 1,669 households etc. The picture becomes even more desolate when one mentions that among these 39,298 households, there were 15,065 or c. 38 per cent which had the use of only one room, in which apart from the family, including even children, there were lodgers staying; of these 15,065 households with only one room which come into question here, 6,953 had 1 male lodger, 4,132 a female lodger; in each of 1,790 households there were 2 male lodgers, in each of 607, a male and a female lodger, in each of 721, 2 female lodgers; 357 [households] had 3 male lodgers.

Source: Preußen: Versuch einer Bilanz: Band 3: Preußen: zur Sozialgeschichte eines Staates. Eine Darstellung in Quellen, *Bearbeitet von Peter Brandt unter Mitwirkung von Thomas Hofmann und Reiner Zilkenat (Reinbek bei Hamburg, 1981), 250.*

Such statistics do not say much about the internal arrangements, type of sharer, their social status, and whether or not they were related to the families with whom they resided (Ehmer 1979: 142–7). Nevertheless, subtenanting and overcrowding were closely linked to class and income. In Duisburg, for instance, James Jackson found that 66 per cent of unskilled families and 50 per cent of skilled families, but only 20 per cent of lower middle-class families, lived in overcrowded conditions as a result of casual lodgers taken in to pay the rent and make ends meet (Jackson 1981; Teuteberg and Wischermann 1985: 319).

Document 4.7 At the Nowaks, Wassertorstraße

The entrance to the Wassertorstraß was a big stone archway, a bit of old Berlin, daubed with hammers and sickles and Nazi crosses and plastered with tattered bills which advertised auctions or crimes. It was a deeply shabby cobbled street, littered with sprawling children in tears.

[. . .]

The living-room had a sloping ceiling stained with old patches of damp. It contained a big table, six chairs, a sideboard and two large double-beds. The place was so full of furniture that you had to squeeze your way into it sideways.

[. . .]

My first evening as a lodger at the Nowaks was something of a ceremony. I arrived with my two suit-cases soon after five o'clock, to find Frau Nowak already cooking the evening meal. Otto whispered to me that we were to have lung hash, as a special treat.

"I'm afraid you won't think very much of our food," said Frau Nowak, "after what you've been used to. But we'll do our best." She was all smiles, bubbling over with excitement. I smiled and smiled, feeling awkward and in the way. At length, I clambered over the living-room furniture and sat down on my bed. There was no space to unpack in, and nowhere, apparently, to put my clothes. At the living-room table, Grete was playing with her cigarette-cards and transfers. She was a lumpish child of twelve years old, pretty in a sugary way, but round-shouldered and too fat. My presence made her very self-conscious.

[. . .]

In these tenements each lavatory served for four flats. Ours was on the floor below. If, before retiring, I wished to relieve nature, there was a second journey to be made through the living-room in the dark to the kitchen, skirting the table, avoiding the chairs, trying not to collide with the head of the Nowaks' bed or jolt the bed in which Lothar and Grete were sleeping. However cautiously I moved, Frau Nowak would wake up: she seemed to be able to see me in the dark, and embarrassed me with polite directions: "No, Herr Christoph – not there, if you please. In the bucket on the left, by the stove."

Source: Christopher Isherwood, Goodbye to Berlin *(1935), 100ff., 105, 120ff.*

As Isherwood's account suggests, and contemporary studies confirmed, lodgers were often young people, and they could be of either sex. In 1885, for example, young single male migrants as a proportion of the adult male population (over the age of 20 years) could range from 68 per cent (Hamburg), to as high as 84.6 per cent (Leipzig); the corresponding proportion of young single female migrants in those two cities being 61.2 per cent and 78.4 per cent respectively (Weber 1899, repr. 1963: 282; Wischermann 1983: 354, 362–3). Fears of sexual impropriety were given added force by contemporary social investigations which showed that it was precisely in households with children that *Schlafgänger* and subtenants were most likely to be found (Friedberger 1923: 39).

After the war, the overcrowded condition of Germany's towns and cities had been exacerbated by the lack of sufficient housing, and by changing expectations. The housing census of 1918 found that the urban centres of the newly established republic faced a shortfall of 1.5 million dwellings. In Prussia alone, the shortfall in towns and cities with populations over 10,000 stood at half a million (StDR 287 1918: 5).

Document 4.8 Interwar Housing Conditions

Migration from the country to the towns, which was estimated at 400,00 persons per annum during the years immediately preceding the war, had already given rise to a housing problem which was characterised by the block system of building and aggravated by difficult questions of landed property and credit.

The many efforts to solve these pre-war housing questions – for Germany can look back on a period of successful and far-reaching housing reform – were abruptly broken off by the war. The balance between supply and demand was seriously upset by sudden changes in both factors. On the side of demand a short setback at the beginning of the war was followed by a marked increase, especially due to the rapid rise in the number of marriages after the end of the war and to movements in population. [. . .]

The effect of the rapid rise in the number of marriages after the war, as compared with the pre-war average, was accentuated by the excessive number of refugees and returned emigrants after the war. [. . .] The actual increase in the number of households from 1910 to 1919 (population census) was 922,305, while the increase in population during the same period was only 584,301. Thus the war, while reducing the number of persons per household, led to an enormous increase in the number of households and therefore in the demand for housing.

The supply of housing followed an opposite course. There was a general setback to building during the war, and since the conclusion of peace the revival has everywhere been slow and comparatively slight. [. . .]

The general result was a rapid and complete occupation of available dwellings, even the smallest and most unhealthy. From 1919 onwards German housing statistics show no figures for vacant dwellings, their place being taken by the figures of persons without accommodation. [. . .]

The industrial area of central Germany may be cited as an illustration of the evils produced by the housing shortage in industrial districts. Thus in Merseburg district the number of new workers engaged permanently since the war was 15,000, and of those engaged temporarily 5,000, while only 1,525 new dwellings were produced. In this district 18,475 industrial workers lived away from their place of work, 10,770 of them at distances of 10 to 15 kilometres, 2,685 at distances of 20 to 30 kilometres, and 435 over 30 kilometres away.

There is no lack of material for completing this gloomy picture by figures or instances of the disastrous hygienic, demographic, and social effects of the housing shortage in Germany. [. . .]

Source International Labour Office, European Housing Problems since the War *(Geneva, 1924), 317–18, 322–3.*

Attempts by housing officials, such as those in Altona, at the beginning of the twentieth century to disguise statistically the *Schlafgänger* system by redefining bed lodgers as full subtenants could not hide from contemporaries the extent to which it continued to exist, even after the war (Niethammer and Brüggemeier 1976: 115; StJB Altona 1928: 314–16). In Berlin one estimate put the number of *Schlafgänger* in the mid-1920s at 44,600 and the number of lodgers at 130,500 (Hegemann 1930: 164). Even though their number was in decline, the phenomenon still caused widespread concern among housing and family reformers about the social and moral conditions said to result from the practice.

Document 4.9 Greifswald Sleeping Arrangements, *c.*1923

Beds. The sleeping arrangements are just depressing. They constitute in the first degree an indicator of material impoverishment. Sleeping facilities, which to a great degree deserve the name 'beds' only superficially and which in part are filled with rags instead of bedclothes, exist for 151 out of 401 inhabitants of the 100 dwellings. That means, when one measures the number of beds to inhabitants, that 62.3 per cent are without their own bed. [. . .] Children usually sleep three and four to a bed, often the parents with two children. Not infrequently children share a bedroom with children of both sexes. The demand made by Rubner "a bed for every German", and the demand by Flügge "whenever possible, a child should have a bed from the age of ten", unfortunately is not achieved here in any way. What A. Kohn wrote on the basis of a survey in 1914 by the Berlin compulsory workers health insurance, where in 35.8 per cent (6,909 cases) sleeping arrangements were inadequate, applies in part here also: "Were the roots for these terrible conditions to be sought only in want and poverty, then help would be effected easily and with fewer resources; but alone in extraordinarily many cases it is not possible even to erect another bed, because there is no space." [. . .]

35 families lacked bedclothes. Even personal clothing was often absent. A sick, almost blind woman lay for weeks totally naked in a bed which had no covering. [. . .]

Schlafgänger system: The *Schlafgänger* system is barely developed here because of the lack of industry. Only in one family was the room rented to three *Schlafgänger*. The family itself slept in a windowless boxroom. In another case, the landlady slept in one room with two female *Schlafgänger*, one of whom suffered severely from tuberculosis. The two beds were put in the service of the two *Schlafgänger* while the woman slept on the sofa. Thus we have here as elsewhere the sad fact that in the case of subletting the tenant always get the best rooms and the landlords suffer more than the tenant. [. . .]

Source: Prof. Dr E. Friedberger, Untersuchungen über Wohnungsverhältnisse insbesondere über Kleinwohnungen und deren Mieter in Greifswald *(Jena, 1923), 34–8.*

The conditions in Greifswald were not peculiar to that town (or that country as Arthur Mearns' *Bitter Cry of Outcast London*, testifies). A survey carried out by the Reich Association of German Youth in 1929 of 200,000 apprentices and unskilled youth showed that more than two-thirds did not have a room of their own; 20 per cent had to share a bed with another family member, and a small number had to share with a lodger (Flemming *et al.* 1988: 101; Sieder 1986: 69–76; Lehnert 1986: 338–41). It is not surprising that in such conditions the individual was 'never alone' (Tucholsky 1929: 118–23). Sharing, either among family members or with strangers, shocked the sensibilities of a bourgeois public and their conception of the traditional 'closed' family (Wirth 1938: 21; Niethammer and Brüggemeier 1976: 122ff.). But even though conditions were in fact worse in the medium-sized cities of the Ruhr, and indeed, *much* worse in the towns of eastern Germany, commentators such as Eugen Diesel focused exclusively on the big city as the cauldron of national and moral decay.

Document 4.10   Urban Poverty in Germany, 1931

One million seven hundred thousand families are without homes of their own, and a fifth of the whole population live in conditions which are very hotbeds of consumption, incest and every kind of vice. In Berlin only sixty-six percent of severe tubercular cases have beds of their own to sleep in; the rest have to share their beds with healthy children and adults, who do not remain healthy for long in consequence. And only one consumptive in a hundred has a bedroom to himself! Every fifth child of the German cities is without a bed of its own; it has to live amid poverty and sickness, immorality, dirt, and coarseness. Thus millions of people exist in conditions of bitter horror, in half-lit dungeons, where six to eight or even fourteen or more human beings are crowded together amid rats and filth. In many parts of the big towns children who do not suffer from venereal disease are actually the exception. It sometimes happens that children are born in unheated attics only to die of cold there, and in many slum dwellings the walls drip with damp, and everything gets covered with mould and rot. In thousands of cases one small room and bedroom has to serve as workshop, kitchen, living-room and bedroom for the whole family.

Source: Eugen Diesel, Germany and the Germans *(London, 1931), translated from* Die deutsche Wandlung das Bild eines Volks *(Stuttgart, 1931), 255–6.*

The discourse on the 'slum' had traditionally been expressed in terms of social hygiene and population policy (see the following chapter), but by the end of the 1920s it had become increasingly influenced by eugenicist debates that purported to show the inability of 'slum'-dwellers to produce healthy and productive families (Weindling 1991: 108; Schwartz 1994; Bajohr 1982; Mitterauer 1983: 100–10; Crew 1986; Pine 1995: 182–3). Although large-sized poor families were common in country areas, reformers focused on the city where the large family of the 'slum' was perceived as a burden and threat to society (Brandt 1931: 72; McElligott 1998: 73, 90–1).

Document 4.11   Unmarried Mother in Berlin, 1928/9

Mother: 32 years old. Concierge and washerwoman.
5 children aged from 12 to ½ a year, all illegitimate, two children already deceased.

The mother came to Berlin from Silesia 15 years ago as a domestic servant. The first illegitimate children were received into care when she took on a position as a concierge in a house in a working-class quarter, she took her children back. There were five more children born, of whom two died of scarlet fever. The father of the surviving children is a streetcleaner, 15 years older than the woman, already a father with 6 grown-up children, he takes no interest in his illegitimate children. He has to pay monthly 40 RM for 4 children, but has been paying absolutely nothing for some time because of illness. The welfare office is looking after the children and pays weekly 18 RM. The woman earns 36 RM from her concierge job, 32 RM are deducted for rent. She works as a washerwoman but irregularly, because she is often ill and has to look after and care for the children. She is receiving help from some quarters.

The apartment consists of one room and a kitchen (window facing the yard). The hall may only be used for access because another two families are sharing it. The room is long and narrow and has a window facing the yard. The whole apartment looks neglected, dirty and unsuitable and is untidy at any time of the day. The woman is slovenly. The children often come to school unwashed and carry with them the dreadful smell of the flat. The woman often has to stay in bed because of pains, and then the eight-year-old has to take care of everything.

The mother is ill a lot. After the birth of the ten-year-old – the child was born in a cold corridor when the mother was on the way to hospital – she started suffering from a serious kidney complaint; she also suffers from migraine. The children are all scrofulous and partly undernourished. For breakfast dry rolls or bread, at lunchtime they eat potatoes with gravy or herring, for supper bread with lard or margarine. [. . .]

These conditions are probably the most miserable I know. There could only be an improvement if the children were taken away. But the welfare office is worried that the mother will produce more children if the responsibility is taken from her. The removal of the one-year-old child, at least, was considered.

Source: Alice Salomon and Marie Baum, Das Familienleben in der Gegenwart *(Berlin, 1930), pp. 42–3, cited in William Hubbard,* Familiengeschichte: Materialien zur deutschen Familie seit dem Ende des 18.Jahrhunderts *(Munich, 1983), 201–2.*

At the time Salomon and Baum published this report, Berlin had 35,699 large families, often with a single parent, living in such conditions (Hegemann 1930: 471–2).

Concern over living conditions in the first two decades of the twentieth century quickly translated into fears regarding social and moral behaviour (Lees 1985: 171–4; Crew 1998). In particular, reference was made to alcohol consumption (and other daily pleasures) and the role it allegedly played in creating the conditions of the urban 'slum' (Horsfall 1904: 163–4; Abrams 1992: 76–81; Roberts 1984; Petrow 1994). The observation that 'very often these people seek for themselves a compensation for a cosy home in superficial pleasures, cinema, alcohol, tobacco, frills etc., and use up disposable income preferably for those things rather than for a healthy apartment in their own and their off-springs' interest' (Friedberger 1923: 43), was widespread at the time. In spite of a wartime decline in the number of Prussia's taverns and similar licensed premises by over 10,000 to 183,155 (LAB 142/1 StB 895), the incidence of alcoholism appeared to rise, according to contemporary studies. For instance, during the first half of the 1920s, the number of registered addicts increased by over 42 per cent at 20 urban alcoholism units spread throughout the Reich (Thilen 1928: 19). To take but one example: Hamburg had 2,233 registered alcoholics in 1,876 households in the mid-1920s, affecting a population of nearly 7,000 living mostly in the city's poorer and densely populated districts (Thilen 1928: 24). Statistical-based investigations carried out by the city medical board combined with modern cartography rendered them visible

Document 4.12 District Distribution of Alcoholism in Hamburg, 1922–7

[see illustration opposite]

Source: Gesundheitsbehörde Hamburg (ed.), Hygiene und Soziale Hygiene in Hamburg: Zur neuenzigsten Versammlung der Deutschen Naturforscher und Aerzte in Hamburg im Jahre 1928 *(Hamburg, 1928), 336–7.*

Underlying contemporary social and moral concerns were economic considerations: what was the cost of alcoholism to the city, and *inter alia*, to the nation? One estimate for 1928 put the total expenditure on alcohol at 4.7 billion marks (Hegemann 1930: 485). And the financial cost to the taxpayer was high, both for treatment and for the attendant mobilization of welfare resources to deal with the social fallout of abuse.

Document 4.13 Magistrat Brandenburg to Deutsche Städtetag

At the moment in Brandenburg 133 alcoholics are under observation from private associations and the welfare office. Of these 68 are supported by the welfare office. 15 of these 68 who have been supervised and supported since 1 January 1924 have been chosen arbitrarily. They have entailed the following costs:
a) financial support.
  [. . .]
  To[tal]: 9,812.79 RM
b) for treatment (Regional mental asylum Görden and Alcohol Treatment Institutes)
  39 cases together amounting to 13,111.80 RM.
Total of a and b = 22,924.59 RM in the years 1924, 1925, 1926, 1927, that means an annual average of 5,731.15 RM.
  Assuming that in the remaining 53 cases the same costs have been incurred, then the immediate financial burden through alcohol abuse in one year is around 26,000 RM. The medium-term damage through destruction of family life, illness, crime etc., cannot be easily calculated in money.

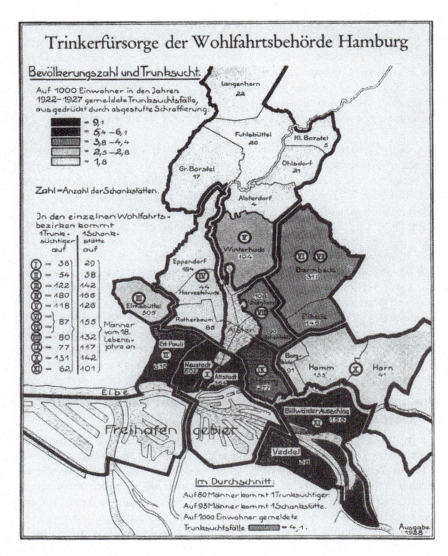

The information is based on the files of the care department of the welfare office. After checking with the relevant female care workers and officers, the calculated sums do not appear to be exaggerated.

Source: LAB 142/1 StB 602, Magistrag Brandenburg to Deutsche Städtetag (12 April 1928).

Such evidence is overwhelming. And yet there was no evidence to suggest that consumption levels were any higher in the city than in the countryside, nor that they were historically higher. Indeed, Michael Grüttner recently challenged the assumptions regarding excessive alcohol consumption, showing that apart from a slight rise in the first half of the 1920s (supporting Thilen's findings), the level declined over the interwar period to between 62 and 68 litres per head of the population in 1937/8; that is, Germans consumed less than half the pre-1914 and post-1945 levels (Grüttner 1987: 235, 267, 273; Dröge, Krämer-Badoni 1987: 161). Indeed, rather than being a symptom of the poverty associated with 'slum' conditions, Grüttner has argued that levels rose when income was both plentiful and stable (Grüttner 1987: 268).

One of the greatest worries was that alcohol abuse inevitably led to criminal behaviour. Contemporary studies purported to show that the crime rate was higher in the city than in rural areas, and that within the city, 'slums' formed the blackspots (Aschaffenburg 1903; Walther 1936: 5–6). The thesis that property crime rates rose with urbanization, and therefore signify a modernization of the urban experience (Zehr 1976: 135, 142), has been convincingly challenged. In a recent study, Eric Johnson shows that neither was there an upsurge in crime, nor were cities 'particularly' more 'crime-ridden' or violent than rural communities in the late imperial period (Johnson 1995). Interwar studies come to conclusions similar to those of Johnson.

In some respects similar to Mayne's argument concerning the 'slum' as a discursive construct, Johnson takes the crime reports of four Berlin dailies in November 1902, to demonstrate how collective experiences of city crime could be shaped by newspaper reporting. While the socialist press was more inclined to report on police cruelty and miscarriages of justice, so-called *Klassenjustiz*, conservative papers focused on property crimes and the misdemeanors of the poor.

Document 4.14 'Raid on Berlin Night Clubs. A "Detective Agency" as Dance Bar', 1922

A large number of officers from the Berlin criminal police yesterday undertook an extensive sweep through several bars in the north, west and south-west of Berlin. Firstly, the business of Lauchert at number 157 Invalidenstraße and another in the Chaussestraße, where dubious clients liked to gather, was sprung and around 60 persons were taken in vans to police headquarters in order to check their papers. Officers then made a surprise strike against two bars in the Goeben- and Steinmetzstraße, after which they paid a call on a low dive in the Kiebelstraße. Everywhere they found wanted persons who had to make an unwelcome trip to Alexanderplatz. The main action of the night-time patrol was a visit to Nr 160 Friedrichstraße. Here, an enterprising mind had established a nude dance bar which he had modestly advertised on the door as a "Detective Agency". Officers met a jolly group of revellers as they suddenly burst in at around 3 am. Landlord, waiters, musicians and clients had to attend the prosaic red house on Alexanderplatz. The bar was closed down and the rooms turned over to the housing office. A raid on a gaming club at number 62 Jerusalemstraße where around 60 persons were caught gambling, formed the finale of the evening. Cards and gaming machines were confiscated, the rooms closed and handed over to the housing office, and the players taken along in order to check their papers. The yield of the sweep was extremely bountiful: a large number of wanted persons sought by the police for some time now, were, as a result, caught.

Source: Berliner Tageblatt, *Nr 118 (9 March 1922).*

It was not only the press that reported such incidents from the city's low-life areas; the film producer Fritz Lang included such a scene in his film, M of 1931, where the police raid a criminal den, the Crocodile Bar.

Social investigation, marshalling all the new and modern techniques of rational science: statistics, anthropology, psychology and sociology, offered a benign – because ostensibly 'objective' – and therefore powerful point of entry into the private sphere of the urban 'slum'-dweller. Over time, a shift occurred from popular social reportage to a discrete language of the 'slum' hardened as 'scientific fact'.

Document 4.15 Social Science and 'Asocials'

[. . .] For these reasons, we continue the work with inquiries into asocial and feckless adults. Such elements are mostly registered as a result of their harmful behaviour to the community and on such occasions are recorded by the police authorities. We therefore transferred our workplace, in continuation of our investigations, directly to the police stations of the district. [. . .] Chief attention was paid to disputes, begging, causing a nuisance, insults, bodily harm, theft, fraud, damage to property, burglary, sexual misdemeanours, and drunkenness. At the same time the work in the police stations revealed the possibility of personal contact with long-standing duty officers in the station, who through personal experiences with reference to their own observations, could enrich our impressions of the lifestyles of the residents and the deplorable state of affairs in the region.

The extracted sections from the files and police incident books were evaluated according to revelant personal and local criteria and, as in the case of [criminal] youth, the culpable's residence and the scene of crime were also exposed cartographically on city maps, as far as they occurred within our area. Together with the youth maps, the other visual accounts of the phenomenon damaging to the community allow us to make further observations about the eventually existing centres of social sickness in the area. [. . .]

As sober as the details are, so are they graphic enough to clearly reveal to us a picture of wretchedness and of depravity, so that further comment is superfluous. No one can doubt that we have discovered here a social danger spot of the worst degree from where other parts of our area are also threatened to be likewise infected.

Source: Notarbeit 51 der Notgemeinschaft der Deutschen Wissenschaft Gemeinschädigende Regionen des Niederelbischen Stadtgebietes 1934/35 *(reprint Hamburg, 1984), 30–1, 38–9.*

This document reveals both the link between the local state (in the form of the police) and academic scholarship, and the process whereby the prejudices of the former were translated into an 'objective' science by the latter. Having identified the dangerous 'slum', respectable society demanded that it should be subjugated, or, at the very least, contained within its own geography.

Document 4.16 Policeman at Entrance to Court Dwellings, Altona-Altstadt, *c.*1932

Source: Landesarchiv Schleswig-Holstein 352/1250.

While the 'slum' was being identified and contained by the authorities, it was also being penetrated by a growing public interest in such areas and their inhabitants during the 1920s. This popular contact helped to construct an image of the 'slum' as a 'dark continent', a site of exotic 'other' and sexual lure. Although the following image is titled 'Oriental Harbour Street', by Gerhart Bettermann, a politically critical artist and sometime member of the vagabond movement in the 1920s (Künstlerhaus Bethanien 1982: 299–320), it is redolent of scenes from Hamburg's and Altona's rookeries which contemporaries often described in the above terms (Danner 1958: 264; Evans 1987: 313), and which Bettermann also studied for his artwork.

Document 4.17 'Orientalische Hafenstraße', 1932

Source: Künstlerhaus Bethanien (ed.), Wohnsitz Nirgerndswo vom Leben und vom Überleben auf der Straße *(Berlin, 1982), 314.*

Meanwhile, based on his own experiences, the English novelist Stephen Spender gave a portrayal of the neighbouring harbour streets that bespoke a wild and exotic landscape.

Document 4.18 Excitement of the Slum: St Pauli

They walked back to the Freiheit, down a side street. Signs for shops and the *Lokale* were written in Chinese. Joachim told Paul of fights between sailors free with their knives. In some streets it was dangerous to walk alone. Someone might throw a handkerchief over your face, search your clothing for valuables and leave you stripped and beaten, dying perhaps in the gutter. Bars were haunted by drug pushers. All this excited Paul greatly.

Source: Stephen Spender, The Temple *(London, 1988), 72–3.*

These seedier parts of St Pauli, straddling Altona's Nobistor, Peterstraße, and the harbour area, were notorious for their nightly low life centred around the numerous dives and brothels, already established before 1890 (Detlefs 1997). The physical concentration of the sexual economy of towns and cities had resulted partly from its regulation by the state. Paragraph 361:6 of the German Criminal Code of 1871 allowed the police to restrict the movement of prostitutes to particular districts, in a similar fashion to laws elsewhere that sought to prevent women 'roaming' the streets (Abrams 1993: 86; Zimmermann 1999: 182–5). By 1892 Berlin had over 4,000 registered prostitutes, many located around the Tauntzienstraße in the centre of the historic city; this figure rose to 7,867 in 1924, by which time prostitutes and bookshops specializing in pornography could also be found in the neighbouring Friedrichstraße. The Wittelsbacherstraße district of central Munich came to replace the Northern Cemetery area as the main centre for prostitution between 1891 and 1914 (Krafft 1996: 48–9). And in Weimar itself, the artist Bruno Voigt immortalized the red-light district centred on 'Potter's Lane' (1932). Indeed, most cities in Europe had established areas for commercial sex, usually contiguous to 'slum' neighbourhoods (Kaufmann 1928: 66; Evans 1976: 113), before 1914.

Document 4.19 Brothels and Districts, Europe, c.1911

[see table opposite]

Source: Abraham Flexner, Prostitution in Europe *(abr. edn, London, 1919), 137.*

In spite of the efforts to segregate them, 'slum' districts were closely integrated into the commercial leisure economy of the city, catering to a marauding mostly suburban population of weekend pleasureseekers (Moreck 1931: 132, 189–90, 194–5; Schär 1991: 127–35, 201ff., 220ff.). There was even a tourist literature on Europe's red-light districts by the end of the nineteenth century. Thomas Cook, for instance, included a sexual topography in some of its guides to Berlin. There was, in other words, a sexual cartography to the city (Schlör 1998: 210–17).

City	No. of houses of prostitution	How loosed	No. of inmates	No. inscribed prostitutes living not in houses of prostitution	Estimated total number of prostitutes
Paris	47	Scattered	387	6,000	50,000-60,000
Vienna	6	Scattered	50-60	1,630	30,000
Hamburg	113	On 8 scattered streets	780	155	....
Budapest	13	Scattered	260-300	2,000	....
Dresden	81	On 32 different streets	293	Few	....
Frankfort	10	Scattered	100 (about)	188	....
Cologne	98	Scattered	194	500	6,000
Geneva	17	Scattered	86	None	....
Rome	22	Scattered	125	100	Over 5,000 known to police
Brussels	6	Scattered	37	145	Over 3,000 known to police
Stuttgart	10	Scattered	22	None	....
Bremen	25	One street	75	None	....
Stockholm	30	On 6 scattered streets	98	228	....

Document 4.20 A Guide to Exciting Berlin

[see illustration on page 86]

Source: Curt Moreck (pseudonym for Konrad Haemmerling), Führer durch das Lasterhafte Berlin *(Berlin, 1931), reproduced in Bärbel Schräder and Jürgen Schebera,* The Golden Twenties: Art and literature in the Weimar Republic *(New Haven and London, 1990), 47.*

Guided by their maps and fired by their imaginations, what did these bourgeois pleasure seekers look for? Heinrich Zille, Berlin's best-known and much-loved caricaturist, who explored the capital's 'hidden back courts' at the end of the nineteenth century, 'encountered' a 'circus' in the solidly poor working-class district of Wedding.

Document 4.21 The 'Slum' as Circus

[see illustration opposite]

Source: Der Deutsche in seiner Karikatur: Hundert Jahre Selbstkritik, *ausgewählt von Friedrich Bohne, kommentiert von Thaddäus Troll, mit einem Essay von Theodor Heuss (Friedr. Bassermann'schen Verlagsbuchhandlung, Stuttgart, n.d.), 83.*

Zille's 'slum' is doubly exotic because of its association with the itinerant circus, thus setting it apart from conventional society. Through its portrayal of semi-naked females and children, it sexualized the experience of the 'wild other' (Lloyd 1991b: 282). At the same time, Zille's composition can be read as an example of what Jill Lloyd in a related context has referred to as the 'Savage within'. Thus the 'slum's' exotic 'other' reflected not the object of the gaze, but the inner being of the gazer (Lloyd 1991b: 268–9).

As in Conrad's *Heart of Darkness*, in Heinrich Mann's novel, *Professor Unrat* (1905), popularized by Josef von Sternberg's film version in 1930, the professor's journey into the heart of the 'slum' is a journey into the inner self. Thus, on arriving at the tingel tangel 'Blue Angel', inhabited by rough working men and disorderly women (Flexner 1919: 189), led by the vampish singer Lola Lola, Unrat is confronted not so much by the actual 'slum', as by his own alter ego.

Document 4.22 Discovering the 'Slum in Oneself'

[see illustrations on page 88]

Source: Josef von Sternberg, Blaue Engel *(1930), Courtesy of Stiftung Deutsche Kinemathek, Berlin*

[Document 4.22 Discovering the 'Slum in Oneself']

The *Blue Angel* suggests to its audience that prostitution occupied a fixed if somewhat ambivalent place in the daily life of the urban 'slum' (Fritzsche 1998: 8–9). Female casual prostitution affected mostly young girls and women under the age of 30 who lived in such districts. Evidence from Munich, Breslau, and Berlin before the First World War showed that the social milieu of the casual prostitute was typically that of the urban lower class, often working on the fringes of the service and leisure economies (Flexner 1919: 19, 55, 58–9, 62–72; Walser 1985: 238). However, factory workers and seamstresses were also heavily represented among casual prostitutes, denoting their economic precariousness (Buschan 1915: 78–9; Krafft 1996: 30–56). Document 4.23 provides some basic information on the backgrounds of 859 women who were registered at the care office as prostitutes in Altona's 'slum' quarters at the beginning of the 1920s.

Document 4.23 Vice Cases 1919, Altona Care Office

Number of cases handled

Unfinished cases carried from previous year	209	cases
Although already discharged the previous year, [the following] were resumed again in 1919	276	"
new registrations	859	"
	1344	cases

Information on the newly registered cases
a) transfers:
Transferred to the Care Office for attention:

1) from the vice police	598	cases
2) children and youth interviewed by the criminal police in sexual cases	24	"
3) from the information centre for venereal diseases	14	"
4) from the hospital skin diseases department	9	"
5) from the welfare department, family support	9	"
6) from prison those women not convicted of crimes of vice	5	"
7) from local welfare departments	53	"
8) from external welfare departments	70	"
9) voluntary	76	"
	859	cases

b) Police aspects:

Of the 859 woman, the following were unknown to the vice police	328	cases
warned once or more times	230	"
had been or were on the control register	301	"
	859	cases

c) Age:

They numbered according to age, 16		years	17
	16–18	"	72
	19–21	"	165
	21–24	"	155
	25–27	"	121
	28–30	"	101
	31–40	"	161
	41–50	"	23
	over 50	"	8
age not determinable			36
			859

23 of the 859 women had a higher or middle education.

d) Education, all others had attended primary, country or village schools.

e) Occupation:

The women had the following occupations:

domestic servants	262
uncertain occupation	10
waitresses	13
artistes	4
factory hands	227
sales assistance	44
craft workers	90
hawker	1
rural worker	2
other occupation	42
housewives without employment	52
girls without employment	29
without details	83
	859

f) Family status etc:

Were born out of wedlock 61 = 7.1%

were single	598
were married	69
were widowed	32
were divorced	47
were separated	96
were without details	17
	859

g) Motherhood.
Among these women were 237 mothers.

150	had	1 child
52	"	2 children
20	"	3 children
9	"	4 children
3	"	5 children
2	"	6 children
1	"	7 children
237		

[. . .]

Source: STAH 424–24 37, Pflegeamt Altona, Appendix to 'Dienstanweisung für das Pflegeamt Altona' (1919).

The number of registered women tripled at the beginning of the 1930s, while the social configuration remained largely unchanged over the interwar period. The fact that cases of casual prostitution rose so drastically in the Depression was recognized at the time as further evidence of the forced 'immoral economy' of the 'slum' (Kaufmann 1928: 64–5).

The following report, in spite of its slant, opens up a complex and rich social history of the culture of commodified sexual activity in the city. Taverns and low-class revue bars were common sites for casual prostitution where it was difficult to distinguish this from the regular activities of the establishment, at least to the outsider (Flexner 1919: 23, 29; Kelly 1987: 252–68). The *Sittenpolizei* (morals police), established in many large cities by the end of the nineteenth century (Flexner 1919: 116), had the task of making this distinction. The officers of this department were few in number, and their reports suggest that they had to demonstrate their general usefulness in the fight for public and national standards. The reports also mirror their mental horizons, revealing a clash of cultures: between that of the 'slum' as 'easy street' and the productive nation.

Document 4.24 Criminal Police Report on Sexual Low Life in Dresden, 1940

The criminal police has known for years – partly through information from the public, partly through their own investigations – that in the wine bars with female service the most immoral conditions prevail and that such bars are places of indecency, as well as sources of infection and the spread of venereal diseases. These bars are for the most part only there for lewd and sexually abnormally oriented men, who act out their lusts in these places. They are only to be regarded as disguised brothels. The conditions described are not only permitted by the proprietors of the bars in their pursuit of profit, but actually promoted in the most unscrupulous manner. They perpetrate aggravated procuring, procuring, hostessing, gluttony, fleecing. They carry out procuring as second nature and for profit, in that through their mediation or through permission and by creating the opportunity they encourage sexual offences. Success on the part of the criminal police has been prevented because the surveillance initiated over many years has come to nothing mainly because of the question of cost, since without a large expenditure in the bars, the arrest of waitresses for prostitution and that of the landlords for procuring was not possible.

The landlords of these licensed premises often lead a life of luxury: they don't work at all, but go hunting and visit bathing resorts.

The waitresses don't follow a productive trade, but instead want to earn money the easy way. Any means is okay by them in order to achieve this goal. Morally, they are to be described as utterly dissolute as a result of their constant relations with lewd men. They are to be seen as veritable prostitutes, mostly between the ages of 20 and 40, and even older. They dress themselves elegantly and are apparitions well-known to us with painted fingernails, made-up faces and bleached hair. [. . .]

The criminal police investigations into the wine bars in question have taken the form of a special action since the beginning of June this year. To date 48 such premises in which sexual offenses by waitresses and procuring by landlords could be proven beyond doubt, have been closed (of which 14 are again open).

58 landlords were charged with procuring.

[. . .]

Up to the present day, 8 landlords have been handed down sentences of up to 3 months imprisonment for procuring. [. . .]

59 waitresses have received fines or prison sentences for hostessing and prostitution in bars.

51 waitresses were committed to the local health authority for examination.

[. . .]

Now a description of the wine bars:

These were scattered throughout all districts, but were concentrated mainly in the inner city. They were mostly very elegantly and very intimately furnished;

a large number however also found themselves in humanly undignified conditions. These must be described as a cultural disgrace. The physical arrangements comprised mostly a main room with one or more separate rooms, whose visual impenetrability was encouraged by the construction of niches or the presence of thick hangings.

Only a small percentage of the Dresden wine bars with female service can be described as respectable. Against these, which have absolutely no [female staff], or at least respectable staff, there can be no complaint. However, those places where, with certainty, there is obviously a questionable female waitress or several – in a few not so large bars up to five waitresses were kept at the same time – were present in order to entice customers, increase turnover, and to carry out sexual favours, must be ruthlessly dealt with in the light of the experiences to date. Such bars do not have even the slightest entitlement to exist in our present-day state.

[. . .]

I myself and those officers I deployed were able to ascertain that when we came into such a bar, each waitress first attempted to sell us not just a glass of wine but one bottle – and as often as possible the most expensive – if we responded to the waitress's suggestions, then we were almost without exception soon led to a separate room. The waitress brought herself a glass so as to drink along, sat herself next to us, in many instances the landlady came too – uninvited and also drank with us. If drinking continued, then the landlady disappeared with the intention of leaving us alone with the waitress – and did not show herself again. The waitress now attempted through all sorts of artful tricks (lifting her skirts, embracing the customers, tongue kisses in the ear, revealing her breasts, fondling private parts, at first through the material etc.) to whip up the carnal passion of the customer. Naturally the waitress took this opportunity to get the client to order more drinks and other extras. If she noticed that the customer was sufficiently aroused and wanted to have sex with her, then the suggestion was made to drink yet another bottle of wine and if it then came to sex, then invariably the waitress demanded further sums of money depending on the sort of sexual act required. The waitresses call this extra payment "stocking money" and very often, in the style of prostitutes, allow this to be inserted into their stockings. As tribute the waitresses also demanded, apart from money, boxes of chocolates, cakes, meat ration stamps, or such commodities and garments which in wartime are now impossible to obtain without a ration card.

It has been discovered that characters with a weak disposition waste huge sums of money in such establishments. Some drinkers after falling into the hands of these vampires have left behind their entire household budget or rent.

The clients come from all sections of the population. In the alcohol-free bars and cafés, they are low-income people: workers, clerks and self-employed tradesmen; whereas the bars where real wine is served are frequented by financially better-off men. There have been occasions when on our arrival the landlord has boasted that senior party officials and army officers frequent their premises. They wanted to give us to understand that we were acting against them without justification. Their bar was prim and proper as far as morals were concerned, otherwise such men would not visit them. Nethertheless, investigations showed the exact opposite.[. . .]

Source: STAM Pol.Dir. München 7953, Polizeirat Wahlrab, 'Bekämpfung der Kuppelei und Gewerbeunzucht in Weinstuben mit weiblicher Bedienung (Dresden, c. Dec. 1940), 1–5.

Wahlrab's report, extending to 13 typed pages, must also be viewed in the context of the war. By the end of 1940, Germany needed all the resources it could muster. According to Wahlrab, the 'slum' dweller was a succubus on the community, a member of an immoral fifth column subverting the mobilization of manpower and sapping its strength (Paul 1994: 15; Schlör 1998: 208–10). It had to be met with the 'most stringent' policing, especially, paradoxically, since Germany's conquest of Europe added to the 'slum' question.

Document 4.25 The 'Other' and Order in Frankfurt am Main

I spoke with Party comrade and Magistrat member Dr Prestel about the trouble that accompanies the presence of the many foreigners in our city. Today, one can no longer speak of a proper surveillance. Dr Prestel reported a case to me, which had taken place in the tavern Maiergustel, in the Kaiserstraße. In this bar a short while ago, some 50 French females resisted being checked by two officials from the welfare office and took on a threatening manner. The officials had to adopt force in order to assert themselves and were almost powerless since other foreigners present took sides with these females. Whoever goes vigilantly about the city can see the antics of foreigners, especially on Sundays in the Kaiserstraße and in the area of the main railway station, which beggars description. In these areas German words are hardly heard any more, since those foreigners employed by the Heddernheimer copper works mostly hang around in Niederrursel where popular entertainments are on offer.

In order to control to some degree this constant swamping by foreigners, I suggest designating taverns which will be exclusively for foreigners and individually naming bars where they will be strictly forbidden entry. Thus a cleaner division will be achieved, so that Germans can be once more among themselves in the bars of the city.

It would be interesting to learn from other cities by means of a questionnaire how their administrations have dealt with the problem of foreigners.

Dr Prestel further reported to me on his efforts in regard to overseeing youth. Here, also, was an increasing deterioration in respect of morals to be reported. A comprehensive supervision is sadly not possible since the manpower for this is not available. The rise in venereal diseases, which is closely linked to the foreigner problem, presents the health department with big problems. The city administration cannot manage in the long run without deploying the most stringent police provisions.

Source: HStAW 483/1652, Der Kreisleiter, Kreisamt für Kommunalpolitik 12/Ko/wa, An das Gauamt für Kommunalpolitik Frankfurt/Main, (22.9.1943, Betr. Monatsbericht für September 1943).

According to the German social historian Lutz Niethammer, writing at the beginning of the 1980s, to counter the threat of the 'slum', bourgeois society embraced welfare policy as a paradigm of social control, a *force douce* as opposed to a *force majeure* (Lüdtke 1982: 348–55).

Document 4.26 On the Making of a New Paradigm of Social Control

The physical threat of the underworld could no longer be ignored as a state of nature on the margins of civilization. On the contrary, it had become part of a growing, instead of a fading, feature of urban culture. Similarly, as in their relations with the indigenous savages of other continents, the middle class answered the challenge of the intramural savagery with a combination of repression and acculturation, often translated into medical terms.

[. . .]

Bourgeois social reform – especially the debate on sociospatial strategies – was an international movement with a constant exchange of experiences, through books, articles, and visits, and even special organizations. [. . .] This exchange was no one-way import into backward countries, but worked in all directions, often legitimizing its position by pointing to an allegedly successful example abroad, exploiting national rivalries in the interest of social reform. The explanation for this phenomenon is to be found in the position of the reformers themselves within their own environment, where they were usually excluded from the ruling class and wealthy establishment, though some of them became quite prominent. Against dominant class interests they were voices in the wilderness, suggesting strategies against social dangers, often personally experienced; a comfortable middle class tended to ignore them as interference with their short-term interests, and only became alarmed by intermittent waves of epidemics and revolutionary upheavals. On the other hand, the reformers certainly did not share the working class's leftist sympathies, which they most often characterized as symptoms of a sick social body.

Their cure for economic class struggle was to introduce a new paradigm of environmental and structural control, stressing the national, spatial, and educational conditions of reproduction instead of the relations to the means of production, social biology as an essential supplement to political economy, social micro-organization instead of political decision or the formation of organizations, and they tried to legitimize their position by technical expertise and empirical research.

Source: Lutz Niethammer, 'Some elements of the housing reform debate in nineteenth century Europe: Or, on the making of a new paradigm of social control', in Bruce Stave (ed.), Modern Industrial Cities: History, Policy and Survival *(Beverley Hills and London, 1981), 137, 150.*

Intervention, however, was more than simply a question of a crudely deployed 'social control'. By the 1940s, the 'slum' had completed its long evolution into the Janus face of urban modernity: it was economically unproductive; raw, disorderly and insolent in its manners; excessive and unbounded in its morals; an alien 'other' residing paradoxically within and outside German *Kultur*, a threat to the social body (Brandt 1931: 76–7). It was thus urban modernity's own 'other'. By identifying it and representing it, the discourse on the 'slum' warned citizens of the dangers they faced when encountering it: the 'slum' not only beguiles Heinrich Mann's Professor Unrat, it destroys him. Thus strategies for its containment and control were in fact surrogates for curbing the 'slum' within oneself.

Rehabilitating the urban body | **5**

The modern German city (or, at least, certain parts of it) at the end of the nineteenth century was not only deemed a threatening place to the social and political order, it was also considered unhealthy for the body. This was a view amply verified for German-speaking Europe by the numerous contemporary statistical and social investigations into urban living conditions that often focused on overcrowding, the inadequate water and sewerage systems, and lack of private sanitary provision (Philippovich 1894: 215–77; Cahn 1902: 460; Röse 1905: 257–61). This picture of the unhealthy city had been lent great force by the outbreak of cholera in the Reich's second largest city, Hamburg, in 1892 (Evans 1987). Moreover, many towns and cities had to grapple with intermittent epidemics of typhus and diphtheria that continued to plague them since mid-century (Spree 1981: 36ff.). The latter resurfaced during and at the end of the First World War, when, together with the impact of the influenza epidemic that gripped the country in 1919, it caused death rates, particularly in the cities, to soar (LAB 142/2, StK 45; Howard 1993).

The outbreak of an epidemic was a dramatic moment when the city appeared to consume its inhabitants. Terrible as these epidemics were, they could be dealt with by the authorities taking extraordinary action. But modern urban life also harboured a potential threat to health that required vigilance on a more daily and mundane level. Ten years before Hamburg's cholera epidemic, the Berlin doctor, Robert Koch, had discovered the TB bacillus, inaugurating a turning point in the medical approach to health and hygiene (Spree 1981: 107; Labisch 1991: 39). Ever since, bacteriology dominated medical and popular theory and this showed how cities were the breeding ground for the spread of diseases.

Document 5.1 The Number of Bacteria in the City's Air

[see illustration on page 98]

The consequences of ill-health went beyond the afflicted individual and any family that person might have. In a contribution to the first German city congress in 1903, Dresden's public health officer, Dr Nowack, provided a graphic financial diagnosis of the impact of poor health upon the local community and the nation at large.

Source: Fritz Kahn, Das Leben des Menschen: Eine volkstümliche Anatomie, Biologie, Physiologie und Entwicklungsgeschichte des Menschen, *Band III (Stuttgart, 1926), 71.*

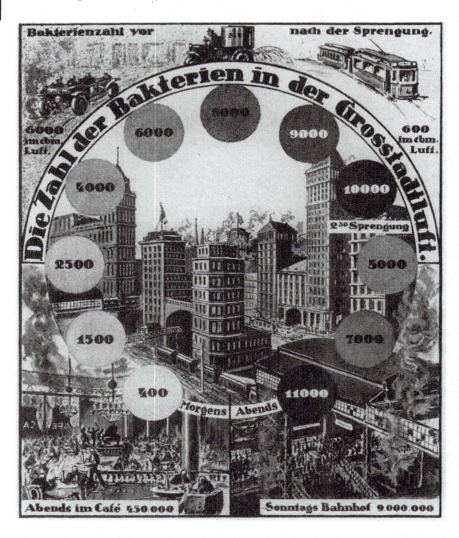

The caption reads: 'The number of bacteria in the city's air. The numerical spheres show the number of bacteria in air cubic metres for the individual hours of the day. One recognizes the utmost importance of street sprinkling for the removal of dust and disinfecting of the air and the dangers to health of all concentrations of people.'

Document 5.2 The Cost of Poor Health to the City of Dresden

The city of Dresden had a population of 400,000 in 1902. According to statistics carefully compiled by regional health insurances, there are 40 to

43 cases of ill-health per death, with 20–22 days off sick. Through illness of its population, Dresden therefore loses up to 12 million marks annually, and because roughly half of the sick are of working age, it loses nearly 6 million marks in wages, both forming a total of nearly 18 million marks.

Equally considerable sums of money are lost with the deceased. Approximately half of them, according to death statistics, are older than 14 years. The 7,000 dead therefore represent a capital value of at least 13 million marks, according to previous deductions. Roughly about a third of these losses have to be considered as avoidable. The natural maximum age for human beings is between 70 and 75 years. If this were reached by all, 13 people per 1,000 would die annually. In reality, however, the death rate is 19 to 20 per thousand. The excess of six per thousand causes a capital loss of approximatly four million marks. In addition, there are considerable sums which arise from looking after the sick and burying the dead, falling to their relatives as well as the public.

In total, therefore, Dresden loses about 22 million marks through ill-health and untimely death, that means the interest of a capital sum of roughly 700 million marks. For Berlin, the equivalent sum would come to more than 100 million marks, for Germany more than 2 billion marks.

Source: Prof. Dr Nowack, 'Die öffentliche Gesundheitspflege', in Robert Wuttke (ed.), Die Deutschen Städte: geschildert nach den Ergebnissen der ersten deutschen Städteausstellung zu Dresden 1903 *(Leipzig, 1904), 452–3.*

As Franz Oppenheimer had found on his medical rounds of Berlin's Eichendorffstraße at the turn of the century, confirmed by Friedberger's study of Greifswald two decades later, and brought to popular attention by Eugene Diesel in his account of poverty published at the beginning of the Depression, poor housing bred poor health; and the bourgeois nightmare was that the sick and contaminated population inevitably passed on its illness to the healthy population (Evans 1987: 116–20; 416–31).

The most common contaminative disease in towns and cities was bacterial tuberculosis, where it was also the single greatest killer. For example, in 1905, there were 45,344 deaths from tuberculosis in towns with populations over 15,000. Even though TB was rife in the countryside, it became synonymous with urban conditions. Official data, however, showed that there was a steady decrease in the incidence of deaths from tuberculosis during the first half of the 1920s, falling from 71,132 cases in 1921 to 55,819 cases in 1925. On a European level where a rate of 20 per 1,000 was considered benign (Kearns 1989: 100–1), the condition in Germany's cities was relatively healthy. Even so, this disease was still pervasive among the urban population during the interwar years and was frequently referred to as 'the national malaise' (*Volkskrankheit*). According to Fritz Kahn, around 1 million persons were permanently ill with TB in the 1920s; and half of those who died in Germany between the ages of 15 and 30 years, were victims of tuberculosis (Kahn 1926: 72, 77–8; Spree 1981: 43). In order to combat the dangers of the disease, a public hygiene campaign was required.

Rehabilitating the urban body

Document 5.3 How Can One Prevent Tuberculosis?

*Captions read: i) Light and air; ii) Outdoor nature; iii) Body culture (exercise);
iv) Toughening; v) Open-air schools; vi) Settlements*

Source: Fritz Kahn, Das Leben des Menschen: Eine volkstümliche
Anatomie, Biologie, Physiologie und Entwicklungsgeschichte des
Menschen, *Band III (Stuttgart, 1926), 79.*

The set of images is instructive, as too is that in document 5.1 (in the latter case, not
least as well for its 'Chicago'-style skyline). Above all, the idea of the 'unhealthy city'
in contrast to the 'healthy countryside' is reinforced. The positive images displayed in
the above document showing how one can avoid contracting TB are offset in Kahn's
book by a preceding sequence of negative images mostly relating to living in the city
(Kahn 1926: 78). Yet statistical evidence showed a marked improvement in the health
of urban populations by the time Kahn published his popular work in the mid-1920s
(SJDR 46 1927: 43; SJDR 57 1938: 43). The decades between the 1880s and 1940
saw a halving of the death rate and an increase in life expectancy for most Germans
(Tietze 1930: 206; Hubbard 1983: 116–18). And this was largely an urban phenomenon (Spree 1981: 46, 117–19, 121, 186–9).

As a member of an influential body of doctors and social hygienists who had
acquired a powerful status in the struggle against 'dirt' since the late nineteenth century
(Spree 1981: 108ff., 122), Kahn had a natural interest in reinforcing such imagery as

part of the popular enlightenment and medical education of city dwellers, considered ignorant as well as unhealthy.

Document 5.4 Combating the Nation's Ill-health

The ideal state reached by education in social hygiene can be imagined as such:

1. Each person must acquire and nurture a clear idea about the value of health.

2. Each person must know the internal system and functions of his body, so that he is able:

a) to identify every fault in this organism or in its functioning even without experiencing pain. (Naturally he should not have to be in a position to diagnose an illness; for that one has a doctor!),

b) to know which influences on the organism he has to ward off in order to avoid malfuntions,

c) to know the influences which are able to enhance the quality and resilience of his body.

3. Each person must acquire a sense of the value of public health more generally. He must learn:

a) what damages the general condition of health of a community (infectious diseases, poor water and air quality etc.), and

b) what can benefit it.

4. Each person must develop total confidence in the science recognized by the state and has to come to the conviction that generally (errors excepted – doctors are human!) only this offers a guarantee to heal sickness.

Before we can reach this ideal state, some time will pass, albeit not as much as one might assume given the apparent great expansion of the task.

Source: K.A. Lingner, 'Einige Leitgedanken zu der Sonderausstellung: Volkskrankheiten und ihre Bekämpfung', in Robert Wuttke (ed.), Die Deutschen Städte: geschildert nach den Ergebnissen der ersten deutschen Städteausstellung zu Dresden 1903 *(Leipzig, 1904), 536–7.*

As we can see, social hygienists such as Lingner and Kahn also endeavoured to show that the environment alone was not to blame for ill-health, and that deficiencies could not be overcome solely by public intervention. By also pointing out that ill-health and disease was often the consequence of a poor or errant life-style, they highlighted the daily responsibility of the individual in the public campaign to improve health and hygiene in the city. In order to reach as wide an audience as possible, city medical officers produced popular pamphlets for the purpose of inculcating good health habits among their residents.

Document 5.5 'How Do I Manage My Daily Routine?'

The captions read:

How do I manage my daily routine?
I rise promptly in the morning,
From my bed of gentle peace
Into my slippers tout suite.
Then spread and stretch my limbs
And so slowly come into being.
My muscles, which are sleepy still,
are methodically drilled.

I force them according to my will,
So that their aim they fulfil.
Begin gently, with little things:
the body forwards, backwards tilt.
Hips still, knees slowly acquiesce,
best naked without a witness!

Then off to wash!

Wash yourself cold!
Warm water makes you flabby and old.
For when the skin is still so limp,
Cold water makes it firm and mint,
for beset by cold stimulation
The muscles are soon awakened.
But water alone cannot suffice!
The skin also needs to be soaped.
So, as portrayed in the sketch, I rub a piece
soft and mild.

Most of the dirt, however,
does not leave by soap and wet,
for it dwells deep in your pores
where all day long one sweats.
How can I ferret the dirt there?
Only with a flannel scrub!
Tightly gripping this I knead
and rub without peace or rest,
thus is the last dirt removed
just like Easter spring cleaning
                    in the home.
So the skin is rubbed down
and thus my toilet is concluded.

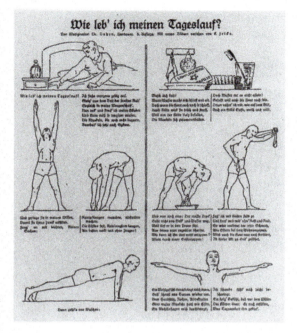

A comfortable feeling spreads through me then,
and I quickly start gymnastics again.
My muscles are hard as iron
from press-ups, roll-ups, and arm turns.
A mood of ease pervades in me;
I poise and feel myself aroused.
A proud feeling, but one that only the volition
of the body serves. It must oblige
what the day's work ordains.

Once I have taken good care of my skin
and my muscles are fully drilled,
so must I clean my teeth
and also groom my hair.
Cleaning teeth must so take place
that we constantly rotate the quill;
so bristles enter into the space
where dregs of food dwell
and through bacteria and ferment
sadly too often putrefy the gums
above all in the night.
So heed my remark:
of greatest good for your teeth
is brushing before dark!

And with only a few buttons unfastened,
quick: slip into your shirt!
Into a shirt with its collar soft and clean,
and whenever possible, sport it open-necked!
The air plays around the throat and chest,
for life is breath.

Avoid all clothing which compels
to constrain the chest, body, feet,
mars the anatomy's slender physique,
and offends our sense of elegance!
With girdles, pointed shoes and their kin
never can you beauty win.

A beautiful shape you only gain
through caring for your muscles;
they lend you grace, shapely lines,
they make you slim like a pen.
The standards of beauty one only finds
in the laws of nature.
Disdain everything counterfeit!

And without neglect
maintain your body and your spirit!

Like a fish in fresh water,
am I. At the breakfast bar
I fortify with blissful zeal
and now nourish my empty tum with a meal.
Allow yourself time in the morn! Avoid haste
when you embrace your day's chores!
With firm plan and calm mind
retire after the day's work!
Already in the evening is laid out prepared,
what one will wear to work on the morrow.
Work tool, files, books, and pen,
each is constantly kept in order
so that even a stranger in the dark
can seize it with a single grasp.

Down your breakfast! Fare you well!
Thus you can go cheerily to work.
View it not as a burden!
The occupation that you have chosen
is the source of your vitality
which blesses you and others.
And creates from this with happy will
the realisation of true happiness.
And when you have completed your task
behold it again to examine
if it is in every way deserved
and does honour to your name!
Then depart for home content and gay
to rest yourself from the toiling day!

And after you have rested in the 'noon,
buoy'd your heart, cleans'd your sap,
wipe away the last trace of workaday
in God's splendid lap!
At play and sport in glorious nature
you'll soon restore your vigour.

Take the saying as a rule:
healthy body, healthy mind!
And punctually make the finish right
Thank your Lord – and say
GOOD NIGHT!

Source: Medical Counsellor, Dr Dohrn, Hannover, n.d. in Adelheid von Saldern ed., Hannover: Stadt und Moderne *(Hamburg, 1989), 148–9.*

In spite of a recent energetic critique (Hennock 1998: 58–74), the view among a younger generation of social historians that such texts contributed to a 'medicalization' of the urban population, thus signalling a shift in the techniques of social control, still holds sway (Labisch 1985: 602ff., 612; Frevert 1985; Steinmetz 1993). Drawing on theories of modernity developed by the German philosophers Norbert Elias and Jürgen Habermas, and, notably, by Michel Foucault in France, these historians argue that the implementation of a programme of health and hygiene constituted what Reinhard Spree calls a 'hidden curriculum' designed to 'civilize' and 'discipline' the urban mass (Spree 1981: 159) by means of an 'inner colonization', as the individual internalized externally defined norms of behaviour (Peukert 1986: 305–17).

This process also reflected the concerns of particular interest groups – and government at all levels – with an interest in developing what Foucault memorably referred to as the panoply of 'modern technologies of power that have life as their objective', and through which the authority of the medical profession and government was both legitimated and confirmed (Foucault 1979: 152; Spree 1981: 138ff.; 160; Frevert 1985: 651–2; Rodriguez-Lores 1991: 63–75). Among the chief protagonists in this process were the new breed of urban medical officers who embodied both the profession and the state, and who had the task of delivering public health policy at the local level, from street cleansing to immunization of children (Sachße and Tennstedt 1988: 15–38; Ritter 1986: 17–130; Weingart et al. 1988: 116). Their work placed them in the vanguard of the nation's carers.

Document 5.6 The Purpose of Local Public Health Care

However often each individual has experienced for himself and through others, what a great, inestimable possession is [one's] health and however simple and evident it therefore should seem that everyone looks after and safeguards one's health – the worries of everyday life and the indolence of the population keep us far from reaching our goal. Again and again the importance of public health care must therefore be emphasized, the implementation of necessary steps has to be called for and its immediate benefit has to be explained. Firstly for the individual, then also for the family, the community and the state.

As these groups are made up of individual human beings, so too from the sum of individual welfare develops one, all-encompassing health care.

Of course it will not be possible immediately to transform weak into strong, poorly disposed into well-endorsed, or frail into healthy individuals. But as much as neglect and ill-health, deficient diet and constant over stimulation can lead the strongest to degenerate and wither; so, on the other hand, planned exercise of and looking after of one's strengths, sensible toughening up, suitable diet and careful protection from ill-health, are able to strengthen a weak constitution, to improve a deficient one, to waken a torpid one, and finally to cultivate in children and grandchildren a strong, resilient race.

Source: Prof. Dr Nowack, 'Die öffentliche Gesundheitspflege', 446.

There was, nevertheless, a limit to the extent to which a concerted and totalizing health and hygiene policy could make its influence felt. This was due not just to the lack of political authority, but also to the absence of an effective administrative infrastructure to implement Spree's 'hidden curriculum', especially before 1914.

Both only came about after the founding of the Weimar Republic in 1918. At the end of the First World War the urban mortality rate had risen sharply, affecting especially infants and the elderly. There was also widespread fear of a collapse in the moral and psychological condition of city dwellers, in particular, among youth (Richter 1919: 17–18, 24–6; Cimbal 1922: 37–42). The conditions at the time thus necessitated the creation of a welfare infrastructure and the new republic lent it political authority (Miller Lane 1986: 295; Ambrosius and Hubbard 1989: 116–26). After 1918, health and welfare offices were established throughout Germany, pioneered by the larger cities and towns.

Document 5.7 Urban Welfare Offices

Questionnaires were sent to 530 towns with over 10,000 inhabitants, of which the majority were completed and returned in spite of the difficult times, even from the Rhineland. It appeared, however, necessary for the description of the typical situation to limit the research for this study initially to the large cities. Of 84 cities with a population over 50,000, 68 completed questionnaires, that is 79 per cent, could be analysed. [. . .]

[. . .] one particular question was asked first: Does a welfare office exist there? Does a youth office exist there?

These questions, but even more, the answers, show us how much we are involved in an organisational restructuring which has partly been already completed. Of the 68 cities, 57 have have welfare offices; of 52 cities, 20 have independent youth offices, and 32 have ones affiliated to the welfare office. With these changes, great social policy progress has been made. The river of war welfare hollowed itself a broad bed and swept away many legal constraints; the postwar period has widened the bed. [. . .]

Source: LAB 142/1 StB 3774: Marguerite Wolf, 'Entwicklungstendenzen in der kommunalen Frauenarbeit', offprint from Die Frau *(August 1923), 1–2.*

Marguerite Wolf wrote this article nearly four years after the first welfare offices had been established. In spite of her optimistic tone, the document reveals the sluggish and uneven pace of progress, largely due to the political and financial situation of the Republic. But there were other factors too which hindered not just the creation of an administrative infrastructure, but also the impact of policy. The social and cultural practices of a large part of the population for whom welfare was intended, also placed limitations on the extent to which the state could deliver its 'hidden curriculum' by the end of the 1920s (Peukert 1986: 313). Nevertheless, the project as such was never abandoned. Indeed, during the Third Reich every effort was expended to show just how completely embedded the ordinary citizen was within the pedagogical framework of the welfare state (Doc. 5.26).

The development of a welfare state after the First World War has been viewed as part of a long-term process of modernization of German society, leading to its more rational organization (Habermas 1987, 2: 522ff.). During the republican era, the municipal share of expenditure on welfare (excluding housing) was greater than that of either the Reich or the *Länder*, denoting the importance of urban social policy (Terhalle 1930: 569–70). Welfare in the city, therefore, formed a constitutive moment in the development of urban modernity. But in the aftermath of war, it was seen by those involved more as an attempt to establish a 'social contract' aimed at integrating social outsiders, and implicit in the 'fresh start' heralded by the republic (Peukert 1991: 130–40). One of the key elements in this contract was housing provision.

Document 5.8 Elisabeth Lüders, 'Why Germany Is Building'

Germany is building all these new apartments because otherwise innumerable Germans would be doomed to live in crowded, tumble-down old buildings, unfit hygienically and morally for human beings. Germany is building because there are a million German families without homes of their own. Germany is building because there are still thousands who are living in stalls, in leaky mansard apartments, in cold, dark cellars, in thin wooden shacks or old railroad cars. Germany is building because the people who are living in these crowded and insanitary hovels are deteriorating both mentally and morally; because their children must go to rack and ruin, not only physically but every other way; because such miserable living quarters are the breeding-ground for embittered revolutionaries and enemies of the state who are daily in danger of coming into conflict with the laws of the land and of wreaking their vengeance on society. Germany is building because its rehabilitation primarily requires a large and healthy population, able and willing to work, for only a vigorous people can undertake to shoulder successfully the heavy burdens of the war and to heal its many wounds. Only a people with sufficient room to live and breathe can be ready and able to participate energetically in the work of international enlightenment and cooperation. For its own sake and that of the world, Germany is trying to provide homes for its people and to give them a feeling of reassurance and strength which comes from possessing homes of their own, where the finer things of this life are not forgotten and from which they can draw the moral force for peaceful work in union with their brothers in other lands.

Source: Marie-Elisabeth Lüders, 'Why, and How, Is Germany Building? The Motives and Methods of Germany's Extensive Building Program', in Passing Through Germany *(Berlin, 1930), 92–8.*

Before 1914, more than 80 per cent of Germany's housing had been constructed privately, or through housing cooperatives, while only about 10 per cent had been public supported, roughly the same share as in Britain (vom Bruch 1985: 61–179; Ladd 1990; Honhart 1990; Daunton 1987). The balance was almost completely reversed in the 1920s. This was partly as a result of the economic difficulties which beset private construction, but mainly because housing was seen as a principal component of social engineering (Sachße and Tennstedt 1988: 138–42; von Saldern 1995: 153ff.). Departing from the massed tenement blocks of the nineteenth century, the geometric and symmetrical layout of the new housing estates, and, especially, the rationalized and minimalist internal arrangements of the dwellings themselves, provided the outer form, or shell, for a new urban type: civilized, disciplined, healthy, functional, rational, productive, who had been emancipated through social hygiene from his old urban self: primitive, degenerate, unhealthy, dysfunctional, impulsive, unproductive (von Saldern 1988: 206–11; *idem* 1990b; 55; Flemming *et al.* 1988: 115–20; Peukert 1991: 183–4). Thus the rebuilt city, hitherto a site of crisis, was to be transformed into a laboratory for a new republican citizen (Tafuri 1990: 208–9; Bullock 1978: 338; Crew 1998: 25–31; Mougenot 1988), who in some ways harked back to the classical ideal of ancient Athens.

Document 5.9 New Architecture and New Man

[see illustration on page 110]

Source: Molnar Farkas, 'Raumstudie Mensch-Architektur', Courtesy of Bauhaus-Archiv, Berlin.

The new housing of the interwar years signalled the triumph of technology over nature (Leinert 1925: 199; Schulze-Gävernitz 1930: 231–2). The discourse on social hygiene in the city was thus extended by a technological vocabulary. This was not only a reflection of the managerialist response to the phenomenon of 'the city as sick organism', but was also a constitutive element of the imagined modern urban experience we noted in Chapter 3. Thus the representation of 'urban modernity' in the 1920s was of a technological utopia, a continual technical process of renewal (Lavin 1992: 39, 44, 51).

In this technological vision the city was rehabilitated as a fully productive and integrated organism. In the view of Berlin's chief planner, Martin Wagner, the healthy city would be a smooth mechanism (Tafuri 1990: 200–2, 346), serviced and safeguarded by the new rational(ized) 'machine worker', himself indistinguishable from the technology (Schulze-Gävernitz 1930: 235–6, 244, 247).

Document 5.10 John Heartfield, 'Rationalization'

[see illustration on page 111]

Source: John Heartfield, 'Arbeitszeichnungen und Gedichte aus den Betrieben: Die Rationalisierung marschiert!', Knüppel Nr 2 (Berlin, 1927), 5.
Photograph: Bernd Kühnert, Courtesy Stiftung Archiv der Akademie der Künste, Berlin.

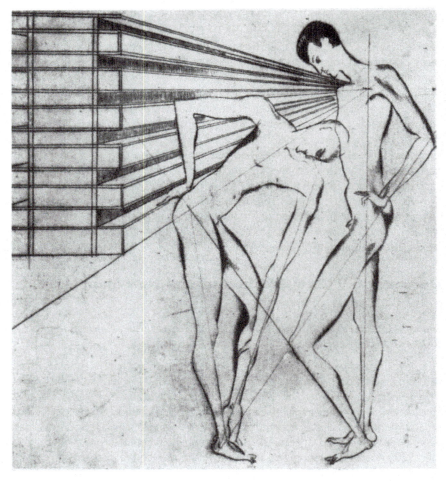

[Document 5.9 New Architecture and New Man]

The rationalization movement of the interwar years was certainly determined by financial considerations of a capitalistic nature as depicted by Heartfield (Brady 1933; Maier 1970; Campbell 1989: 131–2), but it was also in tune with a socially broader and culturally deeper 'spirit of the age', in the words of the Research Institute for Social Sciences in Cologne, that had been in evidence since the turn of the century (Böttcher 1911: 84; Hermann 1990: 313).

Document 5.11 City of Cologne: Rationalization

The city-dweller is not satisfied – as once upon a time – to go for a drink of beer or a glass of brandy on a Saturday evening, or to the cinema, mass sports

[Document 5.10 John Heartfield, 'Rationalization']

events, bathing lidos and parks and the many other things that must serve for entertainment and relaxation. The increase in these life expectations has not merely gripped a small section of the population, but its entirety. The mass of the people confront the leaders of economic and public life with continuously rising demands. The compulsion to squeeze out of every type of activity the most and the best is carried on by all sides. In addition to this, a person's inner attitude is frequently oriented to the functional and plain. The modern person rejects romanticism in word and organization. [. . .] Everything gratuitous is avoided, the functional is emphasized.

2 The representatives of Rationalisation
So it will not surprise us that we are seeing in all areas of human endeavour the shadow of rationalization. That industry and trade have rationalized, does not need to be especially emphasized. It is, however, also [. . .] with the individual household that rationalization must begin. [. . .]

Source: Landesarchiv Berlin 142/I StB 1792/I, Forschungsinstitut für Sozialwissenschaften der Stadt Köln to DST (Mulert), 9 July 1929.

Combining the twin paradigms of biology and technology in an 'ideology of labour' (Prinz 1990: 10–11, 29), the functional modern home was conceived as a machine which would regenerate the family as social capital (Miller Lane 1986: 292–3; Nolan 1990: 549–77; *idem* 1994b: 206–26). Thus the architects of modernity also anticipated that the 'new man' should have a suitable female partner with whom to share his new home, whose presence provided the 'sentimental homestead' as a complement to the sphere of rational(ized) production, what one historian has called, 'functionalism with feeling' (Hilpert 1978: 74–5).

Document 5.12 New Couple and Home

[see illustration opposite]

Source: Molnar Farkas 'Untitled' ('Couple in Front of the Horn House') 1923, Courtesy of Bauhaus-Archiv, Berlin.

Her biological condition would thus soften the hard edges of her own rationalized and functional form (Doc. 5.25), enabling her as wife and mother to nurture her family, while at the same time cultivating the new republican household.

Document 5.13 The Exhibition: Woman, *c.*1931

The Productive Woman
Woman and Reproduction
Woman as Mother
The Household
What must the woman know about food?
Clothing
Woman and body care
Women's Associations
Woman and child in art
Events and lectures

Preface [. . .] The woman as preserver of life constitutes the bridge from the old to the new Being [*Werden*]. An exhibition of 'The Woman' will have to consider especially this biological foundation in the extent of its coverage. Precisely in a period of a falling birth rate it is pertinent to cast the right light on the sanctity of marriage and the greatest value on the female organism – indeed on the development of humankind [*Menschenwerdung*]. [As to the] activity of the housewife [. . .] it is right to answer the question: How does the housewife transform the apartment into a healthy home for the family with the minimal expenditure of labour, time and money?

Source: Landesarchiv Berlin 142/I StB 2337.

This planned exhibition was itself a popular means to educate women in the social (re)production of citizenship, and as such, it indicates how widely cast the discourse had become within a decade of the republic's founding. Nevertheless, it remained the prerogative of professionals to ensure that 'the low expectation in regard to living in the interests of public health and to educate such circles to a better lifestyle with all its effects upon health, cleanliness and the raising of moral standards' (Friedberger 1923: 45), was effectively combated. This broad mission was left to a new profession of female social worker (Sachße 1986: 116–23; Zeller 1987: 101–42; Frevert 1989: 104–6, 159ff.).

Document 5.14 Marguerite Wolf: The Nation's Mothers

Made co-responsible by the constitution, women determinedly face the task of creating the shape and influencing the elements [of social policy]. [. . .]

Women's work in the community, especially caring for the poor and orphans, has a good venerable tradition, and even if there is now fierce competition among different groups – one cannot imagine community life without it. The inquiries into voluntary work by men and women in those areas show the following results: according to new statistics, 77 per cent of voluntary work was carried out by men and 23 per cent by women, in 1923, compared with 82 per cent and 18 per cent respectively, in 1913. Despite the fact, therefore, that in the care for orphans there was definitively a great decline, the proportion of women involved in such work has increased, which provides evidence for the increase in voluntary work by women in the last ten years. Women's volunary work also gained ground in the independent sector. 33 senior officials in orphan care have their own district and instead of two female heads of commission in 1913, we now have 66, although this accounts for only 3 per cent of [their] male equivalents. But the survey yielded one important result, and this corresponds to our daily experience: the increase of paid female employment in all areas of welfare work. Here we find the inverse ratio relating to male employment as in the voluntary sector: 26 per cent male as opposed to 74 per cent female employment. In 1913, 296 women were employed in the care of the poor and orphans, but in 1923, there were 848, nearly a threefold increase. However, in the whole of the social welfare sector, paid employment of women has quadrupled.

Source: Marguerite Wolf, 'Entwicklungstendenzen in der kommunalen Frauenarbeit', 2–3.

While many of these social workers may not have seen themselves as part of a grand design of modernity, they, like doctors, had the job of implementing the 'hidden curriculum' of social hygiene at the mundane level of everyday life. While Weimar population policy may have been influenced by a discourse of 'positive' eugenicism, it is clear from local evidence that its practitioners often expressed ideas closer to the 'negative' eugenicism that characterized policy in the 1930s (Oppenheimer 1931: 100–2; Sieder 1985: 41–5; Weindling 1989: 305–564, passim; *idem* 1991: 108–13; Schwartz 1995: 13–17, 94, 156–70). Sister Ruth Hoffmann, the director of the Care Office in Altona since its creation in 1919, is a good example of the personnel and cognitive bridging between Weimar's modernist project and that of the Third Reich. During the 1920s, her reports on young women were often lined with a tone and language that she would later employ in the service of Nazi racial biologism (McElligott 1998: 77, 84, 226; Koonz 1993; Bock 1994).

Document 5.15 Activity Report by the Welfare Office Section for the Care of the Endangered

Altona, 27 Sept. 1937

Report
on the activity of the Care of the Endangered at the Welfare Office Altona

———————

A welfare agency for those at risk was set up after the dissolution of the Care Office and Girls' Home Hogenfeldweg within Altona's Welfare Office, and the former director of the Care Office and Girls' Home put in charge.
The remit includes:

    I.   at risk welfare: ⎫ for women,
    II. special care: ⎬ men and
                    families with
                    ⎭ children.

I:

1.)	Asocials	workshy, uneconomical, morally at risk, criminally at risk,
2.)	The unstable	who are incapable of organising their life so that they reside within the parameters of the people's community (*Volksgemeinschaft*)
3.)	Mentally weak	who would come under a probation order or who are in need of supervision
4.)	Mentally ill	who draw welfare support, are not a community danger, and among whom, however, children and spouses or family members suffer
5.)	Burnt out old prostitutes	who draw welfare support

| 6.) The unsteady and outcasts | who eventually on the basis of F.Pfl.V. § 20 must be accommodated in open and half-secure homes and with whom the take up of work has to be worked on |

[. . .]

II:

| Special care for separately filed cases | in the event of long-term illness, death, illness in the family, infirmity etc |

Purpose of the Work:

a) Preventative care for those, who through a supervisory hand, advice at the right moment and other help, are brought to or kept to rights, so that they come to an inner and outer calm and thus integrate themselves into the community (*Volkskörper*), the family and their immediate environment.

b) Defensive measures against those who exploit the welfare office [and who] want to live at the expense of the community, or who are so endangered that they either endanger others or who through their life [styles] cause costs that can be avoided.

E.g.:

1.) Educative work through frequent visits and consultations with mothers in whose families the husband cares too little for wife and children. (Aim: Education of mother, viz. women to become sensible comrades.)

2.) Influence uneconomical women towards improvement of the entire household.

3.) Accommodation of unstable girls who have not properly worked since school in a training home.

4.) Cutting off welfare support after thorough investigation of circumstances.

5.) Accommodation of those in need of guardianship in requisite institutes.

6.) Initiation of wardship proceedings in the case of those in need of guardianship or those who must not necessarily be sent to a home, but who nevertheless come under B.G.B. § 6, paragraph 1.

Management of guardianships, since it is proven that success is greater when an experienced person carries out the guardianship. Moreover, a speedy intervention and quicker help is possible when the guardian is an officer of the welfare office. The asocials in particular must be made aware that they will be caught immediately they cause damage again. Frequently a committal to a home can be postponed through intensive association with them.

The asocials, as far as it is possible, are to be allocated forced labour duty.

Also they are to be brought before the welfare doctor so that they do not feign sickness and thus can avoid work.

To list individual work and individual measures is not possible, since they are almost always different in each case and very variable.

Aim of Work:
To achieve an early reintegration of the sick and irresponsible elements and those in need of custodianship into the community through educative work.

p.p.
[Ruth Hoffmann
Senior Carer]

Source: StAH 424–24/37, Organisation und Tätigkeit des Pflegeamts und Mädchenheims . . . 1919–1937

The symbiosis between the individual body as micro-cell and an organic totality underlying Hoffmann's reference to the reintegration of 'social outsiders' into the community was not specific to the development of social hygiene in the Third Reich. The idea of a cellular-biological *Volkskörper* (national body) had been current in utopian thought at the end of the nineteenth and beginning of the twentieth century in Germany (Frecot 1984: 420–38); it also surfaced in the political discussions on the city and citizenship and nation at the beginning of the Weimar Republic, but was rejected elsewhere (Hobhouse 1918; McElligott 1998: 238; Ribhegge 1973). The concept of the individual and the biological whole was, therefore, a paradigm of urban modernity that underwrote the entire approach to regenerating the nation in the interwar period.

Document 5.16 Franz Jung: 'The Part and the Whole'

The individual person, one must assume, is Part of a Whole, of the living environment, of nature, or more exactly, of humanity. One may still think of oneself very much as an individual, but this belonging should not be denied. The Whole is rhythmically determined. It exists outside our consciousness, under its own conditions, in the dynamic of the universe, in its own intensity and essence. It exists nevertheless in our consciousness in the links to ourselves, our experience, to our personal intensity and our personal rhythm, the solitary being experiences it as a pressure and dependence in the midst of his life form, as a weight, against which he himself begins to experience himself. The level of intensity of this link to the vibrant experience of the Whole itself conditions the rhythm, and since rhythm and vibrancy, intensity and resistance, always follow the same dynamism in driving themselves, and reacting to animate the individual consciousness, there develops analogous and according to the level of intensity, sorrow and happiness, hate and toil, restraint and enhancement. It is clear that through this the link itself is not altered, neither toward the one side nor toward the other, neither in terms of community nor of individuation.

Source: Franz Jung, Die Technik des Glücks. Mehr Tempo! Mehr Glück! Mehr Macht! (1923): Werke 6 (Hamburg, 1987), 139.

Rehabilitating the urban body

This quest for wholeness was an expression of modernity, as suggested by Gay in his discussion of the New Sobriety (Gay 1969: 127; Willett 1978: 115–17), underpinning the organization of hygiene that can be interpreted as a model for society *per se*.

Document 5.17 Organic Wholeness of Social Hygiene

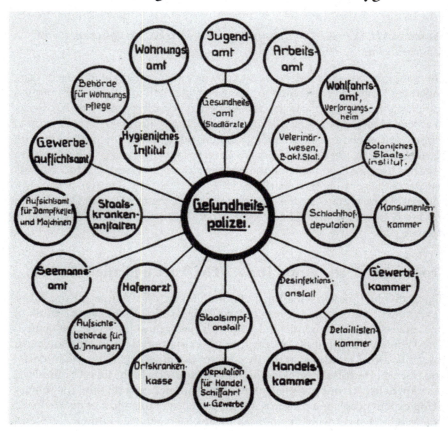

Note: The captions in the spheres refer to the various municipal agencies dealing with different areas of public health, work and welfare; at the centre of these is the 'Health inspectorate' (*Gesundheitspelizei*).

Source: Gesundheitsbehörde Hamburg (ed.), Hygiene und Soziale Hygiene in Hamburg: Zur neuenzigsten Versammlung der Deutschen Naturforscher und Aerzte in Hamburg im Jahre 1928 *(Hamburg, 1928), facing 76.*

The development of German urban society since the late nineteenth century had led to a socially fragmented, politically disoriented and racially weakened nation, as evidenced by the outbreak of war, the subsequent defeat in 1918 and the revolution that followed. It was only a question of political ideology (republican or fascist) that determined where the emphasis would lie. In either case, the technicians of social hygiene sought to reassemble the outer and inner (dis)order of the nation's constituent parts into a new 'wholeness' that stood in equilibrium to itself, society, nature and the cosmos (Wenz-Gahler 1987: 276; cf. Doc. 3.10). According to Gropius, the quest for 'wholeness' reflected a search for inner character (Müller 1987: 254; Prinz 1990: 12–13; Kaes et al. 1994: 683–7), which could only be achieved through training the body and concentrating the mind, bringing both into a harmonious 'total being' (Wolff 1931: 235; Schildt 1991: 168–70).

Document 5.18 Healthy Bodies as Totality

Source: Gesundheitsbehörde Hamburg (ed.), Hygiene und Soziale Hygiene in Hamburg: Zur neuenzigsten Versammlung der Deutschen Naturforscher und Aerzte in Hamburg im Jahre 1928 *(Hamburg, 1928), 177.*

In order to achieve this totality, the state had to provide an infrastructure. In Prussia by the later 1920s the number of primary and secondary play and sports areas totalled 14,503; there were 1,736 outdoor lidos; 117 indoor swimming pools; 9,331 gymnasia;

Rehabilitating the urban body

5,145 shooting ranges; 1,077 tennis courts; 201 racecourses; 895 boathouses; 74 aerodromes; 34 cycle racing tracks; seven motor-cycle tracks; one car-racing track (the Avus in Berlin); 66 stadia (Wolff 1931: 237; Schildt 1991: 168–70).

While the tradition of physical training had its origins in the student movement of the early nineteenth century, it was only from the latter decades of that century and into the early twentieth that physical training and sport as a participative activity developed as a mass phenomenon, especially in the cities.

Document 5.19 Membership of Gymnastic and Sport Clubs* in 53 Towns and Cities,** 1 April 1928

City group		Number of clubs	With a membership level			
			in total		of which youth under 18 years	
			male	female	male	female
A²	T	420	80,396	31,854	28,881	17,544
	Sp	1,592	220,929	40,373	64,492	12,730
B	T	266	51,820	14,851	22,591	9,186
	Sp	845	108,728	21,331	33,707	8,983
C	T	282	50,830	20,135	18,939	10,735
	Sp	900	116,951	20,210	32,370	8,697
A²–C	T	968	183,046	66,840	70,411	37,465
	Sp	3,337	446,608	81,914	130,569	30,410
T+Sp		4,305	629,654	148,754	200,980	67,875

* T=Gymnastic Club, Sp=Sport Club
**11 cities in group A² (=pop. 200,000–500,000, but excludes Cologne, Dresden, Bremen and Bochum); 15 in group B; 27 in Group C.

Source: Statistisches Jahrbuch Deutscher Städte 24 *(Leipzig, 1929), 683.*

During the 1920s, renewed efforts were made throughout urban Germany to harness youth to sports clubs in order to wean them off the street and its debilitating influences, and with some success (Schildt 1991: 181ff.). By 1930 youngsters under the age of 18 made up about half the membership of clubs emphasizing body toughening; and between a fifth and a third of various other sports and athletics clubs. In total, this meant that somewhere between 1 million and 1.5 million youth were involved in these voluntary associations (Eisenberg 1993: 155–6), about a tenth of all youngsters. The level of organization was to rise dramatically under the Nazis, for whom gymnastics and outdoor sport activities took on an even greater role in an effort to toughen up and shape city youth into a physical ideal of the 'German race' (Noakes and Pridham 1974: 355; Klönne 1956: 12–23).

Berlin in particular had emerged by 1914 as the centre of a conscious body culture movement: it boasted its famous lidos at Wannsee, Grunau and Muggelsee; a gigantic closed arena, the Sportspalast; a number of privately owned sport grounds; and 1,200 sports clubs with over 100,000 members. In 1901 the Verein für Körperkultur had opened its own purpose-built amenity, the *Sportspark Kurfürstendamm* in the heart of Berlin's west end. This was the first Air and Light Lido (*Licht-Luft Sportbad*) placing great emphasis on the exercised and toughened body as a temple for a Germanness that denoted a higher culture (Schulze-Gävernitz 1930: 252).

Document 5.20 Sun Club Kurfürstendamm, 1902

Source: Photograph Franz Stoedtner, printed in Berlinische Galerie Berlin, Berlin um 1900 *(Berlin, 1984), 428.*

Berlin's body toughening and sporting activity expanded in the 1920s, when, according to Fischer, around 5 per cent of the city's population belonged to a club of some type or visited, at one time or other, any of its 144 municipal-run sports grounds (Fischer 1992: 28–34, 50–1). A decade later, at the time of the Olympic Games in August 1936, Berlin still had 1,200 sport clubs with around 200,000 members, about the same level as in the 1920s (Fischer 1992: 51).

Much of the iconography of the body from the turn of the century placed emphasis upon a masculine form that drew its inspiration from ancient Greece (Doc. 5.20). Exponents also tended towards a romanticized, conservative, *völkisch* ideal of the 'German body' and its oneness with nature, as Adolf Brand's photograph 'Nordic Race' demonstrates (Berlinische Galerie Berlin 1984: 426). The film *Ways to Power and Beauty* (*Die Wege zur Kraft und Schönheit*, 1925), for instance, projected an image of the city as dark, divisive and threatening, countering this with the athletic form and organic wholeness of the 'German body' under the open skies of a regenerative mother nature (Monaco 1976: 137; Frecot 1984: 420–1). Such a contradiction between the modern city and a Germanic body ideal was *de riguer* in the Nazi iconography of the body during the 1930s (van der Will 1990). In the 1920s a number of nationalist sporting competitions (*Kampfspiele*) were staged by 'völkisch' sports associations, in Berlin in 1922, Cologne in 1926 and Breslau in 1930. The first two had been staged demonstratively after Germany was excluded from the Olympic Games in 1920 and 1924 (Fischer 1992: 74). The explicit aim of these *Kampfspiele* was to demonstrate a particular German physical prowess and fighting spirit, welcomed by the right and ridiculed by the left.

Document 5.21 Healthy Body, Small Intellect

[see illustration opposite]

Caption reads: 'In a healthy body resides a healthy intellect, when sometimes only a small one.'

Source: Herbert Marxen. Courtesy Stadtmuseum Flensburg.

The American cultural historian Peter Gay has described the movement of body culture, especially during the Weimar Republic, as a conservative 'hunger' for the organic whole in the face of modernity, that is, as anti-modern (Gay 1969: 84, 101), although this need not be the case (Docs. 5.18, 5.19). The importance of exercise for the physical and psychological welfare of the mass of the city population is suggested in *Symphony of a City* and *Kuhle Wampe Or To Whom Does The World Belong?* (1931), where the directors include lengthy scenes of outdoor sporting events and competitive games. In *Symphony of a City* the sports scenes are shown as bridging divisions within the urban population as it comes together in a huge people's festival, almost suggestive of sporting spectacles in the Third Reich (von Saldern 1992). In *Kuhle Wampe* the emphasis is on proletarian sport. In 1922 a Working Class Gymnasts' Competition had been held in Leipzig, and in 1925, the first International Workers' Olympics were held in Frankfurt (Fischer 1992: 74; Müller 1993: 108). These events stressed the regenerating powers and comradeship of sport, themes that were echoed in *Kuhle Wampe* in conjunction with the coming class struggle. After having excelled through sport, the proletarian youth stream back into the city to conquer it.

Document 5.22 'Sports Song'

Coming from the full courtyards
Dark streets and embattled cities
you find yourselves in unison
to struggle together.
And learn to triumph.
And learn to triumph.

Source: Kunstler Kollektiv (Berthold Brecht et al.), Kuhle Wampe, oder wem gehöhrt die Welt? *(1931), in Wolfgang Gersch and Werner Hecht, eds.,* Berthold Brecht Kuhle Wampe: Protokoll des Film und Materialien *(Frankfurt am Main, 1981), 57–8.*

Like Peter Gay, Wilfried van der Will associates the concepts of *Ganzheit* (wholeness), *Einheit* (unity), and *Bindung* (cohesion) of the body cult with the antimodernism of the nationalist right (van der Will 1990: 20). But when seen in the context of the city at the beginning of the twentieth century, these concepts can be equally linked to more progressive and democratically enlightened body groups, such as Adolf Koch's Institute for Body Culture, a socialist-reform organization within the nudist movement of the 1920s.

The nudist cult had spread rapidly among city dwellers after 1918, so that Berlin had at least seven nudist clubs and Munich five in 1924. It attracted mainly younger people of both sexes from the new middle classes, mostly white-collar employees and professionals such as teachers, as well as young proletarians (Berghaus 1988: 211). This movement was spurned by those who claimed to follow an 'authentic' body culture. Thus the Reich Committee for Physical Exercise complained of a nudist exhibition in September 1927 that 'There was little or nothing to see of authentic body culture. [. . .] There were primarily [endless] nude photographs, mostly from the rhythmic gymnastic dance. The schools of Hellerau, Bode, Wigman, Mensendieck *et al.* had each displayed their pictures on special stands. The border between pure gymnastic and sport training of the body and of hygiene was crossed in this exhibition.' (LAB 142/1 StB 4240)

Document 5.23 Adolf-Koch-School: Naturist Body Culture

Source: Courtesy Landesbildstelle Berlin.

The difference between the nationalist and socialist or avant garde approaches lay in their understanding and representation of the body: as a means for reforming urban social conditions and seeking reconcilation of the inner and outer spirit in rhythmic harmony with others, or as a finely tuned machine in the racial struggle (conducted on both economic and physical levels).

Document 5.24 A Police Official's Attitude Towards Nudism, 1926

[. . .] the increase of nudity in comparison to the prewar period is acknowledged, but one can have serious doubt as to whether this is more immoral and corrupting than the titillating semi-undress of the good old days. Its contemporary appearance can be attributed to the influence of sporting activity on the one hand, and, on the other hand, to an expression of regression into childhood; a process that in my opinion heralds a [general] recuperation. It must also be noted that exactly under the influence of certain circles promoting nudist culture, the female type has transformed from the fat harem ideal into the slim thoroughly exercised female type, a process that undeniably from the perspective of health and racial hygiene is to be welcomed. This, as in the case of the above-mentioned regression, will contribute to the physical and psychological recuperation of the nation after Germany's unprecedented severe fate. Apart from this it seems entirely impossible to repress by way of police and punitive measures these type of phenonema that correspond to general principles of lifestyle.

Source: STAM Pol.Dir. München 7420, Pol.präs. Tgb. 58/82.II.Th.Z.26, Krim.polizeirat v. Behr.

Attitudes towards the body movement remained fairly ambivalent throughout the interwar period (Reuter 1986: 410).

While the male body continued to represent a temple, the female body during the 1930s came to symbolize the German *Heimat* in which the male temple might be erected. Thus by 1936, Leni Riefenstahl could depict the rationalized and trained female body as part of a total rhythmic aesthetic representing a healthy citadel of the people, in contrast to the unaesthetic city of the Weimar Republic with its false rhythms (de Ras 1986: 413–15; Labanyi 1988; Matthews 1990: 25, 28, 32, 42–4).

Document 5.25 Nazi Idealization of the Body

Source: Courtesy Stiftung Deutsche Kinemathek, Berlin.

As we have suggested, the project of attaining rational perfection of morals at the very least remained incomplete, and was paralleled by the equal failure to achieve perfection of the body as temple, either as product(ive) or as mother. Such images of modernity or its antithesis remained representations of ideal types, rather than social reality. The same can be said of the attempt consciously to modernize urban society through social policy. This too remained a fiction.

Document 5.26 Cultural Film of the City of Nuremberg

Party Comrade Kaufmann imagined the flow of the film along the following lines: that one starts from the position of a German person and a German family in the community and that a particular family of a particular community will be shown: certification of birth, vaccination of the child, registration for school, first day at school, lessons at school, participation in the local authority supported Hitler Youth Home, leaving school, beginning of apprenticeship (possibly in a municipal office), marriage, birth in the new family, honorary work of the head of family in the community, death of a member of family, cases of sickness and corresponding care by the community; use of the model municipal institutions (hospital, Kindergarten, swimming baths, sports ground, theatre, concerts, parks). In this way the all-encompassing responsibility and care of the community can be explicitly expressed each time. Different members of the family are to take part in the run of the action; only the exceptionally good institutions are to be shown.

Source: BAK NS25/1267 Hauptamt für Kommunalpolitik,
A.04683/42–Dr.Mi/Gö to Firma Wien – Film – Abteilung Kulturfilm zHd.
v. Herrn Direktor Lebzelter (26 Mai 1942), Betrefft: Kulturfilm über die
Stadt Nürnberg.

In the midst of war the ideology of a welfare state had clearly become an important propaganda instrument, at the very moment when it was in fact diminishing as an everyday reality for the urban population. The ravages and deprivations of war meant that undernourishment was widespread by 1945, as it had been in 1918.

Document 5.27 Hard Facts on Health

[. . .] Our visitor will notice also the yellow faces of many of the people, the sluggish pace with which they cross the road in the face of oncoming traffic, and above all, perhaps he will notice the darkening shadow beneath the eyes of the Hamburg children. All these signs spell one word – 'hunger'. Following closely in the footsteps of hunger comes disease in many guises.

[. . .] In May 1945, the people of Hamburg had considerable reserves left to them at the end of the war in view of the comparatively good rations they had been receiving. Nevertheless the callousness of the Nazis and their legacy in health matters can be clearly seen in their treatment of T.B. cases. Cases of T.B. were expelled from the hospitals, given hard labour or sent into industry until they died. The Nazis considered these unfortunate people as being little more than human scrap which should be used until it qualified for burial. Having been turned loose from the hospitals, and denied in many cases even elementary human care, these people wandered amongst their healthy fellow beings sowing the seeds of future infection with which the officers and their German counterparts have now to cope.

Despite the lowered resistance of the population owing to shortage of food, T.B. alone, among the infectious diseases, has shown an increase. The gravity of the present position can be clearly seen from the following figures: In 1944, there were 1,676 fresh cases of T.B. reported as compared with 4,372 for the first 5 months of 1946, and on the 1st July 1946, the total number of cases in Hamburg reached the serious figure of 15,983. This represents an increase in six months of about 33 per cent.

In this context the effect of unhygienic housing conditions cannot be overlooked, but behind all other factors hovers the spectre of malnutrition. [. . .]

Emergency steps have also been taken with regard to the inmates of mental hospitals and sufferers from hunger oedema. The former were not previously classified as hospital patients by the German authorities and they received only the normal consumer ration. As these people had no means of augmenting their rations and as their condition was deteriorating it was agreed that they should receive an extra 800 calories a day from 1st June, 1946. During the week ending 31st July, 1946, 12 people died from the effects of hunger oedema and during the same week there were 1,189 cases altogether in hospital. During the month of May, 12 cases of hunger oedema, all in men over 40 years of age, were reported among 3,250 German workers at a British Ordnance Depot. A survey of employees at the Hamburg gasworks, held on 13th July, 1946, showed 90 cases of hunger oedema among 2,200 employees. It is difficult, if not impossible, to know absolutely the total number of hunger oedema cases in Hamburg, but they are estimated at 10,000 cases. Adult cases of hunger oedema, treated in hospital, receive 2,527 calories daily.

It is clear that this disease is not confined to the members of any particular social class or form of employment. There have been six cases among the medical staff of the university hospital and recent sufferers include the dean of the university.

[. . .] Nevertheless, as may be expected, the declining resistence of the people shows itself on all sides. Reports from firms and from branches of the civil administration are unanimous in reporting among their staffs lack of energy, exhaustion, poor memory, abnormal liability to make mistakes, poor concentration and general lack of efficiency. [. . .]

Source: 'Hamburg Today: Hard Facts on Health', in British Zone Review (31 Aug. 1946), 14.

Thus Allied health administrators in 1946 found themselves echoing the concerns of an earlier generation of Germans. The previous half-century of attempts to combat a crisis-ridden urban nation through advancing the healthy and efficient body, had all but disappeared in the debris of postwar Germany. In 1918, at the end of the first disastrous war, it had been hoped that society could be more closely bound through the new welfare paternalism to the republican state. In 1945, therefore, the rebuilding of the body as a means to a spiritual and mental rehabilitation of the German people was added to the long list of tasks for national reconstruction. And as in 1918 and 1933, there was more continuity than break. For as in the case of the 'economic wonder' of the postwar period, one of the prime aims of rehabilitating the urban body during the 1920s had been that of achieving a cultural transformation of the economy based upon technology and a 'rational activism' (Schulze-Gävernitz 1930: 243) that expressed itself not only in efficient production, but also in a higher level of consumption.

Capitals of consumption | 6

By the turn of the century, Germany's cities had become complex economic organisms based upon production and commerce. This development was part of the fundamental transformation taking place within the industrial economies of Europe in these years. A long period of falling prices and a considerable expansion in trade in the last quarter of the nineteenth century had brought a moderate affluence to many ordinary citizens, who used their disposable incomes to acquire material goods, or to lose themselves in one of the many popular entertainments of the period. The last quarter of the nineteenth century thus saw a massive expansion of commercial enterprises catering to the demands of this new monied class. In Germany, as throughout Europe in this period, cities had become the new capitals of this conspicuous consumption. Berlin in particular emerged as the epicentre of the new consumer culture.

Document 6.1 'Conspicuous Consumption'

Luxus! Palast! A strange mixture of splendour, beauty and art with *nouvelle-richesse*. Such is the note of the new fashionable Berlin. It expresses itself in the subtle temperamental colour-schemes and decorations of such establishments as the Hotel Cumberland, which rises in the midst of tall, snobbish, overladen private palaces – monuments of a sort of German Victorian period. All this is the creation of a wealthy middle class. Countless shops cater, not to necessity, but to luxury. Enormous flower-shops that riot with blooms like an acre of paradise, 'delicatessen' shops in whose wide windows are spread model tables that would have startled Lucullus, haberdashers' shops, milliners', tobacco, art and bookshops – though the last two the true German considers as among the necessities of life. Confectioners abound; their windows are decorated with an elaborate architecture of marvellous cakes – creations of master-bakers who work with fervour, like artists of the Renaissance!

A mere commercial wine-bottle, a park bench or electric lamp may be designed by some famous craftsman; the great department stores – Wertheim's, Tietz's, or Kaufhaus des Westens – are strange, yet vital, creations of a new art. The striking posters which shout and gesticulate, and hypnotise the eye in the Untergrund Stations [sic] are the result of art and intellect applied to advertising. Through what they have created rather than borrowed, one catches glints of the intense vitality, aspiration and national faith that burn in the people of Barbarossa. These things are the bright sparks flung off by a dynamo engendering stupendous forces.

Source: Herman Scheffauer, 'The City Without Night: Berlin 'Twixt Dusk and Dawn', The Pall Mall Magazine, No. 251, Vol. 53, (March) 1914, 280–1.

Scheffauer's account of Berlin is evocative of our image of Europe's *fin de siècle*, when luxury prevailed over sense. It is suggestive with its references to department stores, subterranean transit systems, advertising, and glut of material goods, of the emerging mass consumer culture of urban modernity, which, according to Lynn Abrams and Kaspar Maase, dissolved older cultural patterns based upon parochial and class solidarities (Abrams 1990: 178ff., 185; Maase 1997: 58ff.). Their argument is that as more and more people participated in the new commercial consumerism, this activity led to a homogenization or universalization of behaviour and tastes, in spite of the fact that, paradoxically, it was based upon an individualistic appetite, or was located within the 'private' sphere of the family (von Saldern 1988). Social relationships, especially in the cities, were henceforth located within a nexus defined and mediated solely through money (Harvey 1985: 165, 229; Frisby 1985: 87–90). Writing at the time, Germany's 'father' of sociology, Georg Simmel, argued that the very existence of an individual in the modern city depended 'at any moment' on his or her monetary connection with others.

Document 6.2 Money

If all economic transactions are based upon the fact that I want to have something which another person possesses at the moment and that the other will transfer it to me if I transfer something to them which I possess and which they want to possess, then it is obvious that the second link in this two-sided process will not always occur when the first appears. There are innumerable times when I will desire object *a* that is in the possession of person A, while the object or service *b* which I am willing to give for it is totally unattractive to A; or perhaps the mutually offered goods are desired by each side, but the quantities with which they correspond to each other does [sic] not permit an immediate agreement through direct equivalence. Therefore it is of the greatest value for the attainment of our goals that an intermediate link be inserted in the teleological chain, one into which I can convert *b* at any time and which can, in turn, be converted into *a*. [. . .] The generally recognized means of exchange becomes the transit point for all bilaterally binding transactions, and thus reveals itself, like the examples mentioned above, to be an extension of purposive action, in the sense that it is a means to obtain the desired objects, indirectly and through a public institution, that would be unattainable through my efforts aimed directly at them. Just as my thoughts must take on the form of the generally understood language in order to advance my practical ends by that roundabout way, so my services and possessions must enter into the form of monetary value in order to serve my continuing volition.

Source: from the 'The psychology of money', in David Frisby and Mike Featherstone, Simmel on Culture *(London, Thousand Oaks and New Delhi, 1997), 234.*

While a number of academics draw on the contemporary argument that money was the 'great leveller', loosening the old class hierarchies of nineteenth-century industrialism (Roßbach 1916: 33; Dittrich 1939: 16; Neundörfer 1961: 5–6; Harvey 1985: 168; Abrams 1990: 184), some observers at the time were less certain. Critics of urban Germany's early consumerist capitalism, such as Gustav Landauer, could agree with Simmel that money had come to symbolize relations between people, but they also argued that it alienated the city-dweller through individuation, and created inequalities that were expressed in the differing levels of consumption (Landauer 1920: 103, 134). Nevertheless, the German urban world, according to Simmel, revolved on the triple axes of money, goods and services (Frisby and Featherstone 1997: 246). Nearly three decades after Simmel, Werner Sombart offered his own brief analysis of the principal characteristics of this new commercial capitalism.

Document 6.3 Consumers

What characterizes [. . .] consumers in the late-capitalist era and distinguishes them from those of the past is, firstly, that they are mainly persons with medium or small incomes; secondly, that they are town dwellers, chiefly from the cities; and thirdly, that in deciding their needs, they are increasingly dependent on business people, such as producers and traders.

From these characteristics of the consumer coupled with the peculiar conditions of capitalist production and markets, as well as from the general life-style of the period, the particular consumer needs for the capitalist era can be explained, which will be the subject of the following.

A prime and typical feature of this consumer need appears to be:

1) the frequent change of consumer goods. On the one hand, this is a consequence of a consumer's desire frequently to change the world of goods surrounding him; on the other hand, this is due to the necessity to change as a result of revolutionary technology.

The capitalist entrepreneur has a lively interest in constant change. Therefore he has invented many tricks through which he forces us to change, even against our wills, to new consumer goods. One of the best known tricks of this kind is fashion, which today has been completely conquered by the capitalist entrepreneur.

A further trait of satisfying consumer needs in late-capitalism is

2) the acceleration and thereby the shortening of each act of satisfying needs. The facts are well known: we complete a journey in a sixth, tenth or twentieth of the time one needed in the past; Goethe sat at the table for three hours, the

American clerk eats in ten minutes; it took an hour to smoke a long pipe, a cigarette takes five minutes, and so on. The result of this acceleration is that more needs can be satisfied, or often the same need several times over, in the same time span (let's pretend that the satisfaction of needs over longer or shorter periods remains essentially the same). An intensification of consumer needs takes place. In order for satisfaction to be completed more quickly, production and transport must undergo the same acceleration.

The reasons for this acceleration in the field of consumption are the following: first, there is a universally growing feeling that time is valuable, which drives the contemporary person to speed up; time is for him a valuable item. For this reason, 'he has no time'. Goethe had the 'time' to sit at the dinner table for three hours, the clerk in New York doesn't because he has something better to do than Goethe. Secondly, capitalist interest directly leads to haste: the acceleration in the act of consumption means the acceleration of capital turnover, and thus a profit rise. Thirdly, the pace of each individual is determined by the pace of the machinery with which he is aligned: if I want to use the underground, I must not exceed a certain time limit when entering and leaving the train.

The final characteristic shaping consumption during late capitalism is

3) the collectivization of consumer needs, i.e., the increasing tendency to meet needs 'collectively'. The collectivization of consumption can be seen in nearly all areas. The most important are:

a) Educational resources: increase in state schools, libraries, museums.

b) Healthcare and hospital services: increase in hospitals, mental asylums and infirmaries.

c) Places of recreation: increase in theatres, concert halls, cinemas.

d) Hostelries and refreshment: increase in restaurants, hotels, boarding-houses.

e) Household utility: increase of the collective supply of water, gas, electricity.

f) Transport: increase in trains, trams, steamships; but also postal services, photography and telephones.

Source: Werner Sombart, 'Kapitalismus' in Handwörterbuch der Soziologie, *edited by Alfred Vierkandt (Stuttgart, 1931), 258–77, here 271.*

As Sombart noted, the bulk of Germany's modern consumers by the 1920s, in contrast to the privileged few of the late imperial period, comprised lower-income groups who had effortlessly adapted to the consumerist modernity of the city (Leinert 1925: 178–9). Indeed, they were themselves the product of this modernity. Between 1907 and 1939, the proportion of the economically active population working in the tertiary sector rose from a quarter to a third (overall this sector also accounted for about a third of national income by the latter date). Many of the people employed in the sector worked in public and private administration, and in commerce and trade, mostly in clerical and technical positions; or were employed as retail assistants; or found employment in the new burgeoning leisure and sports industries (Petzina *et al.* 1978: 55, 67, 82). In commercial and manufacturing cities such as Hamburg, Frankfurt am Main, Karlsruhe, Leipzig, Münster and Munich, white-collar employees constituted as much as 40 per cent of the economically active population. Berlin, with its public and private administrations, banking and financial institutions, retail and leisure outlets, was described by Kracauer as the city of 'white collar culture' par excellence (Kracauer 1971a: 15).

The members of this new subaltern class not only serviced the new commercial economy, they reproduced it through their own private patterns of consumption. An inquiry by the Reich Statistical Office into spending patterns among urban households between March 1927 and February 1928 showed that the families of white-collar employees and tenured officials (*Beamte*), after allowing for food, spent more on personal hygiene, clothing, household goods, holidays, and leisure and recreational activities than did their working-class counterparts.

Document 6.4 'Other Necessaries' as Percentage of Total Household Expenditure, 1927–8 (Socio-occupational status)

Item	Worker's family	Salaried employee's family	Official's family
Rent	10.0	11.5	12.0
Equipment, upkeep of dwelling	3.9	5.5	6.4
Heating and lighting	3.6	3.5	3.7
Clothing and linen	12.7	12.6	13.9
Personal toilet	0.8	1.0	0.8
Hygiene	0.6	1.6	1.8
Insurance	7.9	7.8	3.2
Education	2.0	2.9	3.7
Amusements and social gatherings	0.9	1.5	1.3
Sports and journeys	1.1	2.2	2.5
Transport	1.2	1.2	1.1
Trade union and other contributions	2.3	1.3	0.9
Taxes	2.5	4.4	4.6
Rates	0.1	0.3	0.3
Allowances and presents to persons outside the family	1.5	2.5	3.6
Other expenses	1.2	2.6	3.7
Total	52.3	63.2	65.5

Source: International Labour Office, 'The German Family Budget Enquiry of 1927–1928', in International Labour Review *22 (1930), 530.*

The annual surveys carried out during the later 1920s by trade unions representing commercial and clerical employees underscored in greater detail the above results (AfA 1928: 202, 287; Triebel 1987: 109; *idem* 1991: 112–35). Given the relatively small incomes – the average monthly income of the 546 salaried households in the Reich Statistical Office study was around 390 Reichsmark – the sums put aside for recreational pursuits and consumer goods would not have been very large. The budget surveys referred to above showed that the average white-collar employee spent about 12 per cent of his monthly income on clothing. These purchases were made possible by the development of stylish but affordable mass tailoring that became a hallmark of the period, and is curiously absent from discussions in the specialist literature (Westphal 1992; Lauterbach 1995). The smart employee went to the menswear departments of the big chain stores of Tietz, Wertheim's and Grünfeld's, to get off-the-peg suits, blazers, slacks, and, in summer, the distinctive boater (Mosse 1987: 126ff.).

Document 6.5 Mannequins

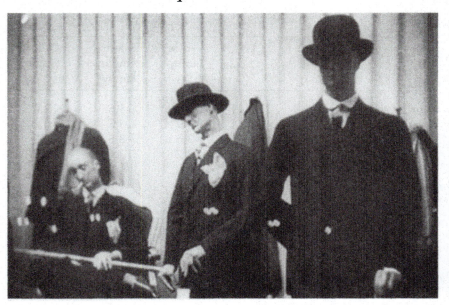

Source: Walter Ruttmann, Berlin: Die Sinfonie einer Großstadt, *1927.*

After having made its debut in Paris in the mid-nineteenth century, the department store had quickly spread across Europe's urban landscape by the last decade of that century, becoming a symbol of consumerist modernity (Miller 1981). Significantly,

Germany's most famous department stores had their origins not in the big city, but in the smaller provincial towns of their founders: Landshut (Grünfeld), Stralsund (Wertheim), Gera (Tietz), Wismar (Karstadt), Margonin in Posen/Zwickau (Schocken). From their humble beginnings as drapery and haberdashery stores in mid-century, they had developed into large commerical enterprises by the late nineteenth century, conquering the larger cities of the Reich, including finally Berlin by the beginning of the 1880s (Fuchs 1992: 191). By 1907, the Tietz brothers (separately) had 27 branches throughout Germany, including the imperial capital, while their competitors, the Wertheims, had three stores in Berlin by the mid-1890s (Mosse 1987: 119–24, 190ff.; Lenz 1995: 51–2; Ladwig-Winters 1997: 11–18). During the 1920s, firms such as Karstadt and Schocken continued to expand their network of branches, and increased the size of their individual stores (Lenz 1995: 68, 108; Fuchs 1992: 191–3).

In 1895 there were approximately 120 department stores, a figure that seems to have quadrupled by 1913, with a turnover of nearly 300 million marks (Shaw 1992: 176). By 1933, there were 1,432 department stores throughout the Reich, employing 116,209 persons, and with an annual turnover of 1.5 billion marks, or around 7 per cent of all retail sales; and in spite of Nazi legislation preventing the opening of any new stores after 1934, those that existed continued to flourish (Gellately 1974: 44; Gurland et al. 1975: 52–3, 145; Lenz 1995: 45–6).

Document 6.6 Retail Trade, by Size of Establishments, 1933

Persons employed per establishment	Establishments		Persons employed	
	Number	Per cent	Number	Per cent
1	416,644	49.4	416,644	21.7
2 and 3	345,387	40.9	774,998	40.4
4 and 5	51,156	6.1	221,209	11.6
1 to 5	813,187	96.4	1,412,851	73.7
6 to 10	20,810	2.5	150,174	7.8
1 to 10	833,997	98.9	1,563,025	81.5
11 to 20	5,957	0.7	83,913	4.4
21 to 50	2,379	0.3	73,274	3.8
51 to 100	747 ⎤		51,580	2.7
101 to 200	303 ⎬		41,884	2.2
201 to 1,000	213 ⎟ 0.1		79,363	4.1
1,001 and over	15 ⎦		23,824	1.3
Total	843,611	100.0	1,916,863	100.0

Source: A.R.L. Gurland, Otto Kirchheimer and Franz Neumann, The Fate of Small Business in Nazi Germany *(New York, 1943, reprint Howard Fertig, New York, 1975), 144.*

The new and modern department store attracted the growing subaltern class of employees as well as the affluent bourgeois citizen. Customers derived pleasure from the innumerable items available under one roof; and perhaps, at the same time they might have been awed by its grand cathedral-like hall behind the ornate glass fronts of the store (Crossick and Jaumain 1999). Indeed, the central hall of Tietz's department store in the Leipzigerstraße gave the effect of a central nave with the ascending double row of stairs leading to an imaginary altar (to consumption).

Document 6.7 Central Hall of Tietz Department Store, 1910

[see illustration opposite]

Source: Landesarchiv Berlin Rep. 806/1950, Courtesy Landesarchiv Berlin.

At the same time, the department store was not unlike a fair or zoo (Chicago even had one called *The Fair*): an exotic place that functioned as a mass spectacle that could also excite sensually. It was not unusual for contemporaries to claim that shopping on this scale was morally corrupting (Spiekermann 1999; Ladwig-Winters 1997: 27; Williams 1983: 265; Abelson 1989).

Document 6.8 Inside the Department Store

[see illustration opposite]

Source: Karl Hubbuch, 'Der Traum der Tietzmädchen' (1921), Courtesy Myriam Hubbuch.

To a late twentieth-century eye, the style of the late nineteenth-century department store may appear as a rather stolid exponent of imperial architecture with its heavy ornamentation. Yet the design, and especially its internal layout, broke with tradition, creating a new style. Indeed, until the 1930s, Tietz, Wertheim, Schocken and Karstadt, with their twin emphases on contemporary styles and technologies, were harbingers of an architectural modernity that mirrored the commercial modernity of the period (Mosse 1987: 123; Ladwig-Winters 1997: 84; Fuchs 1992: 193; Lenz 1995: 103–7).

[Document 6.7 Central Hall of Tietz Department Store, 1910]

[Document 6.8 Inside the Department Store]

Document 6.9 Luckhardt Brothers Competition Entry, 1928: Alexanderplatz Shaped by Commerce

Source: Courtesy of Bauhaus-Archiv, Berlin.

Like so many other modernizing innovations of the period, the department store altered the physical landscape of the city and the mental landscape and habits of its residents (Mosse 1987: 391; Lenz 1995: 28; Sigsworth 1990: 45–9). Thus when the new Wertheim store opened in 1894 in Berlin's Leipzigerstraße, it caused a sensation. Designed by Alfred Messel, Germany's most progressive architect at that time, in the 'grand style', it was 2,800 square metres larger than its contemporary, the Reichstag. When the company opened another branch at Moritzplatz in 1914, Kaiser Wilhelm II, who was the first European monarch to enter a department store, was suitably impressed. He is reputed to have remarked: 'We live in an era of commerce'(Stutzer 1917: 80; Ladwig-Winters 1997: 54–5).

According to Warren Breckman, the department store also gave an impulse to the modernization of society by creating a population of consumers who were 'equal before the cash register' (Breckman 1990–1: 485, 490). This was, however, the illusion that the department store cultivated for its customers (Ladwig-Winters 1997: 44–5). Indeed, the department store, with its rigid price system and explicit oppulence, underscored existing class segregation and created new inequalities by adding yet another, closed, zone to the urban landscape. Moreover, individual branches of the same chain might attract a different type of clientele. Thus Grünfeld's ultra-modern store on the Kurfürstendamm was favoured by members of Berlin's media and fashion world, while its older and more traditional store in Berlin Mitte was patronized by Hindenburg, Ebert, von Papen and other 'old-fashioned' luminaries (Mosse 1987: 124, nn. 60, 61). Indeed, there is little evidence to support the idea that the department store 'universalized' the tastes or spending habits of urban Germans in this period (Gellately 1974: 48–9).

The department store as a motif of urban modernity became a powerful construct in the political rhetoric of those who opposed its large-scale commercialism, and apparent Americanizing influence upon the republic in general. For such critics, not only did mammon's 'dirty lucre' now occupy the central institutions of the nation (Poor 1976; Ladwig-Winters 1997: 55; McElligott 1998: 136), it also threatened to overshadow God in the city.

Document 6.10 Money and God in the City, 1881, 1926

[see illustration on page 140]

The caption reads: Before, the neighbouring building with its gable height and simplicity of its facade, had been tactfully subordinated to the church. The vulgarity of the Dresdner Bank's new construction not only assails the church with its ill-proportioned height, but also through its flaunting columns, which are insolently higher-placed than those of the church.

Source: Werner Hegemann, Das Steinerne Berlin *(Berlin, 1930), 189.*

By closing the distance between the photographer and the object in the later photograph, Hegemann was able to manipulate the appearance of scale between the bank and the Hedwigskirche, thus lending force to his point. In spite of its demonization as 'unGerman', the department store did not fade from the urban landscape after Hitler came to power, though, inevitably, Jewish owners of these stores did (Mosse 1987: 329, 373).

The conflation of anti-Americanism and anti-Semitism also surfaced in a left-discourse on consumerist modernity. As suggested by Sombart, modern urban consumerism was organized on the basis of a successful servicing of needs. It was also based on a successful exploitation of desires. Berthold Brecht and Kurt Weill captured this aspect of modern urban consumerism in their operetta 'Rise and Fall of Mahagonny', staged in 1929. Through the exploits of the chief protagonists, an unsavoury trio of small-time confidence tricksters, who are stranded after their getaway car breaks down in the wilderness, Brecht and Weill offered a thinly veiled critique of what they saw as an Americanized Weimar consumerism. One of the protagonists, Frau Begbick, decides on the course of action.

Document 6.11 The Town of Mahagonny

Good, then we'll stay here. It occurs to me: if we cannot get up above, then we'll stay here below. Look, all the people who come down from there say that the rivers give their gold reluctantly. It is a terrible toil, and we can't labour. But I have seen these people, and I tell you, they give up their gold! You get gold easier from men than from rivers!

Die Hedwigskirche an der Südostecke des Friedrichs-Forums
nach einer Aufnahme von 1881.

Die Hedwigskirche 1926

Früher hat sich das Nachbarhaus mit seiner Gesimshöhe und der Einfachheit seiner Schauseite
der Kirche taktvoll untergeordnet. Der protzenhafte Neubau der Dresdner Bank erschlägt die
Kirche nicht nur durch seine übermäßige Höhe, sondern auch durch seinen Säulenprunk, der
frech höher als die Säulenvorhalle der Kirche gestellt wurde.

[Document 6.10 Money and God in the City, 1881, 1926]

That's why we will build a town here
And call it Mahagonny
That means: town of temptation!
It should be as a snare
That is put up for edible birds.
Everywhere there is effort and work
But here there is fun.
After all it is the pleasure of men
Not to suffer and to do everything.
That is the meaning of gold.
Gin and whisky.
Girls and boys.
And a week here is: seven days without work
The great typhoons don't come this far.
But the men without worry
Wait smoking for the coming night.
Every third day there are fights
With yells and crudities, but the fights are fair.
So put this fishing rod in the earth and raise this piece of
Linen so the ships passing here from the gold coast can see us.
Erect the bar table
There under the rubber tree.
This is the town.
And this is its middle
And it is called: 'Hotel of The Rich Man'

Source: 'Aufstieg und Fall der Stadt Mahagonny: Act 1: Grundung der Stadt Mahagonny', Bertolt Brecht, Stücke 2 (Frankfurt am Main, 1988), 336.

Brecht's trio of confidence tricksters can be taken as representative of the entre-prenuers of the new capitalist leisure industry. They do not engage in production, but syphon off the valorized labour of proletarians (those who dig the gold). They have also been given foreign names, which, like the reference to the rubber tree, suggest the externality of Germany's modern urban-based consumerism. The Jewishness of *Dreieinigkeitsmoses* (Trinity Moses), and the fact that it is the female partner Leokadja Begbick who has the idea of establishing *Mahagonny*, echo contemporary discourses on the degenerate and feminizing influences of 'Jewish' commercialized leisure and consumption upon the city.

As we noted above (Doc. 6.8), popular discourses on consumerism added to the material appetite a sexual dimension. In particular, the gaze looms prominently as a mediating moment in what has now become widely known as the 'erotic barter' (Elsaesser 1986: 45; Doane 1990: 66; Abelson 1989: 67–75). In the morning sequences of Ruttmann's film, *Berlin: Die Sinfonie der Großstadt*, for instance, we see a male clerk pause before a shop window and light a cigarette, he glances at it, then moves on; the shutters lift on another shop to reveal female forms displayed in a lingerie shop; the sexual purchase alluded to here is even more evident in the following drawing by Kurt Weinhold where the sexualized commodification of the female form in a *revuesque* display is opened out on to the street.

Document 6.12 'The New Window Display'

Source: Kurt Weinhold, 'Die neue Auslage', c. 1929–30, printed in Reinhold Heller (ed.) Art in Germany 1906–1936. From Expressionism to Resistance: The Marvin and Janet Fishman Collection (Munich 1990), 150.

The thinly veiled eroticism of the male gaze is, however, countered by the gaze of a female passer-by (Petro 1989: 192). Ruttmann takes the metaphor of the consumer's gaze further in another street sequence of his film when a man and a woman are shown sauntering along the Kurfürstendamm, pass each other, without apparently taking notice, stop on either side of a shop's corner display window, glance momentarily at each other, and in the next sequence are seen walking off together. Film historians have usually referred to the woman as a prostitute (Chapman 1971: 37), though Gleber has recently challenged this assertion (Gleber 1997).

The relationship between modern consumerism and gender is made repeatedly throughout the 1920s, as it is later in Britain (Mort 1995). One of the features emphasized by contemporary image makers was its apparent feminizing influence. Thus Curt Moreck noted in his *Guide to Exciting Berlin* (1931) that effeminacy among men increased with their sartorial elegance and the luxuriousness of their environment (Moreck 1931: 148). Male shop assistants, in particular, were prone to this apparent loss of masculinity, as suggested in a biting caricature by Herbert Marxen of a 'shop man' published in the magazine *Jugend* in 1930.

Document 6.13 The Shop Man

[see illustration on page 144]

The caption reads: Will this evening dress please? Madam, it could be the ground for a divorce.

Source: Herbert Marxen, Courtesy Stadtmuseum Flensburg.

In some respects, these artists were commenting on traditional patriarchy's experience of urban modernity, a theme we will explore in Chapter 8. What is also clear is that much of the imagery suggests something more than simply blurred genders. The crowd of west-end consumers in Jeanne Mammen's painting *Berlin Street Scene* (1929) is androgenous and thus allegorizes not only the fluidity of gender as a result of consumerism, but that of Weimar society *per se*. Thus consumerism transmutes metaphorically into the democratizing tendency of the republic itself. But representations of consumption were also used to reinforce gendered (and, *inter alia*, class) differences in a more prosaic way that anticipates the relationship between marketing, politics and gender in Germany's post-1945 economic boom (Carter 1997).

Document 6.14 Three Friends: Him, Her, Electrola, 1929

[see illustration on page 145]

Caption reads: Him, Her, Electrola

Source: Bärbel Schrader and Jürgen Schebera, Kunst Metropole Berlin 1918–1933: Die Kunststadt in der Novemberrevolution, die 'Goldenen' Zwanziger, Die Kunststadt in der Krise *(Berlin and Weimar, 1987), 186.*

Ironically, few of the new consumer class of white-collar employee or shopgirl could have afforded such an item. They had to content themselves with a cheaper surrogate version of modernity available to them momentarily in the bars, revues, and *Kinos*. For as Brecht and Weill's *Mahagonny* suggested, the city was the site of transitory gratification.

[Document 6.13 The Shop Man]

[Document 6.14 Three Friends: Him, Her, Electrola, 1929]

This was nowhere more strongly emphasized than in the cinema which spread quickly from the turn of the century to the mid-1920s, mostly in towns and cities. In 1910, for instance, there were 480 cinemas in 33 cities, nearly a third of these (139) in Berlin; Hamburg had 40, Leipzig had 31, Munich had 28 and Königsberg had 18 (Werth 1910: Anhang). By the mid-1920s, a quarter of all cinemas were in the 48 large cities of the Reich. In general, between 50 and 60 per cent of the business arising from cinema attendances of over 3 million was being conducted by cinemas in the larger towns and big cities (Monaco 1976: 20–1; Welch 1990: 28–32; Führer 1996: 742–7).

The cinema audiences were often young, and mostly drawn from the new lower-middle class of tertiary sector employees (Altenloh 1914: 64, 69, 88, 92; Peukert 1987: 210). In particular, the 'shopgirl' was said to have been fatally attracted to this screen Hollywood, though Patrice Petro is more sceptical (Petro 1997: 45–7). Indeed, the findings of a survey of young working women in 1929 showed that nearly half could not afford the price of a ticket, which, for instance, ranged between 60 pfennig and 1 mark 40 pfennig in Munich (Führer 1996: 758–66).

Kracauer called popular films 'asylums for the homeless' because they provided their audience with an *ersatz* experience, textually flattened, lowbrow and 'American', the codeword for a modernity emptied of content.

Document 6.15 Films as Asylums for the Homeless

Under pressure from the ruling class, they become asylums for the homeless in an overarching sense. Apart from their actual function they contain another: to keep the white-collar employees away from the desired place of the upper class, and to distract them from critical issues, which they hardly register anyway. As for the present film production, I have shown in two essays that appeared in the 'Frankfurter Zeitung', 'The Little Shopgirl Goes to the Cinema,'[1] and 'The Present Day Film and its Public', how nearly all of the current production legitimates the status quo by averting attention from its deformities as well as its fundamentals; that it drugs the mass with the simile glamour [*Similiglanz*] of the socially fake elite.

Note: [1] See Levin 1995, pp. 291–304. The second is not translated, but see ibid., pp. 307–20, 323–8.

Source: Siegfried Kracauer, Die Angestellten. Aus dem neuesten Deutschland *(Frankfurt am Main, 1971), 98–9.*

Yet surely the point also must be that cinemas were not only asylums for the urban rootless, but also places where city dwellers had their urban experience reflected back to them, as I will suggest below. The scale of cinema-going in Germany during the 1920s (though not as great as in France or the United States) has led historians to speculate on the cinema as an integral part of the modern urban experience. In particular attention has focused on the cinema's universalizing impact upon its audiences (Abrams 1990: 286; Maase 1997: 112).

This claim now looks somewhat thin after having been subjected to a probing examination by the Hamburg social historian Karl Christian Führer (Führer 1996). Führer dismisses the assumption that the development and spread of early cinema into a mass industry, by the mid-1920s, meant that audiences were subjected to the same universalizing experience of values. The different sizes and types of cinema attracted different social classes. Thus the large modern Palace of the West in the Kurfürstendamm attracted a more middle-class audience, while the smaller houses in less smart areas were frequented by a younger and more proletarian clientele (Führer 1996: 742–5). Not only did cinemas vary in size and style, they also offered vastly different programmes, smaller ones often showing local or *Heimat* films on inadequate projectors that produced a very different cinematic experience (Führer 1996: 758–66).

The consumerist hedonism and sexualized materialism of the interwar years have been made familiar to us through the paintings of such Weimar artists as Max Beckmann, Georg Grosz and Karl Hubbuch, or the novels of English visitors, such as Stephen Spender or Christopher Isherwood. Its roots are to be found before the First World War, though representations of it are less familiar to us (the work of Robert Musil or Arthur Schnitzler apart).

Document 6.16 The Pleasure Dromes: Berlin Café Society

Berlin has become a city of Epicureans. Pleasure has been reduced to a philosophy, a cult, a system, brilliant, prodigal, *mondaine*. [. . .]

The corner of Friedrich Straße and Unter den Linden is the focal point of life of the so-called Friedrich-Stadt – the old central city over which the spirit of Frederick the Great broods. What would that bluff and spartan old warrior-king say to the modern Babylon that has usurped the street that bears his name? – this vortex of riotous pleasure, mad extravagence, modern sham, light and laughter?

World-famous cafés of an older day occupy these corners. Their interiors are packed with Berliners and provincials. They sit smoking at little tables and watch the vivid street-life through the great panes of plate glass. They fondle tall glasses of dark-smouldering Münchener, cups of balmy coffee or glasses of Russian tea. Smoke lies lazily in streaks and layers above their heads. Through this mist music pulsates for eighteen hours out of the twenty-four.

I was drawn into the swift and narrow aorta of the Friedrich Straße. Sober old-established firms stand cheek by jowl with insolent flaunting temples of gaiety, cafés and gigantic restaurants. [. . .]

Between ten-thirty and eleven o'clock the theatres pour forth a flood of people, laughing, chattering, criticising. No one thinks of going home. There must first be a glass of wine or beer, or chocolate, or a slice of rich cake and whipped cream. For this (costing about 3*d.*) one may sit for hours in the most sumptuous cafés and listen to their superb orchestras. Perhaps it is only a modest snack of hot sausage, potato salad and beer at Aschinger's. Clerks, students, young bloods, citizens, elderly epicures, the honest burgher and his wife, the elegant cavalier and his lady, flock to the innumerable restaurants. Rathkellers, bars, *paläste* and cabarets fight with light, colour and music for the favour of the public. Rivers of life tumble through the street. The Friedrich Straße bubbles. The multitude is hungry and thirsty for food, for drink, for music, for light and life. The hunger of modern multitudes. [. . .]

But the undisputed queen of the night is the *Palais de Danse* – the first establishment of the new order in Berlin. Its fame has been flaunted abroad in the world. To tourists and provincials its very name is redolent of sin, splendour and expense. It is the golden throne, the over-gorgeous frame in which her scarlet majesty loves to sit, pale and haughty in a sun-burst of diamonds. Though the respectable citizen sometimes takes his wife to gaze on the whirl of life, yet it is properly the meeting-ground for the nocturnal élite of Berlin. It was erected in 1910 at the cost of six and one-half million marks. Every night in the three hours of its greatest activity some thirty thousand marks' worth of champagne is consumed within this palace of the senses! Before its doors there are always groups of curious, watching the arrival of florescent [sic] beauties of the night. [. . .]

Source: Herman Scheffauer, 'The city without night: Berlin 'twixt dusk and dawn', The Pall Mall Magazine, No. 251, Vol. 53 (March 1914), 277–9, 284, 286, 289–90.

Scheffauer's account fits a common pattern of fascination with the city night, especially among visitors to the city (Schlör 1998: 248–58). In the following document, written contemporaneously with that by Scheffauer, the evening perambulations of a bank clerk in Hamburg, and his encounters with the other principal of urban modernity, the shopgirl, suggest a slightly more humble experience of consumerist pleasures, rather akin to those found over the same period in Britain (Davies 1992: 102–8); indeed, in this account, consumerism's surface is pithily portrayed.

Document 6.17 The Young Male Flaneur on the Jungfernstieg

The 'Young Man' develops his real existence along the Jungfernstieg only after business closes. There he can even ignore the Dresden Bank with a light heart – for there his view searches only for the eternal female. He perambulates with an inexhaustible stamina – now from the Hermannstraße to the Gänsemarkt, – and he allows his gaze to flit. There the brunette – here the blond. In front of Kempinski's he collars Posto. Firstly, it is not such a bad thing and it lightens the preliminaries; secondly, one likes to appraise Kempinski's dog, for the beast is a gem, and Kempinski likes it; thirdly, from Kempinski's one has the entire Alster Arcades in view – and [the shop and office girls] are just about the fount of Hamburg beauties – so we are 'in business' – [. . .].

In Neuer Wall and Hohe Bleichen conventicles form, partly mixed, partly unmixed. Both streets are of course premier thoroughfares – and in Hamburg too the young lady is favoured in the specialist shops. If they have connected, then, according to disposition and the generosity of the young man, a conferral takes place in front of Kempinski's, or in Neuer Wall or Große Bleichen, or, on the other hand, especially if it is late in the month, then it is off direct to the self-service restaurant and café. Even there, according to circumstances, it can be nice, especially because he is protected from any unanticipated cravings by his consort. She has to announce beforehand what she wants, and then an equally affectionate as determined *Ritardando* is delivered always with discretion.

Those who think of pilgrimming to St Pauli follow the route via the Colonnades – in order to have a lovely summer evening through an inspiring landscape of hills, valley and water *per pedes apostolorum*.[1]

But not all young men are so blessed by fate. After an extended stroll, many must dine solo in the private supper rooms, which only distinguish themselves from the luncheonettes by the numbers eating.

At 10 p.m. the Jungfernstieg is empty. Only in front of the Alster Pavilion sits a wall of life – beneath laurel and palms – and feeds itself on sorbets, Mazagran or pils.

Note: [1] St Pauli was already, by the turn of the century, renowned for its entertainment dives and sex tourism; see Chapter 4. The reference to 'a landscape of hills, valleys and water' is ironic and refers to the tall buildings and canals that characterized the commercial district.

Source: Triton, 'Der Hamburger, "Junge Mann": Auf dem Jungfernstieg', in Großstadt-Dokumente, *Vol. 39, ed. Hans Ostwald (Berlin, n.d.), 19–20.*

The city, through its various leisure institutions, from cinema to café, offered the visitor the prospect of consuming the big-city experience as lifestyle itself. In particular, its fashionable west end came to symbolize worlds distinct from the sedate and solid province. In Georg Pabst's film *Diary of a Lost Girl*, the small-town burghers visit the city. As they sit sipping sparkling wine in a haunt of the *beau monde*, the apothecary Mehnert turns to his employer's wife, whom he is trying to impress, and boasts, 'Dear lady, here you can see what goes on in the big city'. When Fritz Rasch, the actor playing Mehnert, spoke these words, he was also addressing the cinema audience, who consumed their celluloid *Döppelgänger* in the more popular films (Maase 1997: 113).

But, like the department stores and cinemas, the experience of the city through its café society remained highly differentiated, in spite of the 'weekend' surge into the west end or the 'slum'. The modest petit bourgeois, though not the clerk, sought his pleasures in less ostentious cafés and wine bars, while the members of the working class remained on their own pleasurable turf (Dröge, Krämer-Badoni 1987: 103ff., 114–16). Here, away from the 'rush and glitter' of the west end, popular entertainment took the form of vulgarized vaudeville, collective sing-alongs, brawls and sexual

Capitals of consumption

ventures. This was the world of the 'common man', brought to cinematic life in 1930 by Josef von Sternberg's *Blue Angel*, which, incidentally, allowed a mass audience to 'read' Heinrich Mann's novel visually.

A British diplomat, the cosmopolitan and *bon viveur*, Harold Nicolson, had been a regular visitor to Berlin during the interwar years, living in the Brücken Allee between 1927 and 1929, when he had been Counsellor at the British Embassy. Nicolson later recalled the 'rush and glitter' of Berlin's café society, but 'It was not the Berliners themselves who most frequented these palaces of delight; it was the tourists and the business men from Dortmund or Breslau' (Nicolson 1948).

Nicolson's provincial businessmen, like Pabst's small-town apothecary, flocked to the attractions of the city during the interwar period. Since the middle of the nineteenth century Europe's state and regional capitals, spas and resorts, had been enjoying the patronage of wealthy visitors. By the end of the century, the big cities, exuding the excitement, power and vitality of the new nation state, were clearly more popular destinations than the favoured spas of the nineteenth century (Jordan 1990: 147–54; Steward 1999: 123; Peniston-Bird 1996: 404–5). The war and revolutionary turmoil interrupted Germany's tourist trade, but its 1913 level and pattern were more or less re-established by 1922.

Document 6.18 Tourism's Ten Main Destinations, 1913–31

	1913	1923	1925	192	1928	1929	1931
			in thousands*				
Cities							
Berlin	1,430	1,210	1,593	1,746	1,683	1,633	1,201
Hamburg	630	476	556	658	730	686	405
Frankfurt a.M.	500	403	582	606	609	594	392
Cologne	482	240	300	387	581	516	413
Leipzig	304	635	426	403	456	454	324
Munich	572	671	817	810	869	856	674
Spas							
Wiesbaden	192	75	123	157	159	152	115
Baden-Baden	–	55	72	90	99	96	69
Bad Nauheim	35	28	36	39	41	42	31
Homburg v.d.H.	–	8	8	8	9	10	9

Figures are rounded up or down to nearest decimal point.

Source: Statistisches Jahrbuch für das Deutsche Reich, vols. 1926–32.

The majority of urban Germany's tourists were domestic visitors. Foreign travellers on average rarely exceeded a tenth of the total number of tourists (Schwarz 1993: 100–6). Many of those who visited the city did so for business reasons. For the actual tourist to the modern city with all its associations, it provided a consciousness of a new type of *Heimat*, or sense of belonging between province and city (Peniston-Bird 1996: 435–6; Enzensberger 1996: 130). This is emphasized in Ruttmann's film of Berlin with its repeated images of travel to Berlin, arrival at hotels, and visits to the city's sights. The same can be said of Erich Kaestner's *Emil and the Detectives*, turned into a film by Gerhard Lamprecht in 1931, where the young hero Emil's visit to the big city becomes the bridgehead between the old and new *Heimat* (Doc. 6.28).

City populations were exhorted to sally forth and discover the old *Heimat* by taking weekend trips into the countryside (Schulze 1921: 2–6). During the 1930s, most of the one- or two-day excursions organized by the Strength Through Joy branch of the Nazi-dominated German Labour Front, and which formed the majority of KdF tourist activities by 1938, sought out such fabled rural destinations (Schoenbaum 1967: 104, 106). Such imagery was used extensively by the Nazi tourist authorities in a specifically 'vacation discourse' that privileged a bucolic fantasy of a German *Heimat* rooted in the soil of the nation (Cross 1993: 119; Schwarz 1993: 89–95).

Document 6.19 'Visit Happy Germany', 1936

Source: Uwe Westphal, Werbung im Dritten Reich *(Transit: Berlin, 1989), 58.*

However, in contrast to a British predeliction for the seaside resort or the Alpine regions of Germany and Austria (Walvin 1978; Cross 1993: 114; Peniston-Bird 1996: 376, 381ff., 412–17), the urban tour continued to draw the visitor during the Third Reich. Between 1933 and the summer of 1939 tourism in general grew by two-thirds, but by an astonishing 90 per cent for the 33 cities that constituted the chief tourist destinations by that date (VStDR 1940: 28–31).

Document 6.20 Summer Season[a] Tourism, 1934–7

Destination	1934	1935	1936	1937[b]	1938/9[c] 1932/3
	in thousands of visitors				
50 cities	3,812	4,355	5,358	6,119	+87.6
200 small and medium towns	2,593	2,838	3,437	3,688	+42.7
220 spas	2,619	2,668	3,950	4,303	+65.6
30 seaside resorts	507	564	924	1,036	+60.6
Total	9,531	10,425	13,669	15,146	+68.3

[a]) 1 April to 30 September; [b]) 56 cities; 285 small and medium towns; 465 spas; 94 seaside resorts. [c]) 33 cities; 149 small and medium towns; 183 spas; 35 seaside resorts.

Source: Statistisches Jahrbuch für das Deutsche Reich, *individual volumes 1935–8;* Vierteljahreshefte zur Statistik des Deutschen Reichs, *Vol. 49 (1940), 30.*

Tourist guides, with their emphasis on landmarks and monuments (whether celebrating past kings and heroes or civic institutions), also helped towards constructing national identity, an especially important factor during moments of political fluidity or uncertainty (Peniston-Bird 1996, 367ff., 374ff.). This could be combined with economic considerations, especially where tourism might be one of the few recourses to financial wellbeing. Thus Halberstadt in Brandenburg, a picturesque town of just under 50,000 inhabitants, sought to capitalize on its chequered history as a means to overcome its economic difficulties.

Document 6.21 Halberstadt

The town administration and citizens have attempted to overcome this situation [economic downturn] with all the available means to hand since the coming to power of National Socialism. Thanks to the energetic support through the decrees of the government, it has also been possible to bring a halt to the pauperization [of the local population]. We continue to work untiringly to provide employment for the thousands of still unemployed people's comrades. It is, however, difficult to attract industry here because the town, to its misfortune, has remained overlooked by the development of rail, water and motor-ways. Thus the importation of raw materials and the carriage of finished goods is made difficult and expensive.

The celebration on the occasion of the 800th anniversary of the Reichstag in 1134, when Albert the Bear was invested with the fiefdom of Nordmark, also takes place in the context of our efforts to improve the unfortunate position of Halberstadt's labour market. The town's illustrious historical past inspires us to stage an event on a grand scale. The old beautiful town of Halberstadt will be known once again in the German fatherland. Strong participation from all over Middle Germany is anticipated. We hope thus for an improvement in the economic conditions of the town.

The town has made every effort so that the 800th anniversary of the founding of the Brandenburg-Prussian state at its place of birth appears especially dignified and popular (*volkstümlich*). The unemployed and recipients of welfare will receive a meal from municipal resources – they get 1 RM as well, so that they can joyfully take part.

You will see from these lines, Highly Esteemed Minister President [Göring], that everything is being done to commemorate a true people's festival. We would have a very special joy bestowed on our activity, if you, Herr Minister President, honoured us with your presence. Perhaps it is possible for you to come after all, if only for a very short while.

I enclose a few off-prints of the commemorative celebration programme, and nurture the hope that I receive positive news.

With German Greetings and
Heil Hitler
Yours respectfully,
[signature: Martens]

Source: Geheimes Staatsarchiv Preußischer Kulturbesitz, Berlin-Dahlem, Rep. 77/33 Oberbürgermeister Martens, Halberstadt to Hermann Göring (26 May 1934).

Göring declined the invitation.

The idea, alluded to above, of a *Heimat* in the city was promoted in official illustrated guides and brochures, local histories, and through careful advertising with a commercial element (Steward 1999: 126–7; Peniston-Bird 1996: 384–5, 387). In particular, cities marketed themselves as *Messestädte*, congress and trade cities, and to this purpose constructed exhibition halls. Perhaps the most famous of these venues was Breslau's 'Century Hall' designed by Max Berg and opened in 1913, and here depicted on a postcard.

Document 6.22 Jahrhunderthalle, Breslau, 1913

Source: Courtesy Geheime Staatsarchiv Preussisches Kulturbesitz.

Few cities were without an exhibition hall by the 1920s. And Breslau was even planning a second, larger venue by 1924. Trade fairs and congresses, art and technology exhibitions, as well as more regularly hosted prosaic events became common in Germany, as they did across Europe and in the United States, inviting the crowds who came to feast upon what they found there (Hietala 1987: 358–9; Cross 1993: 182). In November 1929, Berlin was host to 21 trade congresses and art exhibitions, 48 concerts and musical evenings, nine associational gatherings, and 27 sporting events, as well as numerous public lectures; in spite of the deepening depression, Hamburg hosted 38 events, exhibitions and congresses (LAB 142/I StB 4923: Bl. 42–6, 79–81, 115, 141–2). The importance of such events remained undiminished by the end of the 1930s. For example, Munich, a much favoured tourist destination, budgeted 50,000 marks for its regular menu of exhibitions, an extra 1 million marks for the exhibition *Day of German Art*, 1,206,300 marks for the summer festival, 357,865 marks for the Deutsches Museum, 204,520 marks to promote road and air transport clubs, and spent a further 30,000 marks to advertise these events (BAK R36/564).

Exhibitions were a means of explicitly announcing a city's modernity. Thus Hessen's cultural week in November 1937 made the latest technological 'wonder of the world', the television, its centrepiece attraction at the Frankfurt fair (Frankfurter Volksblatt 300, 2 Nov. 1937: 3; Landes 1969: 514). This particular technological innovation, like its 'sister' medium, the radio, was overwhelmingly an urban experience (Rosenhaft

1996: 122). The organizers used it like a magnet to draw crowds from Hessen to Frankfurt in order both to trumpet the regime's achievement, and to inculcate a sense of belonging to a larger *Heimat* by displaying 'valuable cultural treasures' of historical interest stored in the city's museums.

Document 6.23 Gau Cultural Week, Frankfurt 1937

Anouncement for the Lorenz-Advertising Van!
Gau
Attention! Attention!

Here is the Lorenz-Advertising Van on behalf of the Gau leadership of Hessen-Nassau!

Between 13–21 November 1937, the first mammoth exhibition of Gau culture will take place in Frankfurt am Main at the festival hall site.
People's Comrades!
Each person will find in this exhibition [. . .] a whole array of exciting and educative objects on display. Daily you will see Radio Frankfurt in its own studio with big concerts, variety evenings, and children's matinees. In the individual sections of the exhibition you will find paintings and sculptures, an interesting press and newspaper stand, a popular stage, the most beautiful books and valuable old documents, musical scores and instruments, and an interesting exhibit on regional peasantry.
In the film section the most modern film technology will be exhibited. And in the radio division as well as the newest radio equipment you will see for the first time a real television in daily operation.
All together in a mammoth exhibition – the Gau cultural exhibition in Frankfurt at the festival hall site from 13 to 21 November, opened daily all day, from 11 in the morning to 10 in the evening; on Sundays and holidays from 10 in the morning.
[. . .]
Source: Hauptstaatsarchiv Wiesbaden 483/10435, Der Propagandaleiter L/Pf. (10 November 1937), Betrifft: Lautsprecherwagen-Propaganda für die Gaukulturwoche Hessen-Naussau der NSDAP.

The success in attracting exhibitions to a city or town underwrote its municipal status as part of a national cultural grid. In Erfurt in 1924, 20 out of 41 events were staged by external associations, including eight from Berlin. Similarly, when Berlin hosted the World Advertising Exhibition in 1929, it not only restated its position as the capital of German consumerism, but emphasized its place in the international network of metropolitan consumer modernity.

Document 6.24 World Advertising Exhibition, Berlin, 1929

Source: Landesarchiv Berlin Zs 369 Nr 1929, 'Berlin konzentriert'.
Photomontage by Vennemann, Courtesy Landesarchiv Berlin.

The development of modern urban advertising during the early part of the twentieth century was one of the platforms for Germany's flight into modernity. The first advertising pillar was developed by a lithograph printer, Ernst Litfaß, in Berlin in mid-century. By 1900 advertising pillars and hoardings had become a ubiquitous feature of the German urban environment. By that date, there were 2,071 pillars and 1,139 hoardings in the 50 largest cities. But within a few years the concentration in towns and cities had become even greater. Thus in 1914 there were 18,631 pillars throughout the Reich, 7,099 of which were to be found in 44 large cities, and almost half of these again in just 24 cities (Reinhardt 1993: 236, 240–1, 253). By this date, advertising was also making a healthy contribution to the urban economy (Reinhardt 1993: 122).

Document 6.25 Advertising Pillars in Eight Cities, *c.*1912

City	Number and type of advertising system	Method of payment	Level of payment in financial year 1912
Berlin	30 Urania pillars	lump sum	45,000 *M*
	1550 advert. pillars	lump sum	54,000 *M;* from 1.7.13: 555,000 *M*

Cologne	40 pillars 85 billboards 1 other type (gallery rails in the main market)	5 *M* annually per m² advert. space, also a share of the gross revenue: 10% for 5 years; at 11% the following 3 years; 12% the next 2 years	pillars & billboard: 9,679,13 *M* Gallery rails: 6,250 *M*
Dresden	194 pillars 6 direction signs	125 *M* annually per pillar	24,108 *M* for the pillars
Frankfurt	135 pillars 35 billboards	37 *M* annually per m² advert. space	46,513*M* for 1913
Hamburg	100 pillars	10–25% of gross revenue without fixed minimum The percentage is determined by the level of tariff	not given
Leipzig	379 pillars 136 billboards	lump sum	95,000 *M*
Munich	118 pillars 94 billboards 2 kiosks and claddings	25 *M* annually per m² advert. space for pillar billboards, 10pf per m[etre] and per week for cladding	43,767 *M*
Stuttgart	65 pillars 56 billboards	lump sum	15,000 *M*

Source: Landesarchiv Berlin 142/1 StB 4879, Karlsruhe Verpachtung der Städteanschlagssäulen, Anlage 617/14: An den Stadtmagistrat Rüstringen (15 Mai 1914).

By the beginning of the 1920s, the advertising pillar had become an urban landmark as familiar to the city-dweller as the department store.

The turn towards more modern means and techniques of advertising from the turn of the century, and in the 1920s especially, represented a desire to modernize the 'face' of the city in accordance with the new times that emphasized its functionalism and a corporate identity. In his self-portrait, Georg Scholz places himself in alignment with other artefacts of urban modernity: the automobile (Mercedes) and an illuminated beacon.

Document 6.26 The Image of Modernity

[*The adverts posted to the pillar refer to beauty* (sei schön), *and leisure and sport* (Tanzabend, Meisterschaft)]

Source: Georg Scholz, 'Selbstbildnis vor Litfaßsäule', 1926, in Jost Hermand and Frank Trommler, Die Kultur der Weimarer Republik *(Munich, 1978), plate 14.*

In most cases advertising employed the latest technology, artistic styles and technical organization. Kurt Schwitters in Hannover, who repeatedly used geometric grids in his work, typified the attempt to influence the civic landscape according to the principles of the New Objectivity. According to the art historian Maud Lavin, advertising thus mediated between avant garde and mass consumerist culture in the cities (Lavin 1992: 39, 56).

Throughout the interwar period, Germany's production of electrical energy far outstripped that of most other European countries, being nearly double that of its nearest rival, the United Kingdom (Landes 1969: 441). But household consumption was not particularly high, and the largest consumers were industry and commercial businesses. Before 1914 only Berlin and Dresden allowed electricity for advertising, while Hamburg was planning to introduce it. After the lifting of wartime restrictions in 1922, lighting in advertising spread quickly, and because it was cheap to consume, neon came to replace traditional bulbs during the Depression (Reinhardt 1993: 312–29). By 1929, Berlin had the largest neon light advertising complex in Europe, with 6,000 lamps fixed upon a 10-ton heavy scaffolding with an area of 360 square metres along the Kurfürstendamm. Berlin was thus the self-styled neon capital of European consumerism.

Document 6.27 Berliner Europa-Haus Palast

[see illustration on page 160]

Source: Gerhard F.W. Schmidt, 'Leuchtwerbung der Markenartikel-Industrie' in Die Deutsche Werbung, *30 (1937), 1128, reprinted in Uwe Westphal,* Werbung im Dritten Reich *(Transit: Berlin, 1989), 89.*

As this image shows, the neon city beams with a brash assurance, in much the same way that Odol mouthwash was supposed daily to instil supreme confidence in its user. For city-dwellers, such modern advertising created a new landscape of literature for the urban masses, speaking storylines from the tops of buildings (Reinhardt 1993: 323–6; Doc. 7.8).

The neon and even more traditional display of modern consumerism was not accepted by all. But in spite of the sometimes fierce attacks by critics against the profusion of 'vulgar signs' (Hegemann 1930: 162; Reinhardt 1993: 238–9), carefully controlled modern advertising could provide visual order and unity. Thus after incorporating a number of neighbouring communities in 1929, the council of Falkensee was 'contemplating the idea of obtaining for ourselves modern means of advertising that will fit the landscape of our community. The community of Falkensee consists of 10 suburbs, under which there are 2 rural, 2 garden estates, and several villa estates' (LAB 142/I StB 3443, Gemeindevorstand Falkensee, 22 Aug. 1929). By means of establishing visual coherence it hoped to create a sense of organic unity to the new community. The idea of organic wholeness could also be applied to Germany's old and new face.

Document 6.28 Old and New Germany, 1926

[see illustration on page 161]

Source: Herbert Bayer 'Dessau Broschure', 1926, in Photography at the Bauhaus, *edited for the Bauhaus Archiv by Jeannine Fiedler (London, 1990), 218.*

[Document 6.27 Berliner Europa-Haus Palast]

[Document 6.28 Old and New Germany, 1926]

The idea of consuming the city as a unified and unifying urban experience of modernity was driven by a new breed of entrepreneur, the 'captains of consciousness' who, however, had not yet come to displace their nineteenth-century counterparts from industry. Moreover, in spite of efforts during the interwar years to rationalize the organization and presentation of a consumer society, a wide variety of advertising practices persisted well into the 1930s (LAB 142/1 StB 3443, Cologne, Rundfrage, May 1932; Westphal 1989: 13; Ewen 1976). Nevertheless, by the end of the 1930s, the foundations of Germany's postwar consumer society had been laid. But some of the claims regarding its epochal changing nature should not be exaggerated. In spite of public appearance, actual patterns or practices of mass consumption and leisure altered gradually, and remained confined mostly to the new class of office and commercial employees in the city.

There was, however, an incipient consumerist ideology that was quickly mobilized for the economy immediately after the war when industry had either collapsed or was restricted by the occupation authorities. Thus in 1945, Sombart's urban-led consumer society soon re-established itself, before taking off from the late 1950s (Ambrosius and Hubbard 1989: 77; Wildt 1995: 23–41).

Document 6.29 Postwar Shopping

Anyone who has heard of Berlin has heard of the Kurfürstendamm. This endlessly long street, with trams running down the middle between small green hedges, is not quite like any other famous street. And now in 1946 it is not even very like itself.

It used to be one of the busiest, gayest streets in Berlin. It catered for all tastes in all ways. It was primarily a shopping street, a slightly more garish version of Bond Street, but many of Berlin's best cafes, restaurants and night clubs were there too, as well as two theatres and a few cinemas.

What of it now? In many ways the Kurfürstendamm has suffered less than other big Berlin streets. The Gedächtniskirche at the end is a grotesque ruin (it was pretty grotesque before), many of the buildings are shattered, but the street is still very much alive. Trams run frequently, there are some cars, many bicycles and many people walking, window shopping or sitting in the sun in the open air cafes. The street seems alive chiefly because nearly every day another shop manages to clear the rubble away, polish the door, get glass in the window and paint up a new sign or a whole wall. And somehow or other they manage to get something to put in the window. In fact in this shopping street, the Berliners can do some shopping again.

Source: British Zone Review *(20 July 1946), 13.*

The ability of Germans to consume had wider implications than simply those of individual materialism (Fromm 1978: 26–7). For 'the fact does remain that until the ordinary German civilian is made to feel that once more life holds something to live and to work for, the country will not attain even a modicum of normality and an abnormal Germany will remain a blot on the map of Europe and a threat to the rehabilitation of Europe and the world' (BZR, 14 Sept. 1946). This idea of a nation of consumers in harmony with themselves and with others was to sit at the very core of Germany's postwar modernity.

7 Tempo of the city, map of the nation

In his essay on mental life and the city, Georg Simmel wrote of the 'intensification of nervous stimulation' wrought by the city upon the psyche of its inhabitants. In particular, Simmel focused on the tempo of the city, and this was determined by its traffic. This was potentially an anarchic disharmonious force when left to itself, but when harnessed and channelled, its rhythms and flows became a positive force, while the parameters of its organization gave shape to the physical environment.

The volume of Germany's urban traffic had been growing at a phenomenal rate since the last quarter of the nineteenth century. The development of new technology allowed for freer and speedier flows of traffic. The most important contribution to revolutionize both the urban landscape and the urban experience was the electric tram, displayed by Werner von Siemens at the Industry Exhibition in Berlin in 1879. The first public electric tramline was opened two years later on a line just 2½ kilometres in length at Lichterfelde to the south of old Berlin. Within a decade, it had quickly spread to most large cities. Indeed, by 1895, 23 per cent of trams were electrically driven, and by the early 1900s, all were electrified (Hegemann 1930: 430; Niederich 1996: 136).

Document 7.1 Berlin's and Germany's Electric Trams, 1904–6

Berlin's public transport – excluding horsedrawn cabs – carried nearly 754½ million people in 1906, or nearly as many as the Prussian-Hessian state railway over the same period. Of this number, 138½ million were transported by the city and ring trains, 481 million by the electric tram-system and the elevated and underground trains, and 135 million persons were carried by the omnibus company.

It is no easy task to transport these huge numbers of people quickly and safely within the city and from city to the suburbs. Without the excellent technical advances made during the last decades in the sphere of local public transport, this would have been impossible. Barely a century has passed since Lafitte operated the first omnibus in Paris (1819), and the first horse-drawn railway was built in Germany only in 1865, to improve the connection between Berlin and Charlottenburg. In 1879 a small electric train was shown in Berlin for the first time at the trade exhibition by Werner von Siemens. Due to his activities, at first more for the purpose of experimenting, the first of all electric trams was built in Großlichterfelde and introduced to the general public already on 16 May 1881. Today in Germany, as abroad, most public transport in the cities is provided by the electric tram. [. . .]

Source: Adolf Weber, Die Großstadt *(Berlin, 1908), 64–6.*

The development of urban tram systems was quite spectacular, and predominantly an urban phenomenon (Teuteberg and Wischermann 1985: 80–2; Niederich 1996: 138ff.). Between 1893 and 1904, for example, the number of Cologne's tram passengers grew from around 11 million to 55.6 million, and by 1930 had nearly quadrupled to 204 million. A more spectacular growth rate occurred in Stuttgart, where the volume of passenger traffic grew sevenfold between 1890 and 1910 (Kölner Verkehrs-Verein n.d.: 30–1; Niederich 1996: 149). The tram's success continued apace in the decade after the First World War. By the early 1930s, there were over 25,000 electric-powered trams in all of Germany carrying nearly 4 billion passengers. By 1938, the 55 largest cities of the Reich accounted for approximately 80 per cent of this passenger traffic (McElligott 1999: 212).

The ubiquitous tram structured the city experience, and brought order to the street (Hegemann 1930: 411–12). Throughout Alfred Döblin's classic story *Berlin Alexanderplatz, The Story of Franz Biberkopf,* for instance, trams criss-cross the author's narrative as they would have criss-crossed the city from end to end. Sitting inside the tram looking out, the city was possibly experienced as a set of impressionistic tableaux that appeared rhythmically as the wagons meandered along the tracks.

Document 7.2 On a Journey through Berlin

The metropolitan person is closely integrated into the tram-system through work and business journeys. The individual traveller gets by with a few lines and the majority with only one, their regular line. They journey on particular trams, always with the very same people, while they surely read their particular newspapers; moreover, it is certainly the case that they only have a vague idea of what daily flits past the windows.

Any journey, for example with the Nr 128 from Britz to Heiligensee, slices through the old, declining Berlin and the new, developing Berlin. Where the stone sea of the metropolis gives way to the southern prairie and the last low houses begin, the tram starts and rolls up the Hermannstraße, propels itself from the level of the old Rollberg, upon which south Neukölln stands, down towards Kottbuser Damm, [. . .] the Hermannstraße itself [. . .] today thronging with people, here and there already with functional facades of new buildings, in between old courts, tenements and human stalls with wild ornamentation from the *Gründerzeit* [industrial period from 1871], right and left, however, there are pleasant connecting streets with harmonious flat-roofed apartment blocks, cinemas and cinema palaces: the new world. The Rollkrug is no longer at the end of the street, but instead the Karstadt skyscraper, and the street rolls muted alongside. [. . .]

The Marienkirche, the Hakesche Markt, Oranienburger Straße, still quiet and noble, here and there lovely old Berlin houses. [. . .] At Oranienburger Tor the tram heads north. The old Latin quarter with student taverns, entertainment halls, appears to have long sunk with time. [. . .] The Chausseestraße, once the scene for days of unrest, is now disturbed only by the streaming traffic. [. . .]

The tram continues on its way: past the Borsig-Tower, the Tegel Gasworks. [. . .] The reflection of the Tegel Lake shimmers upon approach. The old Humboldt Palace visited by Goethe 150 years ago, looms – now the tram rolls into the spring forest. As the forest thins, the tram journeys on a single track through scattered colourful settlement houses towards the Heiligensee. [. . .] somewhere a light, spring blue lake, and then the old village of Heiligensee with its tree-lined avenue and the Havel [lake].

Source: Die Fahrt. Zeitschrift der Berliner Verkehrs-Aktiengesellschaft, *Nr 9 (15 May 1929), 7–9.*

The perception of the tram's tempo changed over time, becoming associated with a slower, almost leisurely picturesque urban rhythm when compared to other modern technologies (Docs. 7.6, 7.17). Its place in the road was fixed by the immutable grids of iron track that snaked through the city. Its rivals by the 1920s, the motor car and bus, were less inhibited and followed a faster tempo. The volume of motorized traffic in German towns and cities had been increasing steadily since the 1900s. Although Germany lagged behind the United States, Britain and France in terms of production and ownership of private motorcars (Landes 1969: 442; Eckermann 1989: 97–100; O'Connell 1998: 19), the number of registered vehicles continued to rise dramatically in all major cities during the interwar period. By the mid-1930s, there were nearly 2 million motor vehicles on Germany's roads, nearly half of them concentrated in the big cities and towns (StJbDS 26 1931: 240). As one might expect, Berlin had one of the highest *per capita* ratios of cars to population. And it was here, notably around the Alexanderplatz, the Potsdamerplatz and the Gedächtniskirche, that the tempo of the city *per se* seemed to be at its greatest (Strohmeyer 1987: 138–9). The automobile, like the electric tram, became a powerful signifier of urban modernity, as is evident from Walter Ruttmann's classic film, *Berlin: Symphony of a city* (Hake 1994; McElligott 1999).

Document 7.3 Automobiles

[see illustration opposite]

Source: Walter Ruttmann, Berlin: Sinfonie einer Großstadt *(1927).*

Ruttmann's film also contains a number of sequences referring to that other icon of interwar modernity, the aeroplane. Like their counterparts elsewhere, early twentieth-century Germans looked to the sky as a highway of the future. The development of early aeronautical technology and its social impact is well documented (Bongers 1967;

Fritzsche 1992). What is less well understood is its close relationship to urban modernity. In early January 1911, at a meeting in Dresden to raise funds for what would be Germany's first Air Show (*Flugtag*), Professor Hallwachs, an engineer and president of the Saxony Association of Air Transport (*Sächsischer Verein für Luftschiffahrt*) explained to an attentive audience of local dignitaries the civic benefits and national virtues of the proposed *Flugtag* planned for May that year.

Document 7.4 Dresden Air Show, 1911

Another objective in establishing air shows here is that they should serve the advancement and the honour of our beautiful city of Dresden. I don't need to explain that to you any further, it is obvious to everyone. Taking a few concrete benefits, the craftsmen as well as all those who have an interest in the aeroplane, whether active or passive, as I have already mentioned, will directly draw rich pickings from the business. Indirect benefits will arise in very many different areas. One has had the opportunity at the recent air show to see which benefits the railway gained by transporting large numbers of people to and from the airfield; this will be more so with a much larger enterprise of the sort we have in mind, and will extend to all forms of urban transport in the city, whether it be the tram, taxi or automobile. Since I have just spoken of railways, I want to again emphasize that since people will come from far and wide because of our undertaking, the railways will naturally earn more. In addition, the transporting of an aeroplane together with all its equipment means that each round trip [has the knock-on effect that it] brings with it an entire train, so to speak. The aforementioned large numbers of people hold out the promise of important benefits for all conceivable quarters of the city, from publican to cigarette manufacturer, from butcher to photographer.

[. . .]

If, as a result of our undertaking, our tacit desire for a permanent airport were to be realized, this will draw flyers and machines continuously under the spell of the city, and it will be an immense gain. But I want to point out that quick action is called for. There is already a string of airports in Germany. If we wait, then we stand to lose the right advantage because of the strong competition; however, were we to act quickly, then the creation of an airport in such a large city as Dresden would have the result that others would fear the competition and for the time being draw back from establishing an airport.

Source: Staatsarchiv Dresden MdI Nr 1507, Bl. 18: Sitzung des Ehrenausschusses für die Dresdener Flugtage im Mai 1911, [Sonderdruck] (13 Jan. 1911).

The Dresden airshow took place in May and lasted a week. It was rounded off with a flight over Saxony, reportedly the first of its type, and aroused a great deal of public interest and excitement. Indeed, soon afterwards, an international race was held, covering a distance of 1,878 kilometres, and its route anticipated the commercial flight paths that were established between 13 cities in central and northern Germany during the early 1920s (Bongers 1967: 22–32; McElligott 1999: 213).

Some of Germany's largest cities financially underwrote the creation of Deutsche Luft Hansa in 1926, in much the same way as they supported the dozen or so regional air consortia that existed at that time. Within a few years municipal financial investment in the company rose nearly fourfold to 8.5 million Reichsmark, accounting for 35 per cent of the company's shares by 1930. A fifth of the company's 65 directors were mayors or leading municipal officers; the lord mayor of Cologne, Konrad Adenauer, was a deputy chairman. Among the largest contributors were Cologne, Frankfurt and Munich, which also had the busiest airports. By the end of the 1920s, the modern-equipped aerodrome had become as much a part of the urban architectural landscape as the department store, and the aeroplane itself, notably the Junker F13 – the first civilian passenger plane – as familiar a sight in the city as the tram or motor car as the number of air passengers rose from just 2,000 in 1919 to nearly a quarter of a million by 1928; half of these went through the gates of just eight city airports (Bongers 1967: 22–4, 27; McElligott 1999: 214–15). In Erich Kaestner's classic children's story, *Emil and the Detectives*, the boy hero Emil leaves his small town on a train; is warned by his mother about the traffic of the big city; follows the thief by tram, on foot and by taxi; and finally returns home a hero by air in a Junker F13 aeroplane.

Document 7.5 Two Junker F13s in Dresden

Source: Bärbel Schräder and Jürgen Schebera, The Golden Twenties: Art and literature in the Weimar Republic *(New Haven and London, 1990), 101: illustr. 33.*

Technological innovations that modernized the urban experience were but one aspect of urban traffic. Animal-drawn vehicles were still much in evidence in 1939, as de Laforgúe shows in his copycat film *Symphonie der Weltstadt* (1939). Similarly, the bicycle had become universal among the working class as an inexpensive and effective means of getting around the interwar city, as the opening scenes in Slatan Dudow's film *Kuhle Wampe oder Wem gehört die Welt?*, testify. And, as everywhere in Europe, people 'walked' the cities in which they lived (Bessel 1989: 163), as Ruttmann shows in *Berlin: Symphony of the city*, where the early-morning trickle of workers soon turns into a flood.

This juxtaposition of technology and humans in the street was a cultural phenomenon that exercised not only sociologists such as Georg Simmel. Painters turned the rush of the street into a new landscape genre (Doc. 7.9); and novelists, such as Robert Walser, inserted their characters into the midst of the swirling bustle of turn-of-the-century city traffic.

Document 7.6 Street Life, *c.*1900

I often walk through the streets, and there I think I am living in a wild, beguiling fairy tale. What shoving and crushing, what a rattle and patter!

What yelling, stamping, humming and buzzing! And everything so squashed together. The people, children, girls, men and elegant women, walk pressed close to the wheels of carriages; one sees in the crowd the aged and cripples, and those who have bandaged heads. And always new streams of people and vehicles. The carriages of the electric trams look like picturesquely filled boxes. The omnibuses crawl along like great hulking beetles. Then there are vehicles that look like great travelling watch-towers. People sit upon the raised seats oblivious to everything that passes, jumps, and moves below. New crowds press their way into the existing crowd, and it goes, comes, appears and proceeds as one. Horses trample, [. . .] And the sun gleams upon it all. It shines the nose of one, the toes of another. Dogs ride in carriages upon the laps of older elegant women. Breasts bounce towards one, pressed into gowns and fashions, female breasts. And one thinks of unknown streets, invisible new and equally overpeopled neighbourhoods. [. . .] what is one really in this flood, in this never-ending stream of humanity?

Source: Robert Walser, Jakob von Gunten (orig. 1909, Frankfurt a. Main, 1985), 37–8.

Here, Walser makes the mental impression of the congested street the central subject under review. Social reportage did the same. 'Berlin was storming homeward from its work. Solid masses crowded the pavements, a stream of trams and crowded motor-buses clamoured along the street. The Stadtbahn, or city railway, thundered across its arches overhead. The Untergrund [sic] engulfed rivers of humanity in the side streets. Shop-girls, clerks, petty bureau-officials, tradespeople, typists – fresh, eager faces, restless and nervous bodies' (Scheffauer 1914: 284). Similarly, crowds jostle and bear down on the viewer in the street paintings of Adolf Birkle, while in Franz Masereel's woodcuts, *City Cycle* (1926), the city is even brought to a halt by the massed crowds on the street. Georg Grosz turned such street scenes into an artform.

These representations of street tumult on the one hand, and a claustrophobic urban space on the other, confirm a received image of the modern city. But it should not go unchallenged. The Bauhaus photographer, Erich Comeriner's evocative photograph of the Friedrichstraße, taken around 1929, when that street's volume of traffic had increased enormously, conveys an altogether quieter, almost tranquil idyll compared with that painted by Grosz of the same street (Doc. 2.15).

Document 7.7 Berlin, Friedrichstraße, *c.* 1929

[see illustration opposite]

Source: Erich Comeriner, Courtesy Bauhaus-Archiv, Berlin.

By the 1920s, the tempo and rhythm of traffic was firmly situated at the centre of textualizations of the urban experience, such as in Döblin's *Berlin Alexanderplatz*, or Kaestner's *Emil and the Detectives*. The volume and tempo of Berlin's traffic, in particular, was the inspiration behind Georg Goldschlag's poem, 'City'.

Document 7.8 City (1931)

Bands of light draw in over boxes of houses
stepped-facades stand upright.
Escalators shovel people from the nights
of the underground onto the pavements.

Shouts. Ringing. Horns and sirens.
Shop windows. Banks. Department stores. Bars.
As tall as a house and smiling with bared teeth
The giant bust image of a film star.

Cigar kiosks. Cafés with halls.
At arc-lights a street crossing.
In a distant tail flight automobiles
in rows of six, unendingly long.

General Motors – Daimler – Horch – Mercedes –
Studebaker – Chrysler – Opel – Fiat – Ford –
with trembling flanks each waits
for freedom and a new speed record.

The light is red. Pedestrian people migrate
across the vehicle fronts at the same trot.

The traffic cop separates one from the other
only with a gesture, like a god of old.

Surrounded by the power of the flood
alone his outline raging in the tempest.
The light turns green. A chaos is unleashed.
Movement lurches onto the open track.

In changing rhythm the mechanism hammers.
Pandemonium and standstill. A lull and frenzy.
Repressed waiting. Breathless panic.
The track closes itself off. And the road is free.

The traffic lights blaze mystically-without-reason.
After 'Halt' follows 'Go' and after 'Go' 'Halt'.

At each streetcorner flow hourly
ten thousand cars over the asphalt.

On the rims of roofs climb incessantly fatuous
the neon advertising for chocolate and sparkling wine.
Here fate is dissipated blank and profitless.
Here one lives, savours and expires.

O city of horsepower and cable,
full of poverty and riches, want and gluttony –
I call you by your names, Babel,
Sodom, Gomorrah – and Jerusalem!

Source: George W. Goldschlag, 'City', in Robert Seitz and Heinz Zucker (eds.), Um uns die Stadt 1931: Eine Anthologie neuer Großstadtdichtung (orig. Berlin, 1931), reprint with a foreword by Ulrich Conrads (Der Bauwelt Fundamente 75, Braunschweig, Wiesbaden, 1986), 173–4.

So pervasive was the idea of tempo as a *leitmotif* of the modern city, that the expressionist artist, Ludwig Meidner, could convey its elemental nature (Lloyd 1991b: 286) without even depicting a single vehicle.

Document 7.9 Südwestkorso Berlin, Five o'Clock in the Morning, 1913

Source: Ludwig Meidner, reproduced in Art in Germany, *102.*

In Ruttmann's *Berlin Symphony* 'sounds become images'. On the first showing of the film, Edmund Meisel, who composed the symphonic score, placed the orchestra in different parts of the hall so as to engulf the audience by the 'conglomeration of all the noises of the metropolis' (Goergen n.d.: 59). The mediation of the city experience through its sounds was repeated in the film versions of *Berlin Alexanderplatz* and *Emil und die Detektive*, where the cacophony of the city soundscape, from car horns to hydraulic hammers, is used to structure and map the urban experience, of Berlin especially. In Kaestner's story, the children traverse the foreign and sometimes bewildering city-scape by orientating themselves by the sounds emitting from it. Indeed, the clique's leader, 'Professor', sounds his horn in order to communicate with and direct the movements of the other members of the gang.

But by the turn of the century, the noise of the city was also being pathologized through its discursive and visual representation. This would include not only the sociology of Georg Simmel, but notably that of other writers too, such as the psychiatrist Theodor Lessing, who made a connection between the tempo and noise of the city and the alleged degenerative nervous condition of Germany's urban population (Lessing 1909: 79–84; Baron 1982). Lessing's pathology of street noise also found its way into the visual arts.

Document 7.10 The Noise of the Street, 1920

[see illustration opposite]

Source: Otto Dix, 'Lärm der Straße, 1920', Courtesy of Akademie der Künste, Berlin.

The putative chaos of traffic was believed to threaten the urban civitas in at least two principal ways. Firstly, the cacophony of urban noises impinged negatively on the collective psyche, resulting in a heightened nervousness and stored aggression that might explode at any time (Radkau 1994: 211–41); secondly, untrammelled traffic, especially of individuals in their automobiles, threatened to spin out of control, resulting in collisions that would interrupt the city's rhythm and flow with adverse consequences for society and economy *per se* (Scharfe 1990: 223, 230–2). As the volume of all traffic grew, the question of how to control and direct it became more pressing. By the early 1920s, urban authorities were defining themselves as 'technicians' whose primary task was to harness modern science in order to bring rational order and control to the street and thus to the city at large (FZ 24 Dec. 1908; Lessing 1909: 85; Hegemann 1930: 432; Scharfe 1988: 214–17; Emsley 1993: 357–81). According to the head of the Psychological Institute at the Prussian Academy for Physical Training, Dr R. W. Schulte, the control of traffic was imperative if it was not to become the nemesis of urban civilization.

Document 7.11 Traffic and Nervousness

For the inner economic status of a metropolis, for the tempo of its *Zeitgeist* as well as for the outward forms through which it reveals itself, traffic and its regulation are of the upmost importance. Development trends, tensions and outgrowths characterize themselves in city traffic in an extraordinary intensive way. The police, as guardians of public order, require thus increasingly special duties which in earlier centuries they only had to carry out on special occasions, but which today comprise such a large part of their duties, that in the public mind when one thinks of police duties today one thinks first and foremost of regulating traffic. Stage and film, radio and school, press and exhibitions have embedded the activity of the traffic police in the new Germany, and especially in the new Berlin, so strongly, that the child's playfight between cops and robbers already has today become our smallest official act: the friendly arm movement of the traffic police. The new Berlin is characterized by a rich mass of life-joy optimism – and by incredible tension and lively precision as well, when one compares it to other European capitals. The tempo and rhythm of our times are embodied in the rapid growth of our traffic, whose regulation poses the Berlin police authorities with extraordinary tasks. The Berlin traffic is difficult to compare with that of Paris, London or New York. The form of the streets in the city landscape offers particular difficulties, which are unknown, for instance, in Paris, with its grand boulevards and squares. Today it is possible to state that the regulation of Berlin's traffic according to its own rules and methods is a largely and thoroughly satisfactory one, even if from the perspective of a technician such as a technician of psychology there are still a lot of individual and small tasks to deal with and the permanent progress necessarily leads to renewed controls, criticism and improvement. The regulation of Berlin's traffic has sought from the beginning to bring the administrative regulation of traffic through psychological laws into harmony with the mental condition of the city population as far as possible.

Source: Dr R.W. Schulte, Leiter des Psychologischen Instituts der Preußischen Hochschule für Leibesübungen, 'Die Psychotechnik im Dienste der Verkehrspolizei', in Das neue Berlin, *1929, Heft 11 (reprint 1988), 224–6.*

With this observation, Schulte articulated the widely held view that traffic, like nature, could be tamed by technology (Schulze-Gävernitz 1930: 231–2, 236–7, 253). An example of the triumph of man over nature can be found in a promotional film made in 1929 by the Berlin Transport Authority, *Rolling Wheels* (*Die rollenden Räder*), a cinematic anthem to technological solutions to the problems of big-city traffic and which found its counterpart in Britain with the GPO Film Unit's *The City* (1939). In most respects, this technocratic approach fits with the New Objectivity, which, in its depictions of tamed traffic, displayed the success of a rational technological civilization in overcoming the elemental impulses of the big city.

Document 7.12 'Spandau Underpass' (1927)

[see illustration opposite]

Source: Gustav Wunderwald, 'Unterpass Spandau', 1927, reproduced in Reinhold Heller (ed.), Art in Germany 1906–1936. From Expressionism to Resistance. The Marvin and Janet Fishman Collection *(Munich, 1990), 151.*

There was good reason to be concerned about the tempo and noise of the street and its psychological impact upon the individual. Traffic accidents had been on the increase since the early 1900s, rising sharply after the First World War to well over a quarter of a million by 1937. More worryingly, the fatal outcome of these accidents took on alarming proportions: rising from 145 in 1907 to 7,636 in 1937.

Around two-thirds of all road accidents took place within conurbations. But while larger cities such as Berlin, Hamburg, Leipzig, Munich and Cologne inevitably took the lion's share of accidents, the big city was not the inevitable arena for the worst statistics. In 1937, for instance, more people were killed in road accidents in the country-side than in urban areas (StJBDR 1938: 241–2). Nevertheless, road deaths became a by-word for the modern urban experience, and were seized upon by its detractors. Attention was paid to Berlin in particular, where, in spite of a slight improvement in the number of road accidents and fatalities, commentators, from Berlin's chief statistician Richard Korherr to Gottfried Feder, alleged that a 'silent war' was in progress that consumed the German *Volk*, especially those in the prime of life (Strohmeyer 1987: 139; see Doc. 2.17).

Document 7.13 Pedestrian Victims of Road Accidents in Berlin According to Age, 1928, 1932, 1933

Age	1928		1932		1933	
	N	*%*	*N*	*%*	*N*	*%*
0–6	n/a	4.2	257	6.5	220	5.9
6–14	n/a	7.2	419	10.5	367	9.9
14–60	n/a	76.5	2,452	61.8	2,286	61.7
60 and over	n/a	12.0	842	21.2	833	22.5
Total	5,564	100.0	3,970	100.0	3,706	100.0

Source: Die Fahrt. Zeitschrift der Berliner Verkehrs-Aktiengesellschaft, *Nr 3 (22 Feb. 1929), 7;* Statistisches Jahrbuch der Stadt Berlin, *Vol. 10 (1934), 150–1.*

In order to slow the tempo and harmonize the rhythm of cities, the new 'technicians' of city life sought to regulate traffic by inculcating in the public an etiquette of the road. This was thought to be all the more necessary given that the cause of accidents was frequently attributed to a lack of road education: for instance, failure to give hand signals, or to indicate if one was turning or changing one's position in the road, pedestrians oblivious of oncoming vehicles and, in particular, fast and reckless driving. National road safety campaigns were launched from the second half of the 1920s. For example, in September 1932 in Stuttgart a four-week action of combating unnecessary street noise and careless driving was staged. The police sought first to educate the public in the proper use of warning signals and the car horn through a press campaign before setting up controls around the city. By repeating such experiments at regular intervals, the police hoped to achieve a general calming of the supposed nervousness of the public. In Stuttgart at least – and the data in Doc. 7.13 suggest something similar for Berlin – the exercise seems to have produced positive results. By 1934 there were fewer traffic accidents and fatalities, and the decrease was put down to fewer frayed tempers among drivers and improved behaviour such as the decline in reckless speeding over cross-roads (where traffic lights were absent) (McElligott 1999: 217ff.). Although emphasis was placed upon self-discipline and consideration for fellow-road users, appeals were also made to self-interest.

Document 7.14 'Think About Where Carelessness Can Lead'

Denk daran, wohin Unvorsichtigkeit führen kann!

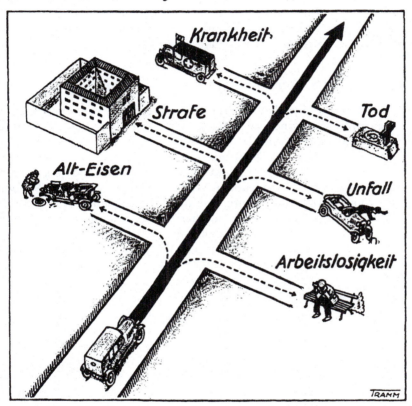

Weiche nicht vom Wege der Vorsicht ab!

Captions read anti-clockwise: To illness; to punishment; to the scrapyard; to unemployment; to an accident; to death.

Source: Die Fahrt: Zeitschrift der Berliner Verkehrs-Aktiengesellchaft, *Nr 3 (22 Feb. 1929), 15.*

Street traffic was not the only cause for concern. In 1928 the Bulgaria cigarette manufacturers of Dresden employed a former world war pilot, Max Wachitz, to fly his single-engine aeroplane, with a siren attached, at 500 metres over Dresden. The brand name of the cigarette had been painted onto the fuselage and wings, turning it into a flying billboard. Wachitz, however, proceeded to strafe the citizens of the city below the 500 metre limit, with irritating results. The director of the municipal zoo complained that animals were being terrorized by the combination of the drone of the engine and the whine of the siren; the pastor of the Church of the Redemption protested that his young pupils were being distracted from their Bible lessons. Dresden's would-be 'Red Baron' finally flew his last sortie when he chanced upon what he thought to be a target audience for Bulgaria Cigarettes.

Document 7.15 Aeroplane Noise

Yesterday, during a funeral at the Striesen cemetery such an aircraft flew low over the graveside mourners at 3.30 pm (according to the funeral assistant: 'Bulgaria'), and a few seconds later after turning beyond the cemetery, even flew over for a second time. The words of the blessing were no longer under-standable over the noise of the siren and the clatter of motors, and the solemnity of the service distressingly disrupted. Witnesses: employees of the Striesen Choral Group, as well as the mourners of the Lehmann family. [. . .]

One is only surprised that at a time when the police authorities thankfully decree strong measures against peace-disturbing clattering of motor vehicles (frequently a result of technical inadequacy), they have not long since already banned the advertising planes which purposefully disturb the peace only to advertise.

signed: Fruesleben

Source: Staatsarchiv Dresden MdI Nr 15123, Bl. 101.

The extension of the city into the countryside through incorporations, and the development of housing estates of the type we noted in Chapter 3, also made radial transport networks imperative by the 1920s. Thus, as the city became more horizontal, so a web-like transport network was spun to hold it together; over it, commuters, like so many thousands of small spiders, could quickly move to the centre (Hall 1988: 119, 121–2). According to transport historian John McKay, the new urban transport networks provided the nerve sinews of the suburban 'spinal columns' that stretched their 'long fingers [. . .] into the countryside' (McKay 1976: 209). And by doing so, they gave a modern form and unity to what might otherwise have been a shapeless landscape of disparate communities.

Document 7.16 Chemnitz

[see illustration opposite]

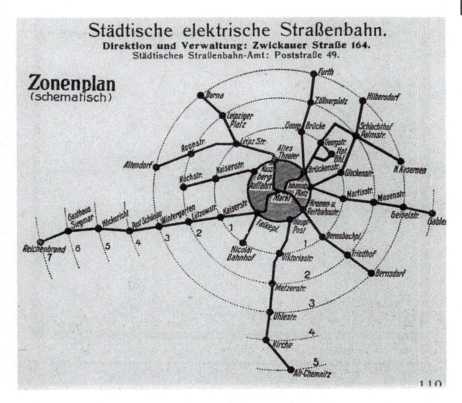

Städtische elektrische Straßenbahn.
Direktion und Verwaltung: Zwickauer Straße 164.
Städtisches Straßenbahn-Amt: Poststraße 49.

Zonenplan
(schematisch)

Source: Verein für Fremden-Verkehr in Chemnitz (hrsg), Chemnitz und
Umgebung: Führer durch Chemnitz *(Chemnitz, Dritte Auflage 1914/16),
119.*

At the same time as the city was being radially connected, Germany's urban transport
companies were also undergoing an organizational modernization rationalized into
unitary publicly owned enterprises. The first of these was established in Altona in
1926, and others soon followed, most importantly in Berlin itself with the creation of
the Berlin Transport Authority, the BVG (*Berliner-Verkehrs-A.G.*), the largest transport
company on the European continent, in 1929 (Lutz 1984: 141–57; Büsch 1960: 89;
Hüttenberger 1989: 369, 386). The BVG offered the Berliner an integrated transport
system that recoded the city's sprawling landscape into a number of simple diagrams,
each dealing with a different reason for journeying in the city.

Documents 7.17 Berlin Transport Maps and Timetable

[see illustrations on pages 182–183]

Source: Berliner-Verkehrs-A.G. Liniennetz *(March 1931), St Andrews
University, University Library Map Collection.*

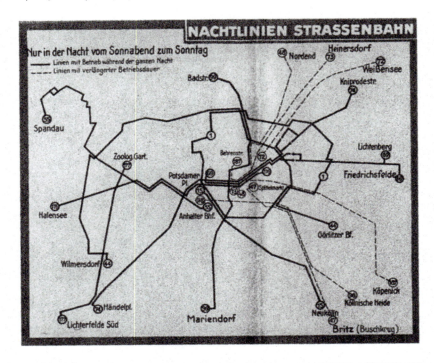

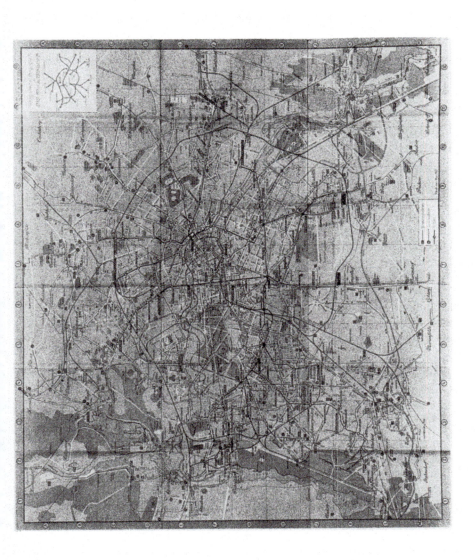

[Document 7.17 Berlin Transport Maps and Timetable]

The map and timetable allowed the individual to render the city – or indeed, any larger space – into a readable grammar, creating a landscape that was easily traversible (Harvey 1989: 31, 254, 265). They also wove space and time in the city into a reticular and geocentric ordered form, or what one sociologist writing in a different context has referred to as *Ordnungsschaffend* (Neundörfer 1961: 9). This existed in another, more obvious guise.

A well-regulated growth and orderly flow of traffic was understood to be a sure sign of the economic wellbeing of the city and nation. The smooth mobilization of goods and people into, from and within the city, without hindrance or upset stood as a metaphor for capitalist circulation (cf. Docs. 6.2, 6.3).

Document 7.18 Alfred Kihn, Metro Journey through Berlin

A parthenon of proud and noble columns
dominate the straits of the crocket-rich stock-exchange

Then business houses. Dark, colossal-fixed
and row upon row of company names.
Offices, warehouses, bales, a battalion of packers.
In a hundred windows scribble industriousness.

The glowing streets, yellow, dusty and close,
in a half-circle formation sweep deep by
with stirred up humans huddled daily
in cut-up rows of babbling coach pulp.

Source: Alfred Kihn: 'Stadtbahnfahrt durch Berlin', in Robert Seitz and Heinz Zucker (eds.), Um uns die Stadt 1931: Eine Anthologie neuer Großstadtdichtung *(orig. Berlin, 1931), reprint with a foreword by Ulrich Conrads (Der Bauwelt Fundamente 75, Braunschweig and Wiesbaden, 1986), 19–21.*

The commuter in Kihn's poem, past whose eyes the city flashes by, was already a well-established figure by the turn of the century. In Ruttmann's *Symphony* commuters queue for streetcars, join and disembark from the city's suburban trains, pour out from underground stations, to stream through the portals of the city's offices and factories. By 1938, 53 per cent of the Reich's 6.2 billion transport users travelled only short and medium distances, averaging a daily distance of 3 kilometres on the tram in Munich and Frankfurt am Main, and 4.5 kilometres in Hamburg, Leipzig and Berlin. If one travelled by omnibus, this usually meant a longer commuting distance, as much as three times that by tram or underground in some cases. In Leipzig, for example, 29 tram and four suburban bus routes carried 185.5 million passengers in 1928. Most of these were commuters who converged on the centre from the suburbs in the west (Leutzsch), south (Connewitz) and north (Wahren). They could expect a journey time of around 25 or 30 minutes. Travel times were even longer, perhaps up to an hour, if one had to cross the city to work.

For some, the commuting experience has come to be viewed as the quintessential experience of twentieth-century urban modernity (Weber 1908, 62–3; McElligott 1995). But apart from sitting in a wagon, what was the nature of the experience? Ruttmann's portrayal is of silent individuation, reinforcing the notion of alienation said to be inherent in both modern capitalism and its urban space.

Document 7.19 Silent Commuters

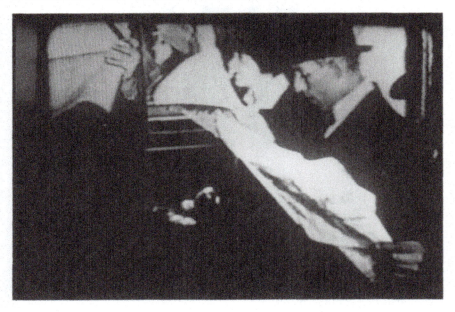

Source: Walter Ruttmann, Berlin: die Sinfonie einer Großstadt, *1927*

As with so much in the representation of the experience of urban modernity, the imagery can be conflicting. Richard Ziegler's *On the Way to the Office in the Underground* (1927) shows a secretary and clerk also commuting in silence. But unlike in Ruttmann's scene, Ziegler has added, in a collage of cuttings from adverts, thoughts to the moment.

Document 7.20 On the Underground, 1927

[see illustration on page 186]

The caption reads: '. . . "you have pasta to eat:/you smile, you make yourself your meal" – "suddenly stands/he before her, the hero whom she had dreamed so fair/and the blood burns her cheeks a fever" –/"the rouge of the worldly woman" – "typist wanted" –'

Source: Richard Ziegler, 'Auf dem Weg ins Kontor in der Untergrund',
reproduced in Art in Germany, *157*

Ziegler's caricature properly calls into question the assumption that alienation is the overriding experience of urban modernity. Indeed, the physical negotiation when boarding or alighting from a tram, train or bus, the silent contact in the crowded passenger coach, the slight brush of limbs or simply an exchange of glances, not only contributed to the sensory inner world of the city dweller, it also shaped a collective world made intelligible through its own silent language.

Germany's modern transport system impinged upon the sensory world of the urbanite in another way too. Throughout the period we are dealing with, city planners and engineers constantly sought to improve transport systems, modernizing and upgrading as technology (and money) allowed. The visual and aural effect of this upon the individual is conveyed in Stenbock-Fermor's account of an inspection of the work being carried out at Berlin Alexanderplatz in 1930.

Document 7.21 Berlin Alexanderplatz

I climb the stairs of the underground station and arrive at Münzstraße. Grey and imposing, embracing the whole left street facade, is the Tietz department store. Flags are flying busily on the roof, flags of different countries, and on the tower rests a globe which shines from the sky in the evening sun.

Behind me is the Alexanderplatz. A square over which 23 different tram and 9 bus-lines cross. Beneath it is a network of many tunnels. Around these roll the electric underground and intercity trains.

What does the history of this square mean in the context of the tasks of today and tomorrow? A monument, the 'Berolina', a final symbol of bygone times, an obstacle to traffic, is gone. The old houses around it, which strangers find romantic because they do not have to live in them, are being pulled down. There is construction and more construction. Tower blocks appear, huge structures, business buildings, offices, shops, restaurants, department stores.

Waves of traffic roar across the square. There are moments when everything is lying as if dead, and moments when a witch's cauldron is boiling. Bus after bus drags itself forward, huge, yellow groaning boxes. Electric trams are ringing and clattering along the rails. Cars are hooting. Black masses of people are moving strictly according to signals, from west to east, north to south, there and back. Policemen in their long blue coats fiddle about with traffic signals on small concrete islands.

Only a few weeks ago the ground was still torn open. It resembled a goldrush town in American films: wooden huts, fences, heaps of rubble and sand, sleepers, wooden planks, cranes, chains, and workers among all of this shovelling and hacking, carrying beams, pushing barrows. The surface closed up again, only some places are still being dug. Wooden fences, however, have been erected and the traffic remains unhindered.

Below ground, all forces have been mobilized. Subterranean passages and stations, an underground construction of phantastical dimensions is growing 16 metres below street level. An unintelligible confusion of beams, girders, pillars and ladders, fills the gorge which is being formed from a concrete box sunk deeply into the ground. An entire forest was cut down in order to restrain this gigantic concrete basin. It rests in ground water and would float if the sleepers and girders did not push it down firmly. More and more masses of concrete, iron and wood are lowered into this gorge and transformed into stairs, platforms, rail tracks, pillars and roofs. The biggest underground station in Berlin is being built here.

The underground highways run into this station from east, north, and south, and later from the west. They overlap each other: the trains will run parallel on two levels.

An engineer led me through a shaft to below the surface. We climbed everywhere. The air is cool. It is quiet. The ceiling trembles from the vibrations of the trains above us. Electric lamps are lighting up the tunnels. The huge iron girders shine fresh and painted red. The walls shimmer green.

We climb out of the underworld and our ears hurt from the noise of the street. The big brick house of the police headquarters lies red-grey and deserted in the background. The houses designated for demolition along the new Königstraße display their naked, scarred walls. A red Romanesque church is situated nearby looking slightly helpless. One will not see it for much longer: housing blocks rise up before it and envelop the Alexanderplatz.

Source: Alexander Graf Stenbock-Fermor, Deutschland von Unten: Reisen durch die proletarische Provinz 1930 (Stuttgart, 1931, reprint Lausanne and Frankfurt a.M., 1980), 132–3.

The surgical incisions into the surface flesh of the city that Stenbock-Fermor experienced in 1930 changed the individual's mental perception of the city, especially as the 'underground city' took shape (Die Fahrt Nr 9, 1929: 8–9; cf. Chap. 3). But this too was a dynamic vista, for here in Alexanderplatz alteration to the physical landscape had been a constant feature since the beginning of the century, although, as we can see from the following scenes, particular landmarks remained intact.

Document 7.22a–d Berlin Alexanderplatz, 1906–33

[see illustrations below, opposite and on page 190]

Sources: a–c) Das große Berlin: Max Missmann, Photographien 1899–1935, ed. Wolfgang Gottschalk (Berlin 1990), 14–17; d) Gottfried Korff and Reinhard Rürup (eds.), Berlin, Berlin: Die Ausstellung Zur Geschichte der Stadt (Berlin, 1987), 475.

It was not just the physical face of the city that altered as roads, underground stations and tunnels came into being. New modern transport technology and its organization, founded upon 'scientific planning', unified the city's fragmented parts, connecting the urban unit to its hinterland. Eventually, through the continued rational expansion of such transport networks, the distant regions of Germany would also be moulded into a unitary whole.

[Document 7.22a (1906)]

[Document 7.22b (1911)]

[Document 7.22c (1925)]

[Document 7.22d (1933)]

Document 7.23 Transport and National Unity, *c.*1928

This unity is especially visible and convincingly shown in the integrated transport of water, land and air. In all areas of modern communications the individual radial transport networks, with their strong concentration around various individual centres, as well as the centre of the Lower Main reveal the transport unity. The names of the different new communications companies such as: Southwest German Radio, Southwest German Air Transport, Southwest German Transport Association, and so on, furthermore in the cultural sphere the 'Rhine–Main Association for Popular Education', which is active throughout the entire region, also clearly express this unity.

Within the transport network of the Lower Rhine, the individual large communities of the satellite towns of the extensive geographical urban crown [cities' crown] gain their special character through their central importance for their [corresponding] hinterland which joins the cities' crown in a variety of intersections.

This cultural, economic and transport technical unity in its combination as well as in its organic structure stands in conscious and crass[est] contrast to the current political and unorganic structure – which administratively subordinates a unified economic area to five different states in grotesque territorial divisions, by which of the 128 enclaves that exist in Germany, about a dozen fall in Southwest Germany. Since the organic economic structure has grown from the pulsating life and in the meantime in spite of all the constraints of particularism, has understood how to assert itself, these two spatial formations exist today:

the unorganic power-political and the organic economic in their contrariness alongside and in opposition to each other.

Nevertheless, the political borders and constraints are in their way of thinking as well as in their practice, in public life, already fully broken and rendered illusory by the spatial changing forces asserting themselves. [. . .]

In all areas of modern communications the individual radial transport networks, with their strong concentration around particular centres, [. . .] reveal the transport unity. [. . .] People, places and states which through the power-political wills and power-political boundaries, have been until now unnaturally and violently hindered in their natural-inclined community life, have been finally brought closer together again by the technology of our day in a matchlessly modern conquest of space and time. Thus a spatial reconfiguration on the greatest scale has been unleashed over all of Germany.

Source: Landesarchiv Berlin 142/I StB 498, 'Zur Deutschen Klein- und Vielstaaterei. Die raumverschiebende Auswirkung der Neugliederung in Südwestdeutschland, dem rheinfränkischen Wirtschaftsgebiet', 1–4.

The claim in this document of furthering national unity may appear odd nearly 60 years after Bismarck's unification of the German states. But in spite of this, Germany was not a cohesive unitary state. Its political and administrative structure was jealously federal; geographically it sprawled uneasily across the continental European land mass; culturally and socially it was deeply divided. The explicit aim, therefore, of a modern traffic and transport system by the end of the 1920s, when the document was written, was to facilitate the integration of Germany that had proved elusive to politicians in the past. A major part of the problem for the modernizers was the apparent lack of a shared national imagination within the population. The aerial film gave a perspective that could overcome this because it provided a visual image of the physical shape of the nation. It reshaped the agglomeration of fragmented spaces, giving a sense of wholeness that was also dynamic. From the air, the disparate land mass of Germany takes shape as a 'living map' of the nation.

Document 7.24 Aerial Film

In its conciseness and great overview the aerial film is already extensively used as an aerial photograph in the German economy. Alongside the static picture, the general public itself has for some time now turned to the motion picture. Thus in many of Germany's cinemas one could see films of cities, bathing resorts, spas, and industrial regions, etc., which were favoured as much for their intrinsic character as a movie as for their primary function of advertising. The impact of such a film can understandably be fundamentally different on one and the same subject. That depends on the type of set-up, the technicality of the film, in brief, the total tempo of a film. One will have success on one's side only if one holds the balance between length and brevity with constantly changing liveliness. In the case of urban photography, for example, one cannot help but show buildings alongside other prominent landmarks. A cathedral, a beautiful church, an old town hall, a house of a famous man, the town walls, ramparts or towers might be shown in a clever way, however, as a sequence they appear as a lifeless composition. For the art connoisseur, these images may appear as a pleasure. But with the cinema-goer we are mainly dealing with the broad mass of the people. Here it is the aerial film which infuses the scenes with life and tempo. No one can escape from the breathtaking tempo with which one can see how one has just passed over the cathedral of a city like a child's toy with little height below one, and in the next moment look up towards the massive towers of human architecture. In quick succession the film allows also the other features of the city to impinge upon one. The full impact of the aerial film allows the eye in the following terrestrial picture to recognize interested individual things. The observer begins to busy himself with these individual things. An interesting journey has developed out of this dry film about architectural attractions of a city, which, however, takes into account the particularities with equal attention. The town planner gets to see in a clear overview the layout of streets, squares, blocks of houses, estates, etc., only through the aerial picture. Similarly, with spas and bathing resorts, only the aerial photograph is in a position to provide a concise overview of location and environs of such a place. With its vividness it arouses the interest of the observers and here also turns the dead images into a lived episode. [. . .]

'*Brevity is the soul of wit*': brief and clearly arranged, the aerial film shows what until now was possible only through sequences of long-winded terrestrial photos, journeys, and inspections.

The film's effect is heightened when it parades before the eyes of the viewer the total object as well as the progress of human technology – in that it allows the observer the experience of the aeroplane with its powerful impressions. It spurs the public's interest in economic processes and circumstances, for the film is never dead and passive, but, eternally energetic, it draws towards these in a rapid tempo.

Convincingly and urgently it leads us to each – if only desired – terrain. The powerful change in the dimensions of objects by land and aerial photography remains unforgettable for the viewer.

Source: Deutsche Lufthansa, Lufthansa Betriebsmitteilungen *Jg., 11, No. 9 (Sept. 1927): 'Luftfilm'.*

The horizons of the urban mental map were thus not confined to its immediate borders. In the opening scenes of Ruttmann's *Sinfonie*, the trains, hotels, air transport emphasize Berlin's centrality not only as *Großstadt* in Germany, but also as a *Weltstadt*. During the 1930s the idea of capital and nation was underpinned by Nazi attempts to capture the technocratic *Zeitgeist* (Brockhaus 1997: 68–117). The new 185 kilometre long Berlin ring road, more than two-thirds of which was completed by December 1938, was not only an achievement of modern technology and planning.

The ring situated Berlin at the hub of Germany by linking it via the 2,014 kilometres of new motorway system to the regions.

Document 7.25 'Roads of the Führer'

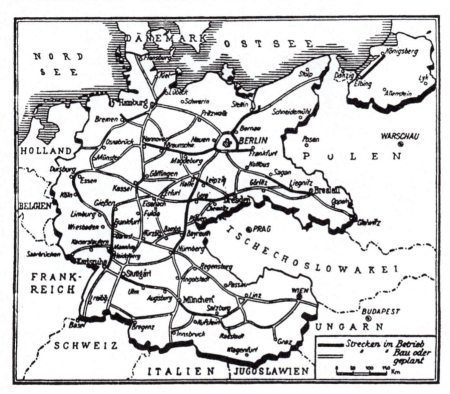

Source: Bundesarchiv Koblenz NS22/493, Frankfurter Zeitung *(8 April 1938): 'Der Spatenstich'.*

To live in Berlin during the interwar years was to be at the hub of a modern world system, connected by roads, trains and air, and at whose centre, in theory at least, was Alexanderplatz, Berlin's own nodal point.

Quite apart from the popular emphasis upon driving as a leisure activity, or road construction's obvious implications for the economy, the road building programme of the 1930s functioned in a way similar to the aerial map, contributing to a new self-awareness of a national and continental identity (Roggatz 1942: 241; Peniston-Bird 1996: 426–30, 445ff.; Brockhaus 1997: 78–81).

Document 7.26 Mercedes Benz, Deeds of World Renown

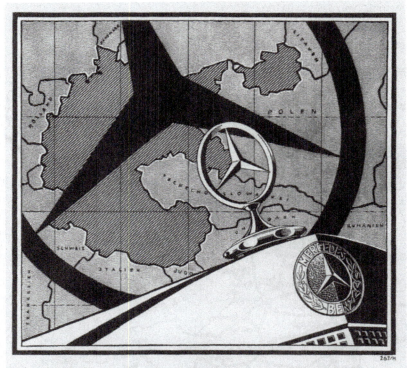

Source: Michael Kriegeskorte, 100 Jahre Werbung im Handel *(Cologne, 1995), 99.*

Proud owners of automobiles would be able to travel beyond the local horizon and connect as individuals within an enlarged German *Heimat*. The motorways of the 1930s, like the *Land-* and *Schnellstraße* of the 1920s, held out the prospect of 'binding the German tribes', as Duisburg's Lord Mayor believed, so that any 'region as a whole can be closely connected to the rest of the Fatherland' (McElligott 1999: 225). Thus through the conquest, first of urban, then of regional space, Germans became 'part of the whole', of the 'mass ornament' (Kracauer) of the nation (cf., Doc. 5.17). But the 'whole' itself was both an expansive and a nebulous concept after 1933. For while technocratic planners of traffic connected individual experiences within and beyond the city according to the current vision of the national goal, they could not always determine the character of those experiences – in spite of efforts to do so – as travellers to Germany learned for themselves.

Document 7.27 'Lessons of the Road'

Driving standards are fair, but lower than in England. One sometimes wonders whether it is a fundamental German characteristic to be insensitive about anybody or anything that is in the way – a certain lack of imagination which causes the German nature to appear callous, ruthless, cruel. Cars do not slow up for dogs or fowls in the road; they ought not to be there, and must move or be run over. It is so suggestive of the reputation ever attaching, in other countries, to German foreign policy. But if an Englishman wishes to begin to understand German instincts in international affairs there is another lesson which he must let the roads of Germany teach him. All of them, except north-wards, lead eventually to that curious barrier resembling a level crossing gate, that national fact of which we English have no experience – a land frontier with foreign country beyond.

Source: The Times *(3 Oct. 1938): 'Lessons of the Road' from the series: 'A Picture of Germany: Everyday Life'.*

Germany's military conquest and occupation of Europe after 1939 altered again the boundaries of the German 'Heimat'. Between the defeat of France in the summer of 1940 and the peak of Hitler's continental power in mid-1942, a compact area stretching from the Atlantic in the west to Soviet Russia in the east with a population of more than 250 million was under German control. The task facing Hitler's technocrats was how to reorganize what their Führer referred to as the 'ragbag of European states' into a rationally structured New European Order, one that would allow the revitalized Germany finally to fit 'organically' at its hub (Stirk 1994). According to an article prepared for publication in the *Rheinisch-Westfälische Zeitung* in March 1942, one of the major obstacles to achieving this aim was Europe's uneven traffic system. Its expansion and reorganization would enhance continental integration and facilitate mobility, for the Germans at least.

Document 7.28 Motorization of the Nation

[. . .] One must, however, take into account that we as a people without space and raw materials, have perforce remained behind in the provision of goods that presume a certain prosperity. This renders difficult perhaps the yardstick to which we must conform in the future. Our existence as a nation of have-nots will finally have found its end after the war. And so too will the calculation, which today is still the chief determinant for acquiring a car, namely the question of economy and utility, lose its significance. A prosperous nation can afford acquisitions for itself suiting hobbies and pleasure at an unrivalled scale. Thus the desire of the German people for foreign places, which has repeatedly shown itself in history in their urge for travel and discovery, can to a great extent be fulfilled through the possibilities offered by the motor car. The government is not interested in a restriction of this possibility; on the contrary, the Führer wants the greatest possible expansion of the motor car; he wants the car to widen the recreational contours for the individual; he wants him to get to know the nearby and distant *Heimat* via the motor car.

[. . .] Over are the times of the out-of-the-way rural idyll, which kept life and its demands, its noise and its daily questions, at bay because they disrupted the muse; the time has come when the near and distant stuff of life have to be controlled by the people who are destined to lead the new European area. The car is an especially pre-eminent means for the conquest of time and space, for the expansion of the horizon.

Source: Paul Roggatz, 'Die Straße im sozialen Wohnungsbau – ihre Aufgaben und ihre Kostendeckung', in Der Soziale Wohnungsbau in Deutschland, *2 Jg., No. 3 (1 Feb. 1942), reprinted in Tilman Harlander, Gerhard Fehl (eds.),* Hitlers Sozialer Wohnungsbau 1940–1945: Wohnungspolitik, Baugestaltung und Siedlungsplanung *(Hamburg, 1986), pp. 239–41.*

As the document reveals, much was being laid in store for a postwar future. The reality was that for the time being, few Germans could look forward to cruising along European motorways, not least because they did not have cars, nor were the European motorways built. In 1939, there was on average in the Reich one motor car for every 52 persons, and it is unlikely that this statistic improved subsequently. Thus, in this respect Germany not only lagged behind countries such as France and the United Kingdom, but also compared unfavourably with the less urbanized countries of Scandinavia. The war itself caused untold damage to both Germany's and Europe's urban and national transport systems. And yet, within months, the reappearance of moving city traffic was seen as a barometer of civil recovery (BZR Vol. 1, Nr 15, 13 April 1946: 8–9; cf., Doc. 3.21); and within a few years of the war's end, the urban dream of mobility either by train or by car across a larger landscape was once again being revived (BZR Vol. 2, Nr 4, 27 Sept. 1947: 7; Eckermann 1989: 158–60).

Masculine women and feminine men | 8

One of the features identified by observers of early twentieth-century life in the city was the challenge to gendered hierarchies of authority. This challenge is seen largely as a result of the long-term structural transformations of Germany's economy and society, and was reinforced by the traumatic experiences of the First World War. Germany's defeat in 1918 resulted in a crisis of masculinity, as it did in other revolutionary societies, while conversely it empowered women. In tandem with the march of 1920s modernity, women emerged from the confines of the home to assert themselves consciously in the public sphere, thereby calling into question the basis of male authority (Daniel 1997: 200–1, 250; Petro 1997: 43; Kaplan 1987: 429–49; Bridenthal 1987: 473–97). This altered state, heralding the 'age of the emancipated woman', seemed to symbolize the experience of modernity in the 1920s European city. As such, it was problematized by contemporaries and widely commented upon. Indeed, the 'revolutionization of the woman' was the title of a book by Erik Ernst Schwabach published in 1929 in Leipzig (Frevert 1999: 88, 98; idem 1989: 166–7; Kaes et al. 1994: 195–219). And the subject was noted in social inquiries of the period. Erich Fromm and Hilde Weiß from the Frankfurt Institute for Social Research, for example, noted the existence of a 'new woman' in their survey of attitudes among blue- and white-collar workers at the end of the 1920s (but only published in the 1980s).

Document 8.1 The New Woman

At the time of our investigation short skirts, silk stockings and the page-boy cut (*Bubikopf*) were the fashion and largely accepted among the population. These fashionable phenomena were connected to the general emancipatory attempts by women; a greater freedom of social position as well as sexual norms can be discerned here as much as the greater participation in sport or women's gradually increasing freedom of mobility. The fashion of the twenties distinguished itself from earlier and later developments in several respects: the conventional distinction between man and woman was as often blurred as the difference between older and younger women, and in general this was about the removal of the individual role differences as well as the accompanying traditional images. This attitude manifested itself most in the *Bubikopf*, less so in the length of skirt and practically not at all with silk stockings, which, in any case, represented for many an unattainable luxury.

Source: Erich Fromm, Arbeiter und Angestellte am Vorabend des Dritten Reiches: Eine sozialpolitische Untersuchung *[1929], (Munich, 1983), 168.*

Between 1895 and 1933, the number of employed women rose from 8.2 million to 11.4 million, constituting just over a third of the economically active population by the latter date. They were, for the most part, employed in a technical, sales or clerical capacity (including in agriculture and domestic services), numbering 1,694,621 by 1933, or 14.8 per cent of the female economically active population. Of particular importance is that they were increasingly young: 47.8 per cent of the female workforce was under 30 years old, compared with 38.8 per cent of their male counterparts (StJDR 1935: 17–19, 26; Pore 1981: 109; Bridenthal 1987: 476, 480, 484–8; Frevert 1989: 176–77, 333–4). What sort of occupations did these young women desire for themselves? And what factors conditioned their final choices?

Document 8.2 The Career Choices of Girls, 1925–9

The career choices of girls are not as varied [as those of boys], nor can they be because the occupational opportunities are lacking.

If one takes into general consideration the economic role of women in employment, [. . .] it becomes clear why it is so difficult to secure an apprenticeship for female school leavers. There are simply few places; they do not exist because the economy until now has had only a limited use for female skilled workers.

A third of all employed persons in Germany are women. There are 11.5 million women who are fully employed. In Prussia, for example, 63 per cent of women in the age group 14 to 21, are employed. The largest group of these young women work in agriculture. That may seem strange to the city inhabitant, but is explained by the largely agrarian provinces of East and West Prussia, Silesia, and Hannover. Two-thirds of the female population of the above-mentioned age group in East Prussia are fully employed in agriculture.

By contrast, a metropolis like Berlin shows a completely different picture, with 50 per cent of 14- to 21-year-olds employed in industry; a similar picture holds in the Rhineland, although the type of employment is different because different industries exist there.

In Schleswig-Holstein of this age group, ⅓ are in agriculture, ⅓ in domestic service, ⅕ in industry, ⅙ in commerce.

The career choices of Altona's female elementary and middle school leavers have become, just like the boys, more and more differentiated from year to year. In the period studied, which for the girls is from 1925 to 1929, the number of choices rose from 20 to 45. But also the number of

Undecided

120————————————
258————————————————
264——————————————————
341————————————————————

443————————————————————————————————

has increased, from 120 in 1925 to 443 in 1929 [the lines represent the successive years].

Among the 20 to 45 choices in this period there are five occupations that stand to the fore; they have altered in terms of preference apart from the most popular occupation, that of

Domestic Service

332————————————————————————————

304————————————————————————

337——————————————————————————

375————————————————————————————

286————————————————————————

which has always taken first place and will continue to do so for the foreseeable future, [. . .] It goes without saying that this occupation might also be determined by predilection, but in many cases it is the domestic and economic situation of the parents which makes this solution to a daughter's career desirable.

[. . .]

As the desire to become a domestic servant frequently appears in pupils' index cards, so can one seldom see in them the intention to go into

Factory Work

That this intention does in many cases exist must be assumed, for on finishing school a whole group of girls immediately seek out this work. [. . .] The stifled desire to work in a factory can be partly explained by the dislike among parents and teachers of sending youngsters into this occupation. This dislike is grounded in the worry that the mostly impersonal supervision of the girls in industrial work will make them, in a certain sense, prematurely too independent and so more difficult to educate domestically. [. . .]

Among the occcupations which require a 2- to 3-year training, that of

Dressmaking

281————————————————————————

128————————————————

181————————————————

186————————————————

93——————————

has for years played a major role among girls' choices. [. . .]

During the inflation period dressmakers were relatively busy, like all branches of business, for this reason a number of dauntless ones were still around in 1925, even though a decline, with its attendant unemployment, had, as elsewhere, set in. The impact of this experience revealed itself only briefly in 1926; already in the following year there was a small rise which continued in 1928. Meanwhile the guild has introduced a qualification, for the dressmaking profession, which has suffered acutely from mass ready-to-wear, has need of especially nimble and talented hands if it is to survive. This will inhibit choice

[. . .] in particular, the relatively high level and often persistent unemployment, which has gradually become comon knowledge, will hold it back. Thus the number of choices for 1929 is already so small that dressmaking has had to give up its premier place among the skilled occupations to that of

Salesgirl

131————————————
83——————
73————
124——————
112——————

[. . .]

While in dressmaking demand for places still now by far outstrips supply, the occupation of salesgirl could always absorb more numbers than the original level of choice (at least for the period of training). At any rate, the group of trainee applicants from among those who failed to get into their [first] choice of occupation, has progressively increased.

In

Office Work

148——————————
70——————
63————
107————————
110——————————

the development has been similar to that in sales. [. . .]

It was difficult in the postwar years to interest a young girl in the career of

Hairdresser

34————
69——————
91————————
105——————————
132————————————

Then the *Bubenkopf* [*sic.*] came and a large demand for skilled workers stirred an interest in the job, even though the haircut was relatively seldom performed by them. But crimping and assorted ancillary functions, as well as beauty care, which has increasingly taken root, has meant that the labour market for hairdresser has boomed to some extent. [. . .]

None among the rest of the 30 or 40 career choices of the Altona elementary and middle schoolgirls come anywhere close to the five choices discussed here; not one of the others can garner for itself even 10 'votes'. A notable example is that of cleaner, which in 1925 appeared attractive to 50 girls, in 1930 attracted only 4 girls, since the prospects are deemed so poor.

[. . .]

The career choices in their majority only mirror the opportunities of the available apprenticeships and the labour market, and the [number of] places for training of the particular town where the school and residence of the applicant are. The market situation of individual occupations either fosters or checks the choice; imitative instinct, usefulness, vanity, only come into question individually or in pairs as reasons for career choices. Purely compulsive career choices are infrequent. [. . .]

Source: Anna Eschrich, Berufswünsche der Mädchen und ihre Erfüllungsmöglichkeiten' in Wohlfahrtsnachrichten der Stadt Altona, *Vol. 6, Nr 9/10 (June–July 1930), 98–100.*

As we can see in this particular instance, the labour market and parental guidance conditioned the choice of school leavers rather than the whimsical nature of fashion. Thus in towns and cities industrial production – and to a lesser extent domestic work – continued to draw the largest numbers of young women. Nevertheless female employees in office, shop and commercial enterprises came to symbolize the confident modern urban type of the 'New Woman' distinguished by their modern style (Bridenthal 1987: 486; Grossmann 1986: 62–80; Peukert 1993: 157–75; Huber 1995: 368–87; Usborne 1995: 137–63).

The outward style of the 'New Woman', shorter skirts and bobbed hair, introduced in France by Coco Chanel and popularized in Germany by the dancer Isadora Duncan, has been interpreted by some feminist historians as a consciously aggressive assertion of a new identity (Anderson and Zinsser 1989: 197, 201–2); as the expression of a generational revolt (Usborne 1995: 138–41, 167ff.); or as a response to the dictates of the emerging rationalized system of production (Grossmann 1993: 139–40). Meanwhile, a younger generation of feminist literary and art historians have focused more on the representation and lifestyle of the 'New Woman' of the art and media world of the 1920s (Meskimmon and West 1995; von Ankum 1997).

Document 8.3 The New Woman: Sylvia von Harden

[see illustration on page 202]

Source: Otto Dix, Portrait of the Journalist Sylvia von Harden, 1926, reproduced from Eva Karcher, Otto Dix 1891–1969 *(Cologne, 1992), 145.*

But one should be careful not to read too much into the lifestyles of a few and extrapolate from these the traits of a generation. Indeed, Renate Bridenthal asked: 'How true to life was the image of the promiscuous flapper? How new was the "new woman" of the twenties?' (Bridenthal 1987: 491).

Indeed, the majority of the so-called 'New Women' came from working-class or lower-middle-class backgrounds. They were usually employed as secretaries, typists or telephonists in offices, or as assembly-line workers in factories, and alongside men from similar social backgrounds, whom they often partnered (Frevert 1989: 182–85).

The daily experience of the proletarian 'New Woman' in the city under such conditions was depicted with poignant force by Sladan Dudow through the character

[Document 8.3 The New Woman: Sylvia von Harden]

of Anni Bönike in his film *Kuhle Wampe or Who Owns the World?* (1931). When Bertolt Brecht and Ernst Ottwald wrote the script for *Kuhle Wampe*, unemployment was topping the 4 million mark; Anni had to strive on behalf of the family as well as to cope with the pressures and consequences of her love life which had produced an unexpected pregnancy.

Document 8.4 The New Woman: Anni Bönike

Source: Sladan Dudow (dir.), Kuhle Wampe oder Wem gehört die Welt?
© *Nachlass Lilly Schoenborn-Anspach, donated by Bernd Kummer.*
(Kunstlerkollektiv Berlin 1931), Courtesy Deutsche Kinomathek Berlin.

The left-wing writer and critic Alice Rühle-Gerstel pointed out in early 1933 how the urbane 'New Woman' 'never became average, never became the mass female' (Kaes *et al.* 1994: 218–19). And yet 'she' inspired a generation of artistic and literary commentators as the prototype of urban modernity, who moved beyond the boundaries of the city (Sackett 1992: 134–5).

Document 8.5 The City Ladies' Hairdresser

[see illustration on page 204]

Source: Anton Leidl, 'The city ladies' hairdresser in the country', Die Jugend, *Nr 18 (May 1933).*

Representations of the 'New Woman' of the 1920s, as depicted here by Leidl's caricature, may have exercised a subtle influence upon academic discussion to date. Yet such images are but one theme within a richly textured discourse on the 'new woman' and gender relations during the interwar period (Petro 1997). While some males were clearly intimidated by the 'New Woman', some were not, as Fromm and Weiß's study of attitudes among blue- and white-collar workers shows.

Der Großstadt=Damenfriseur auf dem Lande!

Document 8.6 Male Attitudes to the 'New Woman' Fashion

Question 323: How do you like the present fashion [for short skirts and stockings]?
(1) 'Good, it is practical.'
   'Why not?'
   'It is not a question of finding it good or bad. It is practical.'
   'Yes, but not because of its erotic features, but because it is more hygienic.'
   'I'm not prudish.'
   'Short skirts, yes. Silk stockings, yes. Short skirts allow the female form to be recognized (shape of the legs). This is necessary if we want to have a perfect race. Shapely legs indicate a good construction of the pelvis.'
   [. . .]

(4) 'Everything in moderation!'

'Yes. That is, up to the calf. It allows for freedom of movement and does not stir up dust.'

'As a fashion, I don't like it, but it is practical.'

'In summer, comfortable; in winter, flu.'

'They could be a bit longer.'

(5) 'I detest it.'

'Awful!'

[. . .]

Question 324: Do you like the *Bubikopf?*

(1) 'When the *Bubikopf* is properly taken care of it looks very good.'

'Yes. It allows more room for individual taste.'

'Yes. The *Bubikopf* is an advancement compared to the "good old days" [of the imperial period].'

(2) 'No. Long hair is the most beautiful asset a woman has. Take it away and the majority look like scarecrows.'

'No. A woman should make herself look beautiful with what nature has given her.'

'No. The manly hairstyle is not amusing when a women adopts it.'

'No, because this type of artificiality spoils so much of what is simple and beautiful about our women and girls.'

Source: Fromm, Arbeiter und Angestellte, *170–1.*

Nearly three-quarters of Fromm's sample of 534 respondents, who were interviewed in 1929, came from urban milieux, predominantly from Frankfurt and Berlin. They were overwhelmingly male, and of those, 64 per cent were blue-collar workers (predominantly skilled), and 29 per cent white-collar employees; 41 per cent of the cohort were between 21 and 30 years old, and 41 per cent between 31 and 50 years; and 60 per cent were married (Fromm 1983: 81–3). Thus it is clear that the majority of interviewees were finding it easier to accept the changes in the appearance and style of women than is sometimes believed to be the case.

As we saw in Document 8.2, career officers found that most teenagers were encouraged by their parents (and the career officers themselves?) to choose occupations that would prepare them for later marriage and motherhood (Peukert 1987: 239–41; Frevert 1979: 94). Few women of the older generation of Weimar feminists would have disagreed with Professor Friedberger's dictum that 'The physiological condition of a woman is pregnancy' (Friedberger 1923: 111; Pore 1981: 74, 104; Usborne 1992: 58). By the beginning of the 1930s, the social and economic position of women was being redefined by the conservative discourse on women, the family and the urban social order. Even ostensible liberals such as Erich Kästner wrote what were essentially conservative texts on the ideal female type (*Fabian*, 1931). But it was not just men who were defining women's role. Indeed, Rühle-Gerstel was no doubt disappointed to find that many of the young women identified as 'New Woman' were actively adopting a more 'traditional' feminine identity by the beginning of the 1930s, and that they were seeking this in marriage and motherhood.

Document 8.7 'New Motherhood'

Caption reads: 'Mothers-to-be can find advice and help at the pregnancy advice centres.'

Source: Gesundheitsbehörde Hamburg (ed.), Hygiene und Soziale Hygiene in Hamburg: Zur neuenzigsten Versammlung der Deutschen Naturforscher und Aerzte in Hamburg im Jahre 1928 *(Hamburg, 1928), 444.*

Friedberger's comment on women's physiological destiny, and the attempt to manipulate motherhood, have to be set against the wider context of a stagnant marriage rate and general fertility decline, worryingly matched by rises in illegal abortions, illegitimate births, divorce and the incidence of venereal disease, all of which were seen as particular to the urban sphere (Theilhaber 1913; Burgdörfer 1934; Usborne 1992: 87, 89, 91–4; *idem* 1995: 154–5). In actual fact, Germany's record was no worse than that of other countries (Mitchell 1978: 28). The social status of women throughout Europe regressed as a result of legislation concerning their economic rights in the Depression (Anderson and Zinsser 1989: 209–14). In Germany their position was further undermined as a consequence of Nazi efforts to reassert the authority of the patriarchal family (Kaufmann 1988: 94–7; Frevert 1989: 207–39). The spaces between rhetoric, law, and the reality of women's urban experiences, however, still remain to be interrogated (Schoppmann 1996).

From the turn of the century, members of the medical profession, as well as eugenicists and racial hygienists, and church organizations attacked what they saw as a degenerate urban environment that encouraged 'moral corruption' in the city with dire consequences for the nation at large (Evans 1976: 236, 241 ff., 248; Kaufmann 1988: 43–123; Usborne 1992: 63–4). Early sexology propounded that males were by nature sexually polygamous, and this aspect of their sexuality was awakened by the cabarets and *variétés* of the city (Buschan 1915: 95). But the libido of both sexes could be excited by other aspects of urban life. The problem lay with the city itself, whose anonymity, artificiality, and rampant commercialism overstimulated the libido and distorted the balance of nature within and between individuals of the opposite sex (Forel and Fetscher 1931: 113).

Document 8.8 The Pathological Sexuality

One of the most important anomalies of sexual life is an abnormal prevalence of sexual feelings and fantasies resulting in massive and frequent urges for sexual gratification.

It is indeed a reward of education and breeding over many centuries that the sex drive essential for procreation and not lacking in the normal individual, is not the dominant emotion of human feeling, rather [. . .] it merely constitutes episodes in the sentiments and striving of civilization, imparting higher, nobler, social and moral feelings which are distinctive from the primitive, and leaving space for purposeful activity promoting individual interests as well as those of society.

Moreover, it is a requirement of the moral and criminal law that the civilized person carries out his sexual urges within limits in the interests of society especially in respect of modesty and morals – and that he controls these urges under all circumstances when they come into conflict with the altruistic demands of society.

Should this demand not be fulfilled among normally developed civilized persons then the family and state as the bases of moral and lawful society could not exist.

In actual fact, a normally inclined, mentally healthy person, who has not forfeited his level-headedness and reason through intoxication (alcohol etc.), never reaches such a pitch that his entire thoughts and feelings are seized, allowing for no other emotions than a frenzied, lustfully demanding satisfaction, without the possibility of furnishing moral and legal constraints; manifesting himself as more or less impulsive and at the same time, after the completed sexual act, either not satisfied or only momentarily, the enslaved is consumed by the unquenchable longing for new pleasures.

A sexual drive which demonstrates such traits is definitely pathological. Such an appetite can occasionally soar to a sexual passion of such proportions that consciousness is lost, emotional confusion sets in, and in a truly psychological crisis, an irresistible urge to sexual violence follows.

Such psycho-sexual crises are still seldom scientifically researched, although they are of the utmost importance for debate, since culpability is scarcely reasonable in such a mental state where the natural urge is intensified to a pathological level overcoming moral and legal constraints.

For society and the police doctor, who has to make the diagnosis, it is a happy fact that such cases, from irresistible hyper-sexuality to the absolutely worst pathological sexual behaviour, occur only among a certain category of people, the degenerate, and almost exclusively on the basis of hereditary degeneration.

Unfortunately, in modern society, which has many physical and psychic degenerate characteristics, especially in the centres of civilization – their number is very large.

[...]

It must also be acknowledged that among totally unaffected people, the level of libido shows major variations, according to age, condition of physical constitution, life-style, the influence of physical illness, etc. The sexual urge rises rapidly to a significant level from puberty onwards; is strongest between the years of 20 and 40, after which it declines. Married life conserves and disciplines the sex urge.

Intercourse with varying objects of pleasure stimulates the sex drive. Since the female is less sexually inclined than the male, a predominance of sexual lust in her raises the assumption of pathological significance. The city-dweller who is constantly reminded of sexual things and who is stimulated into sexual pleasures, has *ceteris paribus* a greater sexual appetite than the country-dweller. A vicarious soft sedentary lifestyle, diets based predominantly on animal foods, consumption of spirits, spices, etc., have a stimulating effect on sex life.

Source: Richard Krafft-Ebing, Pathologica Sexualis (14th edn, Vienna, 1912), 60–3.

Thus, in a similar vein to the theories of the urban sociologists, sexologists such as Krafft-Ebing viewed the city as a transitory place that allowed for ephemeral contacts between the sexes. Such liaisons threatened the stability of the family, and, ultimately, of the state (Forel and Fetscher 1931: 117–18, 346–7).

For youth in particular, the city was a labyrinth in whose recesses a dangerous sexuality lurked. In the following autobiographical passage, the cultural critic Walter Benjamin describes his youthful experiences of walking through the streets of turn-of-the-century Berlin and discovering the secret and sensual pleasures of unknown spaces in the city which seemed ultimately to 'imprison' him. In this excerpt, Benjamin's urban exploration ends in the discovery of his own libido, illuminated by the presence of female 'otherness' (Forel and Fetscher 1931: 105).

Document 8.9 The sexual labyrinth

But I could think of no other form of revolt at that time than that of sabotage; this, of course, derived from my own experience. I relied on it when I wanted space from my mother. I used it most when doing 'messages', and with a hardened stubbornness which often drove my mother to despair. This is because I had adopted the habit of always walking half a step behind. It was as if I was avoiding at all cost to form a front, even with my own mother. How much I owed to this dreamy resistance when walking together through the city I found out later when its labyrinth opened itself to the urges of sexuality. This, however, with its first fluttering, was not searching for the body but the depraved psyche whose wings shone rotting in the light of a gas lantern, or were still slumbering unfolded under a furcoat in which it was cocooned. I now benefited from a gaze which does not appear to see a third of what it can see in reality. Already at the time when my mother was still scolding me for my dawdling and sleepy strolling, I sensed the possibility, in unison with these streets in which I appeared to be lost, to free myself of her domination. There is no doubt, at least, that a feeling, a sadly deceptive one, to deny her and her and my own class, was at fault for the unparalleled excitement in approaching a prostitute on the open street. It could take hours before this happened. The revulsion I felt when doing this was the same with which a slot machine would have filled me if it had been enough to start it with a single question. And so I threw my voice into the slot. Then the blood pounded in my ears and I was unable to pick up from the street the words that fell before me from the heavily made up mouth. I ran from there, only in the same night – as so often – to repeat the daring attempt. When I then sometimes, already toward morning, stopped in a doorway, I had entangled myself hopelessly in the asphalt shackles of the street, and it was not the purest hands that freed me.

Source: Walter Benjamin: from 'Beggars and prostitutes', in 'Berliner Kindheit um Neunzehnhundert', Walter Benjamin Gasammelte Schriften, IV.1, edited Tillman Rexroth (Frankfurt am Main, 1972), 287–8.

Benjamin's allusion to masturbation touched upon a subject that vexed youth reformers and church organizations – though some such as Forel and Fetscher were more sanguine, viewing it as a natural and brief stage in the sexual life-cycle of male youth (Marcuse 1905: 11; Flexner 1919: 42, 46; Albrecht 1926: 9, 12; Forel and Fetscher 1931: 107–8; Neuman 1972: 279–81). Nevertheless, the signs of moral danger were in evidence on the streets with the spread of pornographic grafitti, and especially in public toilets, where 'through these daubings', according to a report by Munich's police in April 1923, 'youngsters get their first education in a form which is hardly beneficial for their sexual development' (STAM Pol. Dir. 7420). In particular, the spread of trash literature and 'sex enlightenment' films in early German cinema caused particular concern (Werner 1990: 26–54, 86–115; Petersen 1992). For those youth who had the income to purchase any one of the growing number of journals aimed at them, such as *Die Jugend*, they would have found the following sort of advertisement for 'scientific' literature, typical of the period's genre (Lewis 1990: 122), offering 'enlightenment' on the 'nature' of women.

Document 8.10 'The Omnipotent Female: Erotic Typology of Woman'

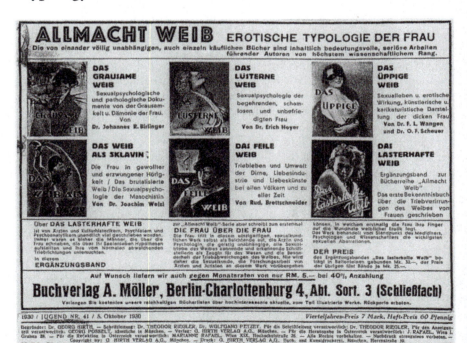

Captions read: top, l. to r.: the wicked woman; the lascivious woman; the voluptuous woman; bottom, l. to r.: the woman as slave; the venal woman; the depraved woman.

Source: Die Jugend, *Nr. 41 (5 Oct. 1930).*

Cornelia Usborne has pointed out that female visibility in the 1920s was underpinned by Germany's demographic structure after 1918, when there was a 'surplus' of 2 million women between the ages of 20 and 30 (Usborne 1987: 81). Many of them did not marry, sometimes because they could not, but also sometimes because they did not wish to (Kosta 1995). This was seen as particularly threatening, since contemporary sexology argued that the female libido was greater and more aggressive than that of males, and according to Freudian psychoanalysis it was 'free-roaming'. Thus modern single women were predatory, with any contact to males sexualized (Bridenthal 1987: 492). The volatility of the female libido threatened the equilibrium of society, undermined the ideal of motherhood and the perfect marriage, whether based on patriarchy or the sort of modern partnership envisaged by progressive social reformers (cf. Doc. 5.13). To paraphrase the feminist sociologist Elizabeth Wilson, by the beginning of the twentieth century, in the male imagination at least, the streets of the urban labyrinth were no longer lorded over by the minotaur, but instead subject to the misrule of a many-headed sphinx with a boundless and destructive libido (Wilson 1991: 7; Theweleit 1987: 63, and passim; Usborne 1987: 100).

The discovery and display of sexuality, while not necessarily exclusive to the city, was nonetheless perceived as an urban experience. Like Benjamin's discovery 30 years before, Stephen Spender only uncovered the secrets of his body (and those of others) when he journeyed to the German *Großstadt* in the late 1920s. Spender recounted his experiences through the character of 'Paul' in his semi-autobiographical *The Temple*.

Document 8.11 The Body as Temple

Entry in Paul's Notebook:
[. . .] I feel as if a new life had begun here in Germany. I do not know precisely in what the newness consists, but perhaps the key to it is in these young Germans having a new attitude toward the body. Although I have never been puritanical in outlook, I confess that till now, whatever I may have pretended to myself, I have always regarded my body as sinful, and my own physical being as something to be ashamed of and to be overcome by compensating and atoning spiritual qualities. Now I am beginning to feel that I may soon come to regard my body as a source of joy. Instead of an obstacle which prevents me achieving satisfactory relationships with others, it may become an instrument by which such a relationship is attained. Perhaps, after all, I may become a complete human being. [. . .]

Source: Stephen Spender, The Temple *(London, 1988), 54.*

But Spender, like his countryman and contemporary Christopher Isherwood, was a 'tourist', and like all tourists, he caught only a small and particular aspect of the city's sexual modernity as gendered boundaries were breached (the same can be said of Virginia Woolf and Vita Sackville-West, both of whom frequented lesbian bars when in Berlin (von Lengerle 1984: 144; Docs. 8.17–18)). The youthful males Spender encountered were 'gentle and soft, the girls sculptural, finely moulded', and he found this 'excitingly "modern"' (Spender 1988: 42). But in many respects, the much-vaunted sexual revolution of Germany's urban modernity was often little more than clumsy experimentation and self-discovery that often resulted in guilt (Marcuse 1905: 6–10). For many German youth sexual experience was a mundane one, traditionally gendered, conditioned by customary family relationships, and often filled with self-recrimination, as Günther Krolzig, a Berlin social worker, found when he interviewed a 16-year-old barber's apprentice.

Document 8.12 Working-Class Boys and Their Girls

I don't get on very well with my family. [. . .] In the past I got on better with my parents. [. . .] Now, by contrast, I am always alone. I usually go away with a friend. Because we were always alone, we wanted to now and then amuse ourselves. Thus, we went to a small dance bar. There I got to know a girl for the first time. I also met her parents, they are very well-off people. Naturally, I told my parents, but they did not comment on this. The girl was only 14½ years old. I never even kissed her. We were just friends. Then I got to know another girl through acquaintances of my parents. My parents did not approve. Unfortunately I was too much in love with that girl to listen to them. So we went out together secretly. We met frequently at her married sister's [apartment]. My girl friend was a year older than me. Her parents live in the south of Germany. We went out for a good ½ year. Now she is back home. I kissed her often and would have gone further, but she said we were too young [for that] and that we could not do that to our parents. I agreed and we thus remained pure. I'm ashamed now that I deceived my parents. Now I will try and avoid having a girlfriend. I would prefer to be with my parents again and thus avoid temptation. Then I can be honest with them. If only I had never gone out with girls.

Source: Detlev J.K. Peukert, Jugend zwischen Krieg und Krise. Lebenswelten von Arbeiterjungen in der Weimarer Republik *(Cologne, 1987), 241–2.*

This particular excerpt is interesting for what it says about attitudes among youth towards their own and shared sexuality, and contrasts starkly with what sex reformers thought young people were up to (Doc. 8.15). As we can see from the account, the proper place for sex was clearly understood to be within marriage. Within the limitations of contemporary sexology this was an important point, for marriage acted as a containing and regulating mechanism for otherwise dangerous libidos (Usborne 1992: 92). This was especially pertinent in the case of women whose sexuality was viewed as both anarchic and destructive, as Document 8.10 illustrates (Buschan 1915: 90–1; Weininger 1903, reprint 1980: 360–2; Forel and Fetscher 1931: 120–1; Kavka 1995: 134; Anderson 1996: 433–53). The monogomous relationship ennobled the male while suppressing female desire, bringing out the (social) good in woman (Andreas-Salomé 1910: 128–33), as recounted in Hugo Wiener's lyrics to the popular song 'Nowak'.

Document 8.13 The 'Nowak', *c.* 1920s

I've got a man many girls would like to have
who always protects me from everything bad;
everyone knows him: Nowak is his name,
it's thanks to him that today I'm a dame.
Whether clothed or completely bare,
Nowak's whole anatomy has got character.
I would have had a bad end long ago
but my Nowak keeps me from debauchery

I could get my pleasures from many things:
I'd love to lie in the gutter;
I'd love to lose myself in booze;
I'd love to rollick with a lady of easy virtue;
I'd love once to exhaust men utterly;
I'd love to smoke marijuana 'stead of 'Memphis'.
I'd have tried morphine long ago
but my Nowak keeps me from debauchery

I'd love to be a vampire when the moon is full;
I'd love to be a fakir's mistress
so when I lie without a mattress
my back will be scratched by the nails;
I'd love to eat oysters in their shells;
I'd love to lose myself with a whale.
I'd planned to do all these things,
but my Nowak keeps me from debauchery

On the one hand Nowak is a blessing.
On the other hand he doesn't let me stir.
There was an advert in the paper:
'Wanted by the management of a night club:
a young girl with a nice disposition
to dance naked before Negroes and Chinamen';
I'd have taken the post straight away
but my Nowak keeps me from debauchery.

Source: Lyrics by Hugo Wiener, n.d.

A screen version of what occurs in the absence of a 'Nowak', or with one who is too weak to contain the female libido, can be found in von Sternberg's film *The Blue Angel*, where the vampish Lola Lola's sexuality is the force that brings down bourgeois patriarchy (represented by Professor Unrat's humiliation and death, see Doc. 4.22). Lola Lola's character combines the 'omnipotent female' presented in Document 8.10 and the 'New Woman' of the 1920s city, revealed in the scene where, clad in a smart (manly) suit of tweed and a felt hat, she is proposed to by the infatuated professor. In a similar vein, but with a different ending, Georg Pabst's film *Pandora's Box* (1929) has the screen character Lulu as both prostitute and new woman (represented as the quintessential *Garçonne* (Doane 1990; Frame 1997)), and, like the female voice in 'Nowak', enjoys having a good time. Like Lola Lola, her sexuality is portrayed as destructive, and must be destroyed in order to redeem the castrated and effeminate male figure of young Alwa, one of Weimar's 'new men'. By way of contrast, in Pabst's other film of 1929, *Diary of a Lost Girl*, Thymian, whose sexuality is first exposed through rape, then commodified and vied for, is finally saved from moral damnation when taken under the wing of the paternalistic and much older Count Osdorff (Schlüpmann 1990). Not only is Thymian redeemed, but so too is the institution of bourgeois marriage, itself depicted ironically by some males as a form of imprisonment.

Document 8.14 Marriage as Prison

We sat in the club, my new friend and me. 'It is sentimental', he said, 'for every now and then I have to think of her. She was a dream . . . '. 'Tell me', said I, coyly, for I had myself, just fallen in love. 'As I saw her for the first time, she sang an aria from Madame Butterfly, her blond hair was flooded with light, I will never forget that. I made her acquaintance; we lived for two years only for each other, in this time I wrote my best stuff . . . '. He went silent, his eyes moistened. I placed my arm around his shoulder. 'What became of her?' I softly inquired. He stood up, took his coat and hat, turned around at the entrance: 'I married her', he said.

Source: Die Jugend, Nr 6 (Feb. 1927).

Clearly, once obtained by the man, a woman lost her allure, suggesting that desire could exist only outside the bounds of marriage (Kavka 1995: 137).

One of the biggest problems facing city authorities was that of venereal disease arising from uncontrolled sex (cf., Doc. 4.23). Buschan alleged that teenagers, in particular, were susceptible to sexual transgressions (Buschan 1915: 74), a view echoed in some interwar writings on youth and sex (Albrecht 1926). It was estimated, for example, that in prewar Mannheim 63 per cent of venereal disease cases among the city's male population were traceable to irregular prostitution by waitresses, servants, and shopgirls (Flexner 1919: 18). In the postwar period, the urban incidence of venereal diseases rose dramatically. The problem fuelled calls for the regulation of the female body, and if found diseased, for its removal from the public space (Flexner 1919:

162–3; Usborne 1992: 84; Davenport-Hines 1990). Women, and young women in particular, became subject to ever tougher and often arbitrary action, especially after changes in the laws regulating juveniles in 1922 and 1926 allowed for their forced commitment to welfare institutions. Here again, is Sister Hoffmann in Altona.

Document 8.15 Anna Th.

We consider educational measures for Anna Th., a text-book example, as completely futile. The girl has been known to the Care Office since 1922, and has almost without exception lived in those areas where risks are considered to be almost accepted. The city, at the request of the Care Office, has paid quite a substantial sum of money for her cure. She has several previous convictions, some of which relate to prostitution. The provincial head should have taken over financing the placement in Neustadt for this severely mentally deficient girl, who, as far as we are informed, has also been certified. The Care Office ensures in all cases in which it is involved that these women are admitted initially to the psychiatric ward of the hospital and then, in consultation with the senior doctor, Herr Dr Cimbal, are transferred to a clinic. Thus the city saves a considerable sum of money, especially because these girls are persistent sources of infectious diseases when they are at liberty.

Source: STAH 424–24 37, Director Pflegeamt Ruth Hoffmann to Magistrat, Wohlfahrtsamt Altona (4 Feb. 1928).

The punitive interpretation of policy under the republic towards city youth and their sexual behaviour became the focus for a controversial stage play by the socialist educator Peter Lampel, *Revolt in the Reformatory* (1927), depicting the harsh regime in homes for errant youth. Such conditions also provided the material for a number of films, including Pabst's *Diary of a Lost Girl*. Together, these plays and films critically reveal a dimension of the perceived crisis of modernity as it affected sexuality in the city, and responses to it. Under the Nazis, there was not so much a break in policy as a hardening of existing attitudes (Crew 1998; cf., Doc. 5.15).

Document 8.16 from a report by Munich's youth police department from the mid-1930s provides a snapshot of 'youth at risk'; what is notable is the relative scarcity of cases of teenage sexual risk.

Document 8.16 Youth and Young Adults at Risk in Munich, 1936–7

Hovering behind the discussions on sexuality during the 1920s was a fear of sexual 'spillage' that challenged an urban order based on a fixed normative sexual hierarchy. This is where, for instance, a masculine *angst* combined the new woman and fashion consumerism with the dissolution of gendered boundaries, a theme painted regularly by Jeanne Mammen (Cooper 1994: 174–8; Lütgens 1997; 96; Bridenthal 1987: 474; cf. Doc. 6.13). The changes of the 1920s seemed to have left urban Germany,

	1936	1937
detained by police	1261	1118
reported by:		
parents/employers	151	56
authorities	151	56
railway station welfare	74	44
self	239	198
Total	1811	1493
Age:		
–12	65	68
12–16	123	68
16–18	193	164
18–21	255	235
21+	1175	958
Total	1811	1493
Reason for Intervention:		
identity/employment check	62	108
morally endangered	150	111
larceny	89	84
homelessness	209	112
suspect venereal disease	115	123
work-shy	153	116
expulsion, breach of injunction	32	23
escape from custody	320	341
runaways/missing (minors)	170	124
begging	70	29
other reasons:		
suicidal	64	73
mentally ill	121	75
various reasons	196	111
in search of work	60	65
Total	1811	1493

Source: Staatsarchiv Munich 7691 Pol. Dir. 'Tätigkeitsbericht der Polizeipflegerinnen in München für 1936 und 1937'.

especially, in a state of confusion: society was turned upside down as far as relations between the sexes were concerned; and individuals were turned inside out as the female's inner male and the male's inner female manifested themselves, as is so wonderfully captured in Marcellus Schiffer's 1920s popular hit: *Maskulinum – Femininum*.

For example, the androgenous style of the garçonne (the woman whose appearance was that of an effeminate man), popular with some young 'New Women' and with lesbian women in particular, upset one stereotype of 'healthy womanhood' (Westphal 1986: 83; Frevert 1990: 107–9; Frame 1997: 26ff.; Docs. 8.5, 8.6; cf., Doc 5.13). The garçonne was mostly associated with the bachelor female (Schlierkamp 1984: 169–79), and in this respect she was threatening on a number of levels, not least for Freud's idea of a free-roaming libido, represented on screen by Lulu in *Pandora's Box*. But in particular the garçonne, through her appearance, represented a hybrid sex: a slightly built, angular female in a 'tuxedo and around her neck a tie' (Schoppmann 1996: 60–1), whose real or imagined existence demonstrated a sexual fluidity that called into question the integrity of gendered spheres of male and female, as the satirical weekly *ULK* displayed on its front cover.

Document 8.17 Lesbian Garçonnes

[see illustration on page 218]

Caption reads: 'Spring 1926: Even the stork is confused!'

Source: Landesarchiv Berlin Zs 73, ULK, Vol. 55, Nr 11, 12 March 1926.

Not all women who subscribed to the garçonne style were necessarily lesbian, as suggested in *ULK*'s depiction. Yet the appearance of 'masculine' women clearly troubled men. In particular, the trouser fashion of the 1930s, popular with many women (Sultano 1995: 18ff.), was unsettling to males, if the following caricature appearing in the glossy 'youth' magazine *Die Jugend* is anything to go by.

Document 8.18 'Trouser Fashion'

[see illustration on page 219]

The caption asks the reader: 'Do you believe that a counter-propaganda is necessary?'

Source: Rubey: 'Die Hosenmode', Die Jugend, Nr 18 (May 1933).

On the one hand, Rubey's caricature seems to suggest that women are duplicitous: they are female but not feminine (Kavka 1995: 124). On the other hand, the message can be construed as reflecting a male insecurity, not so much of masculine women as of feminine men. What the above portrayals suggest, therefore, is a fear that the modern experience of gender in the city was its dissolved boundaries. Yet as Stephen Brockmann has pointed out, the combination of fe/male genders in displays of androgeny might denote also a sexual harmony or wholeness not unlike the quest for wholeness associated with other areas of Weimar modernity (Brockmann 1994: 176; cf., Doc. 5.17).

[Document 8.17 Lesbian Garçonnes

In seeking to explain lesbianism, Johanna Elberskirchen, in her book *The Love of the Third Sex* published in 1904, claimed that there was no such thing as an absolute gender identity (Vogel 1984: 164; Kavka 1995: 130). The logic of her argument was that if there was not such a thing as an 'absolute woman', there could not be an absolute male, a theme contemporaneously pathologized by medicine and psychiatry, and notably by the sexologist Magnus Hirschfeld and his Institute for the Study of Sexuality (Fout 1992; Bridenthal 1987: 493; Sulzenbacher 1999; Doc. 8.20). Thus if women could be men, then it was obvious that men could be women.

Die Hosenmode
Glauben Sie, daß eine Gegen-Propaganda notwendig ist?!

Document 8.19 Transvestite Ball

The 'Misogynists' Ball'. Practically every social group in Berlin has its social club: the fat ones, the bald ones, the bachelors, the widowers – why not therefore, the misogynists? This psychologically curious and socially not exactly edifying human species had a ball a few days ago. 'Grand Viennese Masked Ball' – according to the announcement; the sale or distribution of the tickets was conducted with great care, for the gentlemen wanted to be among themselves. Their venue is a well-known large dance hall. We entered the hall around midnight. There was lively dancing to the sounds of a full orchestra. The heavy cloud of smoke veiled the shimmer of glass, and at first hid the details of the event. We could only make a closer inspection during the dance break. Masks were by far in the majority; tailcoats and ballgowns appeared only occasionally.

But what is this? The lady who passed us just now in a pink tarlar [gown] had a cigar in the corner of her mouth and puffed on it like a dragoon. And she had a blond, only lightly powdered beard. And now she is speaking with an 'angel' in a very low-neckline and tights, who stands there leaning upon bared arms and is also smoking. Those are two male voices and the topic of conversation is equally male; [. . .] So. Two men in women's clothes.

A common clown stands over there by a pillar in intimate conversation with a ballerina and has his arm thrown around her perfect form. She has a blond titian head, a sharply chiselled profile and apparently sexy shape. The glimmering earrings, the necklace with the medallion around the throat, the full round shoulders and arms do not permit any doubt as to her 'authenticity', until she suddenly frees herself with a quick movement from the embrace and yawningly removes herself with a heartfelt sigh in the deepest bass: 'Emil, you are boring today!'. The uninitiated can hardly believe his eyes; the ballerina is also male!

Suspicious, we inspect further. We almost guess that here one plays at reversed worlds; for here a man walked – or rather minced by – no, definitely not a man, although he had a carefully trimmed moustache. The beautifully coiffeured curls, the powdered and made up face with the heavily 'painted' eyebrows, the golden brooch with real flowers that adorns the elegant black gown, the golden bracelets on the wrists and the delicate fan in the white-gloved hand – those are surely not attributes of a man. And how coquettishly he handles the fan, how he dances and turns, how he minces and lisps! And yet mother nature created this doll as a man. He is a salesman in the local large department store, and the ballerina from before is his 'colleague'.

At the corner table over there a large audience appears to be in progress. Several older gentlemen press themselves around a group of ladies with very prominent cleavages, who are sitting with a glass of wine and – from the loud guffaws – are telling none too delicate jokes. Who are these three ladies? 'Ladies!' chortled my knowledgeable guide. Let's see: the one on the right with the brown hair and the half-length fancy outfit is 'Butterrieke', according to her own testimony a hairdresser; the second one, the blond, in a chanteuse's costume and with the pearl necklace is known here under the name, 'Miss Ella on a tight-rope', and according to her a ladies' tailor, and the third one – well, that is the universally famous 'Lotte'.

[. . .]. Surely that cannot be a man? This figure, these breasts, the classical arms, the whole comportment is categorically female!

I was then informed that 'Lotte' used to be an accountant. Today, she – or rather he – is only 'Lotte' [. . .]

By closer examination of those present I discovered to my amazement a number of people I knew: my shoemaker, whom I would have taken as anything but a 'misogynist'; today he is a 'troubador' with a sword and a feather hat, and his 'Leonare' in bridal dress serves me 'Bock' and 'Uppmann' [cigars] in the cigar-shop. I recognized 'Leonore', by her big frozen hands when she took off her gloves in the break. And yes! There is my tie-maker. He is running about in a questionable outfit as Bacchus, and is the seladon [consort] of an unlikely kitted-out Diana, who otherwise works as a waiter in a beerhall. What there is of 'real' women at the ball, escapes public description. At any rate these keep to themselves and avoid any contact with the misogynist men, who also are consistent and keep to and amuse themelves, ignoring totally the winsome female species.

Source: Richard Krafft-Ebing, Pathologica Sexualis *(14th edn, Vienna, 1912), 442–3.*

Flexner estimated the homosexual population of Berlin at the time Krafft-Ebing made his tour to be around 30,000, serviced by a small army of homosexual prostitutes of between 1,000 and 2,000 (Flexner 1919: 30; Ostwald 1906, reprint 1992: 4). When Spender travelled to Hamburg he took the opportunity to acquaint himself with the city's homosexual nightlife, especially in the St Georg district, close to the main railway station, and in St Pauli. In one such bar, the 'Three Stars', he found scenes of sexual dubiety, as same-sex couples intermingled with respectable-looking heterosexual couples and danced to the jazz coming from a band of 'uncertain musicians' (Spender 1988: 74). Such scenes were turned into public currency during the 1920s, as *urbane* homosexual subcultures became popular with 'weekend' tourists (Moreck 1931: 132, 157). Dix made Berlin's most famous and oldest transvestite bar, 'Eldorado' in the Lutherstraße (a new one was opened on the corner of Metz and Kalckreuthstraße in the 1920s), the subject for a painting of the same name in 1922, showing two rather burly ladies in heavy make-up; and Curt Moreck included it in his guide to Berlin's underside a decade later, with a nonchalant caricature of male transvestism.

Document 8.20 Berlin's 'Eldorado'

[see illustration on page 222]

Source: Painting by Paul Kann in Curt Moreck, Führer durch das Lasterhafte Berlin *(Leipzig 1931), 179.*

Such visual depictions and literary descriptions of transgressive genders, and homosexual activity, might have been intended to either shock or titillate a German public, and need to be balanced. Christopher Isherwood, for example, found a more sober scene when he visited the male gay bar 'Cosy Corner' which he found 'plain and homely and unpretentious' (Isherwood 1977: 30). Even Moreck showed up the discrepancy between the surface gloss of *demi-monde* bar life and a bleaker everyday existence of the female lesbian habitués of the 'Olala' bar (Moreck 1931: 166; Kokula 1984: 152).

Yet it was the surface image that struck home at the time. The city produced an emasculated and effete male, symbolized by the weak characters of the young Count Osdorff in Pabst's *Diary of a Lost Girl* and Alwa Schön in *Pandora's Box* by the same director, or Christian Schad's provocative drawing of two naked '*Young Men Kissing*' (1929). These were, therefore, effeminate men lorded over by phallic women, and were depicted by early psychological science of physique and character, as schizophrenes with a retarded sexuality.

Document 8.21 Male Typologies

On the other hand, it is well known to be no rarity to find appearances of overwhelming sexual excitement in acute schizophrenic psychosis. In certain schizoid groups an overstrong sexual impulse is a typical personality symptom. He then has that kind of general affectivity, which is characteristic of the temperamental schizoid [. . .], and which swings abruptly backwards and

forwards between the alternatives of excessive heat, and excessive coldness, and is uneven in the regulation of the impulse [. . .]

After careful exploration we also find among people suffering from schizoid diseases, some with abnormal, or not one-sided direction of the impulse. We find among them and among their relations frequent tendencies to homo-sexuality, and further, cases, without strong sexual impulses, of contrary-sexual types of affectivity – masculine women, and feminine men. Sadism, and the perversions related to it, are occasionally met with, but these things do not hang together with the sexual impulse as such, but with the general schizoid temperament, and particularly with the coldness of the affective life, and the convulsive hunger for stimulation. [. . .]

There is above all the abnormally strong affective fixation on the mother (more rarely also on the father) [. . .]; it is an elective, extravagent tenderness, at a time when normal young people have cut themselves loose from the narrow bounds of the family, and have devoted themselves to other ideals. [. . .]

With many schizophrenes this goes together very closely with the harsh fit-ful, uneven functioning of the regulation of the impulses. Timidity is [. . .] one of the most common characteristics of the late developed schizophrene. It can attain so high a degree that it can hinder altogether the attainment of a sexual end, which is, in itself, very strongly desired. Side by side with this abnormal inhibition we also find, especially in the case of defective post-psychotics, complete absence of inhibitions, cynical brutality, and shameless forms of sexuality.

Source: Ernst Kretschmer, Physique and Character: An investigation of the nature of constitution and of the theory of temperament, *translated from second rev. edn, by W.J.H. Sprott (London, 1925), 89–90.*

In some instances, such people harboured a deviant sexuality that was destructive of society. This is the suggestion in Fritz Lang's film *M* where in a particular sequence, shop windows constantly attract children to their displayed treasures. We know from a previous scene that these windows represent danger to the children. The psychotically disturbed childkiller, Hans Beckert, is attracted to a window display of pocket knives, and while standing there possessed by the flashing blades, he notices the reflection of a little girl. In this scene she becomes part of the display, an object of desire, commodified through her presence in the window.

Document 8.22 Object of Desire

[see illustration on page 224]

Source: Fritz Lang, M *(1931), Courtesy Deutsche Kinemathek Berlin.*

Beckert is a feminine-male defined by his uncontrollable libido and a pathological, irrational and hysterical nature, and as such, when he kills children, it is as a woman (Buschan 1915: 95; cf., Künkel 1934: 142–51; Walkowitz 1992: 227).

Beckert suffers from the 'irresistible hyper-sexuality' and 'the absolutely worst pathological sexual behaviour' that, according to Krafft-Ebing (Doc. 8.7), was caused by the city's over-stimulation. With his libido unleashed, Beckert threatens the regeneration of national Germany in two respects: by his own ambivalent sexuality and by killing the country's greatest asset, female children. In the film, his pathological sexual condition spills over to pitch the urban order into crisis, in much the same way that Beckert's real-life contemporary, the mass sex-murderer Peter Kürten, unleashed a hysterical panic in Düsseldorf (Hüttenberger 1989: 408–12). It was widely believed

at the time that such forces could only be contained by reinstating the dissolved boundaries (Walkowitz 1992: 208–12), and by rebuilding hierarchies underpinned by a reassertion of patriarchal authority.

Document 8.23 The Authoritarian Male

[. . .] many men display in their character a constitutive authoritarian element. In their most inner self they have the deep desire to dispose of a person who is weaker, who will obey and admire them; this need is satisfied by female dependence. Undoubtedly, many workers remained authoritarian in their personality even when in political terms an anti-authoritarian posture was adopted. This is hardly surprising since the authoritarian character is itself a product of history. Although at the time of the survey, that is to say, 1929, the authoritarian personality in its purest and most extreme form was to be found primarily among members of the lower middle class, one could often find it also among workers. Whilst the transformation in the function of the working-class family as well as the typical dismantling of traditional personal contact to managers in the large factory eventually led to a changed attitude towards authority, at the same time developing a sense of solidarity among fellow workers, the powerlessness of the individual in society is nevertheless contrasted by the development of the subordination of wife and children as an important compensatory function, and which could only be relinquished with difficulty.

Source: Fromm, Arbeiter und Angestellte, *183.*

When Fromm conducted his study at the end of the 1920s, traditional authority in Germany, and especially in its cities, was at a crisis-ridden crossroads. Some historians trace this crisis to the beginning of the decade, when defeated German soldiers had returned home to the city only to find themselves displaced by women empowered by revolution in a republic of Sodom (Theweleit 1989: 27; Brockman 1994: 171ff.). But paradoxically in this foreign republic of sex, they found a place, as some of Grosz's critical city works from the early days of the republic show, and displayed here by the Communist artist Bruno Voigt.

Document 8.24 The Boss's Thoughts, 1931

Source: Bruno Voigt, The Boss: Thoughts of a Man Watching an Attractive Woman in a Café *(1931), reproduced in* Art in Germany, *134.*

A surface reading of Voigt's imagery shows the economic underpinning of sexual inequality of the republic's urban experience: money buys male sexual freedom. However if we probe a little further and read the composition's signs, we find the disputed emblems of Weimar's sexualized urban modernity (Lewis 1990: 114, 133): 'Bar', 'Tango', '69', 'paragraph 175 (offset by a foetus just above his head)'; revue girls and champagne. The proliferation of female genitalia and the motif of the eye might underline the Boss's sexual desire expressed through the male gaze; but could also suggest male castration, given the obscured presence of what appears to be a slack – and thus impotent – penis (in the crux of his arm). At the same time, the boss can only envisage the female as the sum of her sexual parts. Voigt's image, therefore, also alludes to the relationship between the sexes as essentially violent (Stekel 1935: 76–7; Theweleit 1987: 171–204; Kavka 1995: 138, 145).

Document 8.25 Graph of Female Violent Deaths 1926–36

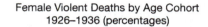

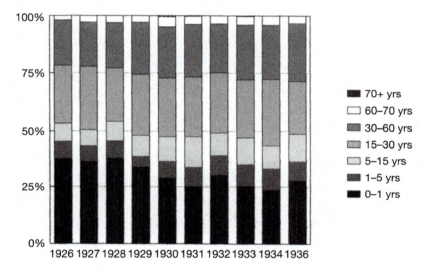

Female Violent Deaths by Age Cohort
1926–1936 (percentages)

Legend:
- 70+ yrs
- 60–70 yrs
- 30–60 yrs
- 15–30 yrs
- 5–15 yrs
- 1–5 yrs
- 0–1 yrs

Source: Relevant volumes of StJbDR
no data for 1935

Source: Compiled from Statistisches Jahrbuch für das Deutsche Reich *(1926–38), in sequence.*

Two contemporary statistical studies of persons convicted and sentenced to death for murder during the six years 1928 to 1933 showed that women formed the majority of 321 victims (181 against 140 males); and, overwhelmingly, the perpetrator was male. As we can see from Document 8.25, the single most vulnerable group of females (excluding infants and toddlers) were young women between the ages of 15 and 30 (StDR 507 Kriminalstatistik 1938: 41). That is, women in their sexual prime. Such violence against women was graphically portrayed by Weimar artists such as Dix, who represented himself as a sex-murderer, that is one who killed for sexual gratification (*Lustmord*).

Document 8.26 The Sex Murderer

Source: Otto Dix, Sex Murderer, Self Portrait, *1922, reproduced in Eva Karcher,* Otto Dix 1891–1969 *(Cologne, 1992), 61.*

The violent representations of sexual lust and crime such as those presented here by Voigt or Dix, that depict the sexual tensions of the 1920s city, have led Beth Irwin Lewis and more recently, Maria Tatar, to read into them a 'sentence of death against women' by anxiety-ridden males seeking to avenge their emasculation (Lewis 1990: 204, 207, 213ff., 220, 224, 226; Tatar 1995: 10–12). According to Maria Tatar

'[. . .] it becomes evident that the representation of murdered women must function as an aesthetic strategy for managing certain kinds of sexual, social, and political anxieties and for constituting an artistic and social identity' [under the republic] (Tatar 1995: 6).

But how reliable are such portrayals as symptomatic of the male response to Weimar's modernity in its gendered guise? Firstly, the murder of women by males was only a fraction of the total of interpersonal crimes, and it declined over the period. Nevertheless, in spite of the few sensational cases that occurred in the second half of the 1920s (Evans 1996: 526–36, 548–61, 572–605; Johnson 1995: 235), its depiction also virtually disappears after 1923. Secondly, not all sex murderers carried out their acts in a sexual frenzy, as purported by medical psychologists, and shockingly popularized by Weimar artists. The perpetrators were less the gory beast favoured by a Grosz, Schlichter, or Dix, than the pathetic figure of a real-life Albert Speckner, tried in early 1912 in Munich for the murder of 11-year-old Frieda Bracher the previous Christmas, and shown here in a courtroom sketch.

Document 8.27 Sex Murderer Albert Speckner, 1912

[see illustration opposite]

Source: Staatsarchiv Munich, Pol. Dir. Munich, 8080; Neues Münchener Tageblatt, *117 (26 April 1912), 5.*

Initially, Speckner's crime was treated as a sex-murder. The press imputed to Speckner the stereotypical predatory instincts of the 'prowling beast' in the urban jungle (MNN 602, 25 Dec. 1911). But as the facts were uncovered, it became increasingly clear that Speckner, who knew Frieda by sight from the neighbourhood, had met her by coincidence and not by design, that sex had not been planned, and that her death had occurred in a panic after she had begun to cry in his lodgings. In spite of archive evidence showing similarities to Speckner's case, art history critics and some historians have been tempted to take the 'psychotic personality' of the urban sex-murderer as represented in artistic works or newspaper reports as a paradigm for the male experience of Weimar modernity (Tatar 1995: Chapter 3; Hüttenberger 1989: 410; Lewis 1990: 115).

The following letter by 32-year-old Johann Eichhorn, a serial rapist under investigation for five gruesome sex-murders committed between October 1931 and late autumn 1937, appears to illustrate this point; but because it dates from the end of the 1930s, it requires us to stretch the paradigm beyond the limits of a 'Weimar modernity'.

Neues Münchener Tagblatt

Nr. *117* vom *Freitag, 26. April 1912*
Seite 5, Spalte 1, 2 u. 3.

Mädchenmörder Speckner vor Gericht.

Albert Speckner

und sein Verhör.

Document 8.28 Johann E., to his wife Josefa

Copy

Munich, 20.7.1939

Pepi!

Despite my dreadful crimes, I have repeatedly tried out of love and sincerity and for our children's sakes, to get on a good footing with you. But you have not found it worth the effort to visit me or even to write a postcard or even to send me word of a last goodbye. And precisely because of this explicitly cruel behaviour – to put it mildly, you have proven what I always believed to be the case – that you never properly loved me and that I was just the means to an end and your right to get money from me. Indeed, the disgraceful behaviour of your parents and your nasty sister Marie should have been enough to stop me from marrying you. But you always knew very well how to use sensual means to bring me under your carnal spell and in this way we had the children. And as soon as these appeared, and I absolutely never refused to match my paternal duties from my earnings, you and yours had the unbelievable cheek to get my wages docked at my workplace. You put a revolver to my heart and forced me to marry you although deep down this was never in my thoughts. And so began my unhappy life. You have not kept in any way to what you and your father boastfully broadcast, especially in financial matters, then your so-called wealth and your dowry were always a deceit. You not only failed utterly in this respect, but also in wifely matters: in cooking, cleaning, etc. you lacked enterprise. With your high and mighty opinions you needed the salary of a government counsellor instead of a poor railway worker with a monthly gross wage of 150 Marks, to pay for the belatedly acquired necessary household goods! I never once saw a sign of your so-called earnings – indeed I had to pay off the remainder of your tax obligations – for which you had spent on your relations and your one-time paramours. Also, I would like to know why you were not afraid of me before? How so often you came looking for me and hauled me from the taverns – did you not have any fear of me on those occasions? But in this respect and in others – the last word has not been spoken. The men before whom you present yourself today as so innocent and nice to demonize me are not, or are hardly, impressed by this. We want to see first how far you have been faithful during our unhappy marriage – whether you have not also been crawling around in other married beds as you used to. Pepi, the day has not yet turned to night, God knows where you and your relations, especially your father, will be this time next year – in this respect you certainly don't have the right to throw stones when you yourself sit behind glass. I reap today in my greatest predicament and doubt such an unearned thanks for the many good things I have done especially for you, which you will never be able to answer for. I know that I have failed terribly and so must pay a terrible price. – But I

do not want your pardon, only justice. Remain at least a truly caring and just mother to the children.
signed Hans.

Source: Staatsarchiv Munich, Pol. Dir. 8008.

How are we to read Eichhorn's letter? Is there not a danger of reproducing the myths generated by a condemned man seeking to justify his crimes or even to comprehend them for himself? As indeed there is a danger of taking as unequivocal a small group of artists seeking to shock; or reading as absolute the discourse generated by critics of Weimar modernity (Evans 1996: 535). For instance, murder between the sexes was generally not *sexually* motivated, but tended to stem from domestic quarrels or was a crime of passion (StDR 433 Kriminalstatistik, 1934: 37; StDR 507 Kriminalstatistik, 1938: 39, 43; Johnson 1995: 217–19; Abrams 1992). Indeed, *Lustmord* constituted only a sixth of the murders between 1931 and 1933, and almost half of these are accounted for by the nine murders committed by Peter Kürten in Düsseldorf, itself an untypical case since such murders usually took place outside the city limits. In fact, only a fifth of murders between 1928 and 1933 took place within a big city, while nearly 60 per cent occurred in country areas (StDR 507 Kriminalstatistik, 1938: 42–3). Thus the big city was only infrequently the setting of the crime (always the setting for *Lustmord* paintings), and rarer still was the empowered woman of urban modernity the victim: she was the excuse.

Women were emancipated under the Weimar Republic, but were they really empowered, and by the same token, men disempowered? There is broad agreement among historians that in terms of women's social and economic position they remained subordinate to men. The same can be argued for their sexual status, in spite of some source material that appears to show otherwise. The unequal relationship between the sexes, especially at the workplace, constituted the subject matter for any number of popular films in the 1920s, for instance, *The Girl from Checkout 12* (1927), or *The Secretary* (1929), both of which took the experiences of the modern urban woman as their focus. Although such films recycled fairytale romances in modern garb, they also reveal the continuing gender inequality of the period, and remind audiences of a 'woman's place' subordinate to that of the man/husband. The following montage by the Berlin-born avant-garde photographer H. Hajek-Halke, suggests that the city may be female, but it is a city shaped by and subjugated to male power.

Document 8.29 Female Asphalt

[see illustration on page 232]

Source: 'Scandal', c. 1932 *ICA Exhibition Catalogue,* Berlin: A critical view of ugly realism 20s–70s *(London, Berlin, 1978),* 33.

Thus, in spite of the challenges to a privileged masculinity after the First World War, we can argue that men were not displaced from their political hold on power, from their economic prerogatives, or from their social status. Indeed, patriarchal authority was restored after 1933, and in spite of its temporary setback at the end of the Second World War, was again consolidated after 1945. For the next 30 years, the female metaphor of interwar modernity disappeared from representations of the city, and strong males recolonized its public spaces.

Files and fingerprints: Indexing the city

The documents in the previous chapters have shown how the city was a place of massed shifting population; a fast-moving and ever-changing environment. The city, and the lives it contained, was neither fixed nor contained by clearly defined boundaries. Indeed, the modernity of the city lay in its mercurial fluidity (Leinert 1925: 241), as Ruttmann's street scenes show only too well. Nearly all commentators on the modern city recognized how urban anonymity offered a refuge for those who wished to 'disappear' into its labyrinthine networks; or presented the opportunity to reinvent for oneself a new identity. For those charged with the task of urban management, such fluidity challenged their authority through evasion, and thus posed a problem of control over the urban space.

In response to this, from the turn of the century, urban technocrats began to modernize traditional means of keeping control, such as the police *Razzia* or swoop (cf., Doc. 4.14), or random identity checks by introducing new rational techniques of urban management (Habermas 1987: 306). Drawing on contemporary technical, scientific and administrative developments, they set out to cocoon the city and its inhabitants within 'a total system' (cf., Doc. 5.17). A prominent role was assigned to a bureaucratic system that created a new urban architecture from paper.

Document 9.1 The Registration

The statistical recording accompanies the Berliner from birth to the grave. If a child is born then this is to be reported to the registry office within a week. Not enough with the entry in the register, without which one is not at all recognized as having been born, a certificate is filled in which shows the age and occupation of the parents, what number child etc. Henceforth, police and church oversee the new-born: the baptism is witnessed, the vaccination, the repeat vaccination, school registration is noted, [as too] school attendance, and the spiritual and physical maturity for military service. Come the day for marriage, so one endeavours with the registry banns to prepare for the statistics, and finally through the signing in the register the issue of a marriage certificate in which again age, occupation, previous family status etc. of both partners is carefully noted. A household is now established; the registration form will acquaint the police, who with devoted precision will note each change of residence, not only with the household itself, but also with its inhabitants, the servants, chambermaids, and lodgers. The police even wish to get to know newcomers personally – and one cannot bequeath to them – and to the statistician – a greater anguish than that left when one moves on without deregistering.

At the same time the tax office puts out its feelers. It carries out an annual census with the simple aim of locating the taxpayer. The office does not rest before it has committed to paper the sources of revenue and income and does not allow one any rest until everything is declared: the profitable activity, the bonds, the life assurance policy, etc. Then one receives one's tax code, and knows how much one is worth to the state. If one is male, then the election office springs into action; it provides election cards, one for every adult. On it is, apart from the tax paid, one's nationality, age, address and date of move. Even whether one is irreproachable or previously convicted, whether one is bankrupt or under legal restraint, is carefully noted.

So one does not think that one can otherwise do or let something be done which escapes statistical registration. What doesn't get noted for the individual, gets noted for the household (e.g. the gas consumed), or for the building (e.g. water), or for the pumping station (e.g. the sewerage). The price of food, which one has invariably to pay, is noted, the rent ascertained. The acquisition of property is registered in detail. A public notice is obligatory for those who are property-owners when property changes hands. Legal processes in which one is involved are carefully entered in the court log. In the case of criminal convictions a large register is opened, in order to record the accused.

Thus the authorities' attention accompanies the Berliner along all his paths; should a contagious disease befall him, the formula is ready, and finally should death remove him from all these recordings, registrations, formulas, even then his corpse will not be lowered into the lap of the earth before his name, age and occupation, size of apartment, the number of persons dwelling there, the cause of death – with small children, how they were nourished – is noted. And the population is so used to such cataloguing that even on the gravestone, one can read mostly chiselled in stone the name, dates of birth and death, often also the occupation and place of origin: the final permanent registration in stone or iron, which seals the statistical earthly existence of the deceased.

Source: E. Hirschberg, Bilder aus der Berliner Statistik *(Berlin, 1904), 1–3.*

Although in this document Hirschberg is extolling Berlin, the register system with its fetish for data had become part of common urban practice throughout Germany by the beginning of the twentieth century (Hietala 1987: 78–83). This system of registration, however, was not intended as a static mechanism for order and control. According to contemporary theories on the modern city, collective life was fragmented, with individuals estranged from one another and alienated from their true self. The statistical index described by Hirschberg allowed for these fragments to be taken up and reassembled into a new whole. As Siegfried Kracauer argued in his influential essay, 'The mass ornament', *regulating* the fragments of society had as much to do with control as *shaping* the urban form. These twin aims of regulating and shaping were thus quintessential elements of Germany's urban 'modernity'. Thus while Hirschberg's statistical system caught the individual as a 'fragmented' part of society on to the register, a further device was needed that would enable the administrator to control and reassemble the whole.

In 1911 a firm in Berlin was commissioned to perfect a register that would provide a 'complete and mechanical overview of all documents in relation to time, place and type for the establishment of lists, compilation of statistics for tax, electoral, conscript duties, military balance, nationality, welfare support, controls of persons, housing, and trade etc., [. . .]'. The authors of the system that eventually emerged, decided, after careful study of the material, to opt for a dual system organized alphabetically and by street. The system was designed to be dynamic; it could grow and change as the circumstances of the individual person and the community altered, while its essential nature and function remained intact. The double register was especially necessary in the case of cities where populations were constantly on the move.

Document 9.2 The Index Register

District
  Street
    House
      [Building]
       [Floor]
        [Apartment]
        Household
         Individual

[. . .] every part [of the system] can be applied, according to need and according to size of place, to any preferred degree of perfection and completeness.

Where, at the first stroke, the material cannot be managed to the minutest division for technical reasons, an expansion can gradually follow.

At any rate, it is better in the long term to go too far than not to go far enough.

Why this is, is shown in the following.

The register presents easily to hand and at first sight administrative, technical and criminologically important information in the form of a constant statistical tabular work.

[. . .]

Where statistics are kept, the statistician – without expending any particular extra energy – is able to create the most wonderful data on age, sex, criminality and many other things, whatever his imagination or practical needs dictate:
[. . .]

On the other hand, the criminologist will have a watchful eye, when the number of white, yellow, red, blue and black register index-tabs in a street, or in a house, or in an apartment, begin to cluster in the persons control column, thus his entire area of competence which we depicted in the basic framework as 'police surveillance, domestic behaviour, wanted poster (personal description), identity check, surveillance of morals, criminal records', is put before his eyes in a locally most complete overview and controllable form.

– This part of the tabular system can be expanded and broadened in a massive way for the cities which share a solely administrative and police service. The means described yield chronologically, spatially and objectively, a complete mirror image of all possible conditions and streets: even the shape of noses, ears, scars and gait, stature [. . .] [of individuals].

Source: Internationale Treuhand-Vereinigung G.m.b.H. Berlin, Das Meldewesen nach dem Tabulator-System. Sein Technik und seine Leistungen in verwaltungstechnischer, statistischer und kriminalistischer Hinsicht (Berlin, 1911).

The efficacy of such a system was put to the test after the murder of 11-year-old Frieda Bracher on Christmas Eve in 1911. The *Munich Latest News* was confident of an inevitable and early arrest because 'Munich has not resigned itself like other cities such as Berlin, Hamburg, London, or even New York, where murders occur more often, and where, because of the impossibility of keeping a well-ordered system of registration, the detection of the perpetrator is rare' (MNN 602, 25 Dec. 1911). And indeed, Frieda's killer, Albert Speckner, was soon apprehended and brought to trial (Cf. Doc. 8.27), as too was the fictional Hans Beckert (Doc 8.22). In *M* the audience is shown the efficiency of the modern index system as both police and the criminal underworld race to track down the child killer (see below).

The system of surveillance portrayed in document 9.2, with its demand for an integrated index, became the model for the administrative grid of the modern German city in the early twentieth century. Not only the police, statistical bureaux, and tax offices, but health and welfare agencies too, favoured such a system. But in order for such a system to be properly effective, the office itself had to be made manageable through the introduction of rational systems of filing and order (Riechenberg 1929; Pirker 1962; Eggenkämper 1995: 229–34). Document 9.3, dating from the mid-1920s, is from a brochure for modern office systems found in the files of the Munich police, who at this time were undergoing a reorganization of office procedures.

Document 9.3 Advert: 'Find it Again!'

[see illustration opposite]

Text paragraph reads: It is important to find things again when catalogues, price lists, prospectuses, books, journals and other printed materials are collected in order to serve – daily and hourly – as source materials. – The most avid collecting loses its purpose when – as unfortunately is the case in many offices – the archive material is hastily crammed onto any shelf, – without care for a quick retrieval through a clearly planned system.

Source: Staatsarchiv Munich, Pol. Dir. 7549.

This image is suggestive of what we have been arguing here: through ordered files the city becomes penetrable, and thus, controllable, to the eye of the administrator. By capturing the individual in the city on to an index card, the modern office system promised to end the impenetrability of the 'urban jungle' (cf. Doc. 4.15). For the system that was being considered amounted to nothing less than an archive of individuals neatly catalogued and contained in brown files. Thus, in an important scene in Fritz Lang's film *M*, the criminal police, gendarmerie and welfare agencies (including psychologists) discuss in a smoke-filled conference how to catch the child killer. During a heavy silence, we hear the voice of the officer in charge of the search, Inspector Lohmann, who remarks:

Document 9.4 The File

There is perhaps another way. Without doubt there already exists a file on the person we believe to be the perpetrator. Certainly, as a severely pathological person, he has had a brush with the authorities. Therefore, all welfare institutions, prisons, psychiatric clinics, and mental homes must be included in the search. We must receive information especially about those persons who have been released as harmless, but who, because of their disposition, could be identical with the murderer.

Source: Fritz Lang, M Protokoll (Hamburg, 1963), 49.

In a later scene we see Inspector Lohmann perusing the case files of sex criminals released over the previous five years. He is certain that somewhere in these files a clue is catalogued which will lead him to the killer, and, of course, there is one (though the criminal fraternity, by deploying their own dragnet, get to Beckert before the police).

The files Lohmann pores over are individual case histories, and include psychological as well as physical attributes of the person concerned. The 'case history' had been developed in Germany during the 1920s by forensic psychiatrists and criminal biologists such as Fritz Lenz in Munich, Rainer Fetscher, a leading public health official in the state of Saxony, and the Tübingen psychiatrist Ernst Kretschmer (Weber 1993; Schwartz 1995). They had stressed the importance of 'following the individual from the cradle to the present' by means of the case history. Using a 'table of life events' that contained minute details of family (past and present) and social milieux, it would be possible to construct a typology of characteristics that would provide a socio-psychological key to the individual (von Rohden 1938: 527, 627–8, 636; cf. Doc. 8.21).

Document 9.5 Human Classification: The Typology

The typology should – and must – not be anything more than a point of reference, a classification [*Ordnungshilfe*], a thread, which should help one to find one's way among the variety of appearances. Fetscher graphically compares the typology with an alphabetical order. As convenient as it is in an index first to conduct a general pre-sorting according to the first letter of the alphabet and then to fix a precise alphabetical order, so is the pre-sorting with the help of the typology convenient in the case of people. [. . .]

Source: Friedrich von Rohden, 'Methoden der Kriminalbiologie', in Prof. Dr Emil Abderhalden (ed.), Handbuch der biologischen Arbeitsmethoden, *Abt. IV, Teil 12 1/1: Methoden der gerichtlichen Medizin und Kriminalistik 1 Hälfte, Band 1 (Berlin, Vienna, 1938), 710–11.*

During the 1930s, the criminal biologist Friedrich von Rohden fused this forensic psychology with the idea of the degenerative type of the 'born criminal', associated with Cesare Lombroso (Mannheim 1965: 226; Schwartz 1994; Pick 1989; cf. Docs. 4.15, 4.24). According to von Rohden, the criminal was the product of the chemical fusion of both innate (biological) and environmental (socio-historical) influences. Thus von Rohden recommended the use of the case history, but recommended also that the characteristics thought to denote the 'criminal type' be recorded. Police and doctors were told to pay attention to: (i) the shape, size and bearing of the head; (ii) the face, cheekbones, profile, chin, presence or absence of buck teeth; (iii) the eyes, their colour, blindness, pronounced stare, far/short-sightedness, squint; (iv) size and shape of ears; (v) irregular teeth, condition of gums, weak jaw; (vi) skin pigment, moles, feminine boundaries of pubic hair; (vii) shape and size of body and arms/legs: whether feminine or masculine, reverse internal organs, absence of some bones, deformities of fingers/toes, club feet; (viii) sexual organs: hyper-hypoplasien; testicles that had not dropped, absence of one testicle; real or pseudo hermaphrodity; secondary opening of male urethra (von Rohden 1938: 640; Ginzburg 1980: 24–8). The details were to be entered on to an index card. In this way, the totality of the individual based on his or her invisible and visible traits was recorded.

Document 9.6 Human Classification: Measuring

[see illustration on page 240]

Source: Gottfried Korff and Reinhard Rürup (eds.), Berlin, Berlin: Die Ausstellung zur Geschichte der Stadt *(1987), 183 © Ullstein Bilderdienst*

The case history, combining personal attributes and social information subjected to psychological analysis, created a map of the individual by being able to explore both the physical and the inner being. It also emphasized the individual's historicity. This was an interesting development because, according to the sociology of the day (Tönnies, Durkheim, Simmel, Sombart), the modern urban experience was devoid of past. Instead, it comprised rootless superficial identities and transitory experiences, making it horizontal and shallow. By contrast, with its stress upon a linear trajectory ('from birth to the present'), the case history restored verticality to the urban experience. And even though it was first applied to those thought to be sick and 'criminal', as a mechanism or sociological tool, it could be extended to urban society at large.

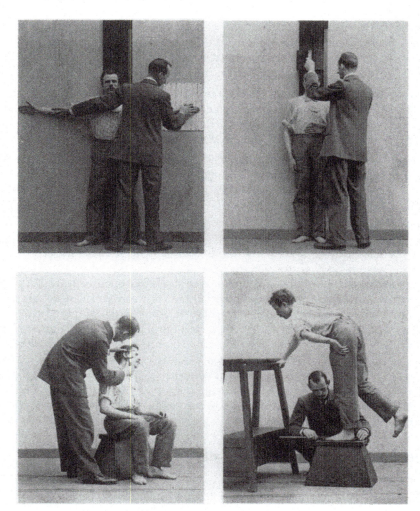

The focus on the individual's visible and invisible characteristics, the emphasis on his or her physical and psychological traits and the influences that shaped these, also provided a key to mapping and deciphering the city. Again, we may refer to Fritz Lang's film *M* for an illustration of this. In a critical scene, the fictional story turns into a public information film as the chief of police (*Polizeipräsident*) explains to the interior minister the methods of the police in tracking down the child killer. Lang contrasts the more traditional and mundane police footwork of door-to-door enquiries, following up dead-end clues and sifting through unreliable public information, with the obviously more modern rational office system (the case file) and forensic science of the laboratory.

Document 9.7 Deciphering the City

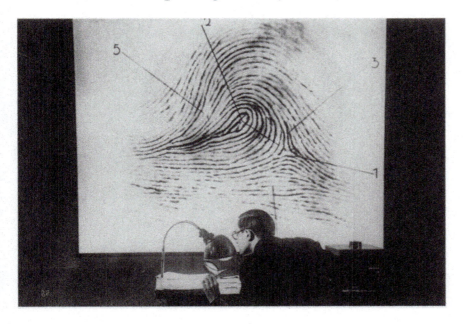

Source: Fritz Lang, M (1931), Courtesy Deutsche Kinemathek Berlin.

The fingerprint not only represents the exclusive characteristics of an individual (Kahn 1929: 229–31). In *M* it comes to signify the control of mass urban society through the forensic scientist's ability to reveal and identify at a glance the city's social pathology in the minutest way. If we refer back to the tabular system (Doc. 9.2), and take into consideration that the police kept an archive of fingerprints, we might argue that what Lang is representing is a *key* to the hidden characteristics of the modern city. Thus even the darkest recesses of the city could be exposed to the technician's eye guided by a rational system founded on principles of science and method.

Referring once again to *M*, two further powerful representations, namely, the police dragnet circumferencing the city, and the gloved hand of Schränker, the leader of the criminal fraternity, extended over a map of the city (cf. Doc. 7.16), signal how the radial vision could contain the city, no matter how large and sprawling, or anonymous, thereby affirming authority's grip.

Document 9.8 Containing the City

[see illustrations on page 242]

Source: Fritz Lang, M (1931).

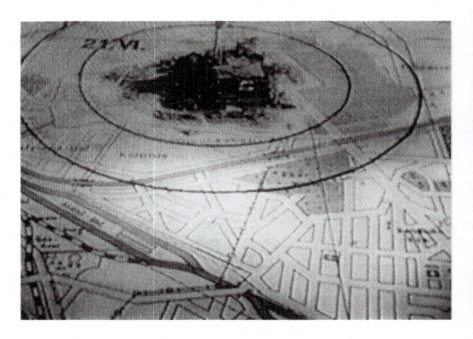

In spite of the developments we have been charting in this chapter, the system of indexing the city did not fall into place overnight, since urban administrations moved only gradually towards its implementation. During the 1920s, the system remained principally a textual one, represented on occasion by works such as that produced by Fritz Lang. Even after 1933, when under the Nazis the technocratic fetishism for registering and indexing the population was driven to its utmost, it eventually collapsed under its own immense bureaucratic weight, according to Gabriele Czarnowski (Czarnowski 1991: 159–61). Indeed, it is probably right to say that an integrated system of registration and indexation was not perfected before 1945, in spite of the obvious potential for such a system after the community census of 1939. The war interrupted any serious work that could be done with this census. But seven years later, it was to provide the Allies with a model for the first postwar census of occupied Germany during the night of 29/30 October 1946.

Document 9.9 Counting the People, 1946

The task of the enumerator will not be an easy one. In pre-war days, the local directory and other sources gave him a complete list of all dwellings with name of street and number. Now whole streets have been wiped out, numbers no longer exist, families are living in cellars or shelters, and considerable care and ingenuity will be required not only in seeing that every household receives a schedule but duly returns it. Fortunately the enumerators are persons with local knowledge who are allotted a small area with whose peculiarities or difficulties they become acquainted well before C[ensus]-day. [. . .]

The total population we know fairly accurately from local records, food cards issued etc., and we know from the labour registration approximately the numbers employed and unemployed and the numbers unable or not available for work, but information on the age and sex distribution, on nationality, on the size of the family, on the number of rooms occupied, on educational status, and on exact occupation is almost entirely lacking. We do not even know how many males and females there are in the British Zone and estimates vary by nearly 10 per cent. The only data available for making an estimate – and a very unsatisfactory one – are those from the issue of tobacco cards! For the numbers at different ages, all we have are some rough estimates for those persons under 18 who receive special ration cards.

Information on all these points is of vital importance for administrative and planning purposes, for forecasting the future population and the future supply of labour, for estimating the number of children for whom schools and teachers will be required, and, together with information on the number of families of different size and constitution (about which no information is at present available) for measuring density of population, overcrowding of families, for planning housing programmes and the location of industry, for estimating the yield of taxes, the cost of social insurance and pension schemes, for estimating food consumption and for fixing ration scales.

Every Division of the Control Commission requires population figures of one kind or another, and every Division has been hampered in its task of administration and control by the lack of information on some characteristics of the population. The great changes not only in the size but in the constitution and distribution of the population in the British Zone since 1939, make the census data of that year out-of-date for most purposes. This census, it may be added, was carried with typical German thoroughness, conscientiousness and promptitude and is a model which many other countries – including some allied countries – might well follow. This augurs well for the success of the present census. The population will, it is hoped, collaborate loyally and truthfully – and all the schedules are confidential and will be used for no other purpose than yielding statistical information – and the staff engaged includes many officials who worked for the census in 1939.

[. . .] The data for each person will then be 'coded' and the code numbers punched on special cards which will be sorted by machinery into whatever characteristic is required (e.g. male persons born between 1910 and 1915) and then passed through tabulating machines which will record the aggregate number in any special group or combination of groups.

Source: J.W.N., 'Counting the people', British Zone Review (31 Aug. 1946), 4.

As the author of this document recognized, the population census was a means both of reimposing administrative order in the absence of physical infrastructure, and of reconstructing the city. The information gathered could be deployed to meet positive social ends through social planning, and ensure its orderly regulation. In this respect 'J.W.N.' shared with Hirschberg, the city planners and social engineers encountered in earlier chapters of this book, the same awe for the power of knowledge in numbers, whose lineage extended back to the census-takers of the late eighteenth-century Enlightenment (Foucault 1972; Glass 1973). At the same time, an analogous awe was reserved for forensic science and new technology as the means to map, expose and contain the dark side of human nature that threatened to overturn postwar society (BZR, 28 Sept. 1946: 14).

Document 9.10 The Stadtpläne: City as Sphere and Grid

[see illustration opposite]

Source: British Zone Review *(20 March 1948), 16.*

The fingerprint, like the radial transport network, or the vision of the organic city, had in part represented a cartesian bio-cellular vision of the early twentieth-century city. Falk's geometric grid of Hamburg, like Sharoun's rectilinear plan for Berlin (cf., Doc. 3.24), offered a technocratic model for comprehending and negotiating urban modernity (Harvey 1989: 240–6). For, like the filing system, this map was both a repository and an index serving urban order, and thereby underpinning the integrity of the nation itself.

16

HANSESTADT HAMBURG

The Stadtpläne

A close up view of the Hamburg Stadtpläne.

IN the summer of 1945, a young and enterprising German engineer, named Gerhard Falk, came to Hamburg from Berlin with an idea firmly fixed in his head of creating an entirely new type of town plan for each of the major cities in Germany. Herr Falk spent two war years in Russia with a German Survey Company, and it was there that he gained invaluable knowledge in the production of military maps, which has since considerably helped him in producing the Stadtpläne (Town Plan).

On arrival in Hamburg, this young Berliner managed, after a great deal of trouble, to acquire a small room over a second-rate restaurant in the suburb of Hoheluft, and it was there, with a staff of six people, working long hours for eight months, that the first town plan of Hamburg, since the war, was drawn up, printed, and ready for distribution to the Germans in June of 1946. Within a very short time all copies of these maps were sold out, and thousands more had to be printed to keep pace with the public's demand. The total number of maps sold in twelve months amounted to somewhere in the region of 70,000, the cost for each map being 3 R.M.

The Hamburg map consisted of eight pages marked alphabetically, and each page was divided into three sections which could be opened separately so as to remove the necessity of unfolding the entire map before examination. The most important factor was the two different scales, the centre of the city having a larger scale and the outer areas a smaller one. This enabled Hamburg to be projected in great detail on to a much smaller sheet than hitherto. That, in itself, may seem a small thing, but it is an extremely important point owing to the acute shortage of paper in Germany today.

The actual method by which this map was produced is a closely guarded secret of the young inventor, the secret now being in the Patent Office in Hamburg.

Briefly, without giving any secrets away, a map of a particular city is placed over a spherical object and photographed by a special camera from above. The portion of the map nearest to the camera appearing in the photograph is in normal scale, whilst the outer areas are in smaller scale. The photograph is then reproduced on to a celluloid sheet and eventually, when all the thousand and one markings of streets, houses and bombed areas have been transcribed in colour on to the celluloid, it is then ready for printing.

With the great success of the Hamburg Town Plan, orders came pouring in from the British, American and French Zones. Most of the orders came from the larger cities of Germany who enquired into the possibility of maps being made for them. Up to the present time, maps of Frankfurt, Berlin, Nuremberg, Düsseldorf, Hannover, Munich and five maps of the Ruhr comprising Essen, Wuppertal, Dortmund, Bochum and Oberhausen-Mulheim have been produced. A special map of Hannover was produced in honour of the Trade Fair and something like 6,000 foreign visitors purchased a copy of the map at a special stall in the Trade Fair. In all, 80,000 maps of Hannover were produced, and sold within a twelve-months' period.

A firm in Birmingham has recently asked whether a map of their city could be made. Herr Falk and his colleagues are, of course, very interested in this, as it would probably mean that his firm would receive a portion of the payment in sterling. Up to the present moment only reichsmarks have been paid for these maps.

The Americans have intimated that they, too, would like a map of the whole of their Zone in the form of a Travel Catalogue, showing hotels, beauty spots and places of interest. This catalogue is primarily intended for the use of American tourists, who may, in the not too distant future, visit the U.S. Zone on sight-seeing tours.

France and Brazil are also negotiating with the Falk Company, and perhaps in a matter of years, plans of cities in the two countries will be produced. Herr Falk now occupies five large rooms in Sprinkenhof Building in Hamburg. His staff has been increased to thirty-five, all of whom are under thirty years of age, and full of enthusiasm regarding the future of these patent Town Plans.

It is now a common sight in Hamburg to see a member of the Police Force, on being asked the way to a certain road or district, produce one of the Hamburg maps.

The Falk Company intends, when the opportunity arises, to open branches all over the world and the inventor predicts that within ten years or so large numbers of foreign travellers will be using his maps all over the world.   A.J.M.

Left: Finishing touches being put to a blueprint. **Right:** Herr Falk, the inventor, examining the Hamburg Stadtpläne.

10 | Conclusion: City *Vaterland*

In recent times some urban historians have argued that a particular feature of modernization was the nationalization of local life, as cities became integrated into the larger constellation of the nation (Ribhegge 1973: 3–4; Harvey 1985: 32–3, 57; Buse 1993: 521). The sources we have been confronting in the earlier chapters of this book, however, suggest that the process was more the reverse as artefacts and practices for organizing the urban experience 'thickened', initiating a new paradigm of modernity that encompassed the nation. In other words, the national whole became the sum of its urban parts (Frisby 1992: 8ff.).

Put into its early twentieth-century German context, marked by war, defeat, and revolution, the ongoing pathologization of urban modernity and its perceived crisis found a parallel discourse on the condition of the national body, on how to cure its inner being by carrying out the necessary surgery of political reform. For, as we saw in Chapter 5, only 'healthy cells' could constitute a healthy body (McElligott 1998: 7).

Document 10.1 Self-Government and Democracy

The political self-government of local life is an asset of the highest value for all of national life. The idea of a decentralized self-determination of the communally corporate organized population is a feature of a good state structure, a pillar of the constitution and national administration [. . .] [a] shared enthusiasm bearing the preparedness for responsibility. Its opposite is the central administration through the state bureaucracy, the extreme of this opposition is the treatment of the communes as public institutions analogous to the principle of the law of guardianship in the previous authoritarian state.

Political self-government, alongside the principle of equality for all *Volksgenossen* [sic] in the participation in public life, is also the second fundamental buttress of the democratic people's state, since only through it can an immediate influence by the population on the process of public administration be practically achieved, which in a [centralized] state bureaucracy is excluded in practice.

Historically, self-government, according to the testimony of the Prussian Interior Minister, for example, proved itself as the 'source of strength' which overcame the collapse of 1806/07.

Today its increased national political significance is due to its role as the only means for the civic education of the broad mass of the people who have come of age through the acquisition of the equal vote.

Source: Landesarchiv Berlin, 142/1 StB 2376 Beigeordnete Albert Meyer-Lülmann, 'Kammer der Selbstverwaltung' (11 Jan. 1921).

In this extract Meyer-Lülmann, who at the time was deputy chairman of the influential Association of Cities, is calling for the modernization of city government in order to free it from its condition of political passivity, associated with the discredited imperial system. The city would be thus transformed into a 'living' school for democracy, consonant with the reality of mass urban society.

Implicit also in Meyer-Lülmann's suggestion is that there must be teachers to bring about the desired change in consciousness; and as we have seen in previous chapters these were to be its civic leaders and administrators. But within a decade, the interim result of the educational enterprise of creating a civic *Vaterland* was less than satisfactory.

Document 10.2 'City and Self-Government', 1929

The meaning of municipal self-government is that the local community regulate their own immediate co-existence. Not the state from above, but the citizenry should administer local matters. The citizen is objectively and personally closest to local conditions. He knows where the shoes are tight. He knows best the economic, social and cultural wishes of the resident population. [. . .]

The lack of civic pride is one of the factors which cause the German to lag behind a few nations in his patriotism. Participation in community matters, which was already poor before the World War, has almost sunk further in the German Republic. Some persons and circles who used to avail themselves as honorary officers, today hold back because of a lack of time and money, and also because of annoyance [with the system]. They all too often leave the representation of citizens to the interest lobbies and professional politicians and this is a grave mistake. If the idea of self-government is not to become a cliché, then the interest of the citizen in his community and its administration must be rekindled and consolidated. In the era of mass transport, modern man is inclined to see himself as a member of the whole and not of the part. He overlooks the tremendous moral and economic importance which municipal government has for all of us and for him in particular. Most people do not realize how closely linked their entire life and fate is with the municipality and its government.

Source: Landesarchiv Berlin, 142/1 StB 1181, Lord Mayor Gustav Böß, Radio lecture (1929): 'City and Self-Government'.

By the time Berlin's lord mayor, Gustav Böß, gave this radio talk, the political modernity of the city was in crisis, but not only because of the apparent apathy that he noted (and, incidentally, because of the very forces of modernity that he briefly alludes to). From 1929 the struggle intensified between advocates of the active city and their opponents, the latter seeing in the modern city a weakened and 'rootless republic', and, therefore, the very antithesis of a revived national community (McElligott 1998: 241). This came in 1933, with the formation of Hitler's government of 'national renewal'. The new regime set about erasing what its supporters had long held to be the degenerate and divisive influences of urban modernity, and, of course, subordinated the city to the unifying control of the centre after passing a statute to that effect in January 1935 (Ribhegge 1973: 15, 18; McElligott 1998: 200, 239). But the new masters of Germany sought national cohesion much as their predecessors had, by nurturing the idea of the organically rooted *Vaterland* in the city.

Document 10.3 Five Years of the German Municipal Statute

On 30 January 1940, the D[eutsche] G[emeinde] O[rdnung] will have been in force for five years. The meaning of this piece of legislation could already be gauged from its announcement on the anniversary of the National Socialist Revolution. It was declared a foundation of the state upon which the reconstruction of the Reich was to be completed. [. . .] The German Municipal Statute was a comprehensive result of municipal political will, which sought broad and far reaching solutions and a secure basis for the further development [of state and society]. [. . .]

The situation in the communal sphere was characterized in the previous century by the term 'self government'. Reich Freiherr vom Stein released the deeply embedded disposition within the German character towards responsible participation of individual people's comrades in their [collective] political fate from the divisiveness of the individualist–absolutist petty principality and made them the centre of a new vital state form. The liberal period that followed, twisted the ideas around into the system of parliamentary irresponsibility, transformed trustworthy popular forces participating in the leadership into anonymous agents of interests and found an especially derisory expression of this false development in the local councils.

National Socialism freed once more the core of the idea of individual responsibility. The German Municipal Statute gave a legal underpinning to a foundation, newly created by National Socialism, upon which the living forces of the local community were to develop their maximum ability under the leadership of the 'Party'.

Source: Bundesarchiv Koblenz, NS25/97: Dr K.H. Patutschnick,
Reichshauptstellenleiter Hauptamt für Kommunalpolitik, 'Meaning and Task
of the Party's Municipal Policy Work (1940)'.

The date of Patutschnick's memorandum is important. For 1940 was the year when, after the defeat of France, Germany planned the reorganization of the European continent into a 'New Order'. This 'New Order' included a comprehensive reorganization of the continent's social, cultural, racial, economic, and political life into a unified and single entity. This ultimate project of modernity (Bauman 1989), took the urban-based 'cells of the nation' as its paradigm to create out of Berlin, Europe's capital city 'Germania' (Reichhardt and Schäche 1998; Lüken-Isberner 1991; cf. Docs. 1.2, 3.20). As Hans Fiehler, the mayor of Munich and party leader responsible for municipal work, confidently predicted in the 31 December 1940 issue of the *Völkischer Beobachter*, 'The German local authorities have at the same time demonstrated inner order, resilience, and drive which will put them in the position also to energetically take on and master the great tasks of the post-war period' (BAK NS25/1215).

The changing fortunes of war, ending in defeat in 1945, denied the German modernizers the opportunity to embark upon these 'great tasks' as far as Europe was concerned. Nevertheless, as James Pollock and others observed in the summer of 1945, there was still in the rubble of the city a remnant of a German *Vaterland*, and here, in 1945, the technocrats returned to complete the uncompleted modernity of the first half of the century (Sywottek 1998: 739).

General bibliography

Archives

Bundesarchiv Koblenz
Hauptstaatsarchiv Wiesbaden
Landesarchiv Berlin
Landesarchiv Schleswig-Holstein
Staatsarchiv Dresden
Staatsarchiv Hamburg
Staatsarchiv Munich

Newspapers and Corporation Journals Statistical Series

Altonaer Stadtkalendar
Berliner Tageblatt
British Zone Review
Deutsche Städtetag in der britischen Zone, Wiederaufbau-Mitteilungen
Die Fahrt: Zeitschrift der Berliner Verkehrs-Aktiengesellschaft
Die Zukunft
Frankfurter Zeitung
Führerschriften
Lufthansa Betriebsmitteilungen
Münchenner Neuesten Nachrichten
The Pall Mall Magazine
Wohlfahrtsnachrichten der Stadt Altona
Statistik des Deutschen Reichs
Statistisches Handbuch für das Deutsche Reich, various
Statistisches Jahrbuch des Deutschen Reichs
Statistisches Jahrbuch für das Deutsche Reich
Statistisches Jahrbuch Deutscher Städte
Statistisches Jahrbuch der Stadt Altona
Statistisches Jahrbuch der Stadt Berlin
Vierteljahreshefte zur Statistik des Deutschen Reichs

Published Sources

Adshead, S.D., 'An Introduction to Civic Design', in *The Town Planning Review* Vol. 1 No. 1 (April 1910), 3–17

Akademie der Künste, *Berlin um 1900. Ausstellung der Berlinischen Galerie in Verbindung mit der Akademie der Künste zu den Berliner Festwoche 1984* (9 Sept.–28 Oct., Berlin, 1984)

Bairoch, Paul, *Cities and Economic Development. From the Dawn of History to the Present* (Chicago, London, 1988)

Bechtel, Heinrich, *Wirtschaftsgeschichte Deutschlands, Band 3: Im 19. und 20. Jahrhundert* (Munich, 1956)

Benjamin, Walter, *Gesammelte Schriften* IV.1, edited by Tillman Rexroth (Frankfurt am Main, 1972)

Bericht über die Gemeinde-Verwaltung Altona in den Jahren 1863 bis 1888, 1863 bis 1900, 3 vols. (Altona, 1889–1906)

Brecht Bertolt, Kurt Weill, 'Aufstieg und Fall der Stadt Mahagonny: Act 1: Grundung der Stadt Mahagonny', in *Bertolt Brecht, Stücke 2* (Frankfurt am Main, 1988)

Chandler, Douglas, 'Changing Berlin', in *The National Geographic Magazine*, Vol. LXXI, No. 2 (Feb. 1937), 131–77

Das große Berlin: Max Missmann, Photographien 1899–1935, edited by Wolfgang Gottschalk (Berlin 1990)

Diesel, Eugen, *Germany and the Germans* (London, 1931), translated from *Die deutsche Wandlung das Bild eines Volks* (Stuttgart, 1931)

Dyos, H.J., 'The Slums of Victorian London', in David Cannadine, David Reeder (eds.), *Exploring the Urban Past. Essays in Urban History by H.J. Dyos* (Cambridge, 1982)

Eisenberg, Christiane, 'Massensport in der Weimarer Republik. Ein Statistischer Überblick', in *Archiv für Sozialgeschichte* XXXIII (1993), 137–77

Evans, Richard J., *Death in Hamburg: Society and Politics in the Cholera Years, 1830–1910* (Oxford, New York, 1987)

Feder, Gottfried, *Die Neue Stadt. Versuch der Begründung einer neuen Stadtplannungskunst aus der sozialen Struktur der Bevölkerung* (Berlin, 1939)

Flexner, Abraham, *Prostitution in Europe* (abr. edn London, 1919)

Forel, August, Rainer Fetscher, *Die sexuelle Frage* (orig. 1904, 16th edn prepared by Rainer Fetscher, Munich, 1931)

Friedberger, Prof. Dr E., *Untersuchungen über Wohnungsverhältnisse insbesondere über Kleinwohnungen und deren Mieter in Greifswald* (Jena, 1923)

Frisby, David, Mike Featherstone (eds.), *Simmel on Culture* (London, Berkeley, 1997)

Fromm, Erich, *Arbeiter und Angestellte am Vorabend des Dritten Reiches. Eine sozialpolitische Untersuchung* [1929], (Munich, 1983)

Gesundheitsbehörde Hamburg (ed.), *Hygiene und Soziale Hygiene in Hamburg: Zur neuenzigsten Versammlung der Deutschen Naturforscher und Aerzte in Hamburg im Jahre 1928* (Hamburg, 1928)

Goldschlag, George W., 'City', in Robert Seitz, Heinz Zucker (eds.), *Um uns die Stadt 1931: Eine Anthologie neuer Großstadtdichtung* (orig. Berlin, 1931), reprint with a foreword by Ulrich Conrads (Der Bauwelt Fundamente 75, Braunschweig, Wiesbaden, 1986)

Gurland, A.R.L., Otto Kirchheimer, Franz Neumann, *The Fate of Small Business in Nazi Germany* (New York, 1943, reprint New York, 1975)

Habermas, Jürgen, 'Modernity – An Incomplete Project', in Thomas Docherty (ed.), *Postmodernism: A reader* (New York, London, Toronto, Sydney, Tokyo, Singapore, 1993), 98–109

Hegemann, Werner, *Steinerne Berlin* (Berlin, 1930)

Heller, Reinhold (ed.), *Art in Germany 1906–1936: From Expressionism to resistance. The Marvin and Janet Fishman Collection* (Munich, 1990)

Helmer, Stephen Dean, 'Hitler's Berlin: Plans for reshaping the central city developed by Albert Speer' (Cornell University, Ph.D. thesis, 1980)

Hermand, Jost, Frank Trommler, *Die Kultur der Weimarer Republik* (Munich, 1978)

Hirschberg, E., *Bilder aus der Berliner Statistik* (Berlin, 1904)

Horsfall, T.C., *The Improvement of the Dwellings and Surroundings of the People: The example of Germany* (Manchester, 1904)

Hüttenberger, Peter, *Düsseldorf Geschichte von den Ursprüngen bis ins 20.Jahrhundert*, Band 3: Die Industrie- und Verwaltungsstadt (20. Jahrhundert), (Düsseldorf, 1989)

ICA Exhibition Catalogue, *Berlin. A Critical View of Ugly Realism 20s–70s* (London, Berlin, 1978)

International Labour Office, *European Housing Problems since the War* (Geneva, 1924)

International Labour Office, 'The German Family Budget Enquiry of 1927–1928', in *International Labour Review*, 22 (1930), 524–532

Internationale Treuhand-Vereinigung G.m.b.H. Berlin, *Das Meldewesen nach dem Tabulator-System: Sein Technik und seine Leistungen in verwaltungstechnischer, statistischer und kriminalistischer Hinsicht* (Berlin, 1911)

Isherwood, Christopher, *Goodbye to Berlin* (1935)

Jung, Franz, *Die Technik des Glücks: Mehr Tempo! Mehr Glück! Mehr Macht!* (1923): *Werke* 6 (Hamburg, 1987)

Kahn, Fritz, *Das Leben des Menschen: Eine volkstümliche Anatomie, Biologie, Physiologie und Entwicklungsgeschichte des Menschen*, Band III (Stuttgart, 1926)

Karcher, Eva, *Otto Dix 1891–1969* (Cologne, 1992)

Kihn, Alfred, 'Stadtbahnfahrt durch Berlin' in Robert Seitz, Heinz Zucker (eds.), *Um uns die Stadt 1931. Eine Anthologie neuer Großstadtdichtung,* (orig. Berlin 1931), reprint with foreword by Ulrich Conrads (Der Bauwelt Fundamente 75, Braunschweig, Wiesbaden, 1986)

König, Wolfgang, 'Massenproduktion und Technikkonsum. Entwicklungslinien und Triebkraftendenzen Triebkräfte der Technik zwischen 1880 und 1914', in idem (ed.), *Propyläen Technikgeschichte* (Berlin, 1990)

Korff, Gottfried, 'Die Stadt aber ist der Mensch', in idem, Reinhard Rürup (eds.), *Berlin, Berlin: Die Ausstellung zur Geschichte der Stadt* (Berlin, 1987)

Kracauer, Siegfried, *The Mass Ornament: Weimar essays*, translated, edited, and with an introduction by Thomas Y. Levin (Cambridge, Mass. and London, 1995)

Kretschmer, Ernst, *Physique and Character: An investigation of the nature of constitution and of the theory of temperament*, translated from second rev. edn by W.J.H. Sprott (London, 1925)

Kuczynski, Jürgen, *Geschichte des Alltags des Deutschen Volkes*, 5 vols., *Vol. 4: 1871–1918* (Cologne, 1982)

Künstlerhaus, Bethanien (ed.), *Wohnsitz Nirgerndswo vom Leben und vom Überleben auf der Straße* (Berlin, 1982)

Lang, Fritz, *M Protokoll* (Hamburg, 1963)

Lasswitz, Kurd, *Bilder aus der Zukunft* (Breslau, 1878), 2: cited in Edwin M.J. Kretzmann, 'German technological utopias of the pre-war period', *Annals of Science*, 3 (1938), 417–30

Lingner, K.A., 'Einige Leitgedanken zu der Sonderausstellung: Volkskrankheiten und ihre Bekämpfung', in Robert Wuttke (ed.), *Die Deutschen Städte: geschildert nach den Ergebnissen der ersten deutschen Städteausstellung zu Dresden 1903* (Leipzig, 1904)

Lüders, Marie-Elisabeth, 'Why, and how, is Germany building? The motives and methods of Germany's extensive building program', in *Passing Through Germany* (Berlin, 1930)

Lupescu, Valentin, 'Sociology of the German small town', *Die Gesellschaft* VIII (1931), 464–71

Moreck, Curt (pseudonym for Konrad Haemmerling), *Führer durch das Lasterhafte Berlin* (Berlin, 1931)

Mullin, John Robert, 'Ideology, planning theory and the German city in the interwar years', Part 1 in *Town Planning Review*, Vol. 53 No. 2 (April 1982), 115–30

Neundörfer, Ludwig, *Auflockerung von Arbeits- und Wohnstätten* (Frankfurt am Main, 1947)

Niethammer, Lutz, 'Some elements of the housing reform debate in nineteenth century Europe: Or, on the making of a new paradigm of social control', in Bruce Stave (ed.), *Modern Industrial Cities: History, policy and survival* (Beverley Hills, London, 1981)

Notarbeit 51 der Notgemeinschaft der Deutschen Wissenschaft Gemeinschädigende Regionen des Niederelbischen Stadtgebietes 1934/35 (orig. edn, 1935, repr. Hamburg, 1984)

Nowack, Prof. Dr, 'Die öffentliche Gesundheitspflege', in Robert Wuttke (ed.), *Die Deutschen Städte: geschildert nach den Ergebnissen der ersten deutschen Städteausstellung zu Dresden 1903* (Leipzig, 1904)

Oppenheimer, Franz, *Erlebtes, Erstrebtes* (1931), pp. 100–2, excerpted and reprinted in Walter Steitz, *Quellen zur deutschen Wirtschafts- und Sozialgeschichte von der Reichsgründung bis zum ersten Weltkrieg* (Darmstadt, 1985),

Peniston-Bird, Corinna, 'The debate on Austrian national identity in the First Republic (1918–1938)' (University of St Andrews, Ph.D. thesis, 1996)

Petzina, Dietmar, Werner Abelshauser, Anselm Faust (eds.), *Sozialgeschichtliches Arbeitsbuch II: Materialien zur Statistik des Deutsche Reiches 1970–1914* (Munich, 1978)

Peukert, Detlev J.K., *Jugend zwischen Krieg und Krise: Lebenswelten von Arbeiterjungen in der Weimarer Republik* (Cologne, 1987)

Photography at the Bauhaus, edited for the Bauhaus Archiv by Jeannine Fiedler (London, 1990)

Pommer,Richard, Christian F. Otto, *Weissenhof 1927 and the Modern Movement in Architecture* (Chicago, 1991)

Poor, Harold, 'City versus country: Urban change and Development in the Weimar Republic', in Hans Mommsen *et al.* (eds.), *Industrielles System und Politische Entwicklung in der Weimarer Republik*, Band 1 (Düsseldorf 1974)

Preußen: Versuch einer Bilanz: Band 3: Preußen: zur Sozialgeschichte eines Staates. Eine Darstellung in Quellen, Bearbeitet von Peter Brandt unter Mitwirkung von Thomas Hofmann und Reiner Zilkenat (Reinbek, 1981)

Rochdale Education Guild, *Report of a Visit to Germany made by Members of the Guild, May 28th – June 12th, 1909* (Rochdale, 1909)

Roggatz, Paul, 'Die Straße im sozialen Wohnungsbau – ihre Aufgaben und ihre Kostendeckung', in *Der Soziale Wohnungsbau in Deutschland* 2 Jg., Nr 3 (1 Feb. 1942), repr. in Tilman Harlander, Gerhard Fehl (eds.), *Hitlers Sozialer Wohnungsbau 1940–1945: Wohnungspolitik, Baugestaltung und Siedlungsplanung* (Hamburg, 1986)

Rohden, Friedrich von, 'Methoden der Kriminalbiologie', in Prof. Dr Emil Abderhalden (ed.), *Handbuch der biologischen Arbeitsmethoden*, Abt. IV, Teil 12 1/1: Methoden der gerichtlichen Medizin und Kriminalistik 1 Hälfte, Band 1 (Berlin, Vienna, 1938)

Saldern, Adelheid von, *Stadt und Moderne: Hannover in der Weimarer Republik* (Hamburg, 1989)

Salomon, Alice, Marie Baum, *Das Familienleben in der Gegenwart* (Berlin, 1930), in William Hubbard, *Familiengeschichte: Materialien zur deutschen Familie seit dem Ende des 18.Jahrhunderts* (Munich, 1983)

Schräder, Bärbel, Jürgen Schebera, *Kunstmetropole Berlin 1918–1933: Die Kunststadt in der Novemberrevolution, Die 'Goldenen' Zwanziger, Die Kunststadt in der Krise* (Berlin and Weimar, 1987)

—— *The Golden Twenties: Art and literature in the Weimar Republic* (New Haven, London, 1990)

Simmel, Georg, 'Metropolis and mental life', translated and reprinted in Karl Wolff (ed.), *The Sociology of George Simmel* (Chicago, 1950), orig. 'Die Grossstadt und das Geistesleben' *Jahrbuch der Gehe-Stiftung,* 9 (Dresden) 1903, 185–206

Sombart, Werner, 'Städtische Siedlung, Stadt', in Alfred Vierkandt (ed.), *Handwörterbuch der Soziologie* (Stuttgart, 1931), 527–33

—— 'Kapitalismus', in *Handwörterbuch der Soziologie,* edited Alfred Vierkandt (Stuttgart, 1931), 258–77

Spender, Stephen, *The Temple* (London, 1988)

Spengler, Oswald, *Der Untergang des Abendlandes: Umrisse einer Morphologie der Weltgeschichte. Zweiter Band: Welthistorische Perspektiven* (Munich, 1923), from the translated edition with notes by Charles Francis Atkinson, *The Decline of the West: Perspectives of world-history,* Vol. 2 (London, n.d., *c.* 1928)

Statistisches Bundesamt Wiesbaden, *Bevölkerung und Wirtschaft 1872–1972* (Stuttgart, Mainz, 1972)

Stenbock-Fermor, Alexander Graf, *Deutschland von Unten. Reisen durch die proletarische Provinz 1930* (Stuttgart, 1931, repr. Lausanne, Frankfurt am Main, 1980)

Stutzer, Emil, *Die Deutschen Großstädte, Einst und Jetzt* (Berlin, Braunschweig, Hamburg, 1917)

Taut, Bruno, *Die Auflösung der Städte* (Hagen i. Westfalen, 1920)

Triton, 'Der Hamburger "Junge Mann"': Auf dem Jungfernstieg'in *Großstadt-Dokumente* vol. 39, ed. Hans Ostwald (Berlin, n.d.)

Tucholsky, Kurt, *Gesammelte Werke* 3: 1929–1932 (Reinbek, 1960)

Verein für Fremden-Verkehr in Chemnitz, Chemnitz und Umgebung, *Führer durch Chemnitz* (3rd edn, Chemnitz, 1914/16)

Walser, Robert, *Jakob von Gunten* (orig. 1909, Frankfurt am Main, 1985)

Weber, A.F., *The Growth of Cities in the Nineteenth Century: A Study in Statistics* (New York, 1899, repr. 1963)

Weber, Adolf, *Die Großstadt* (Berlin, 1908)

Weber, Max, *The City*, translated by Don Martindale, Gertrud Neuwirth (London, Melbourne and Toronto, 1958), 65–6, orig. in *Archiv für Sozialwissenschaft und Sozialpolitik,* 47 (Tübingen, 1921), 621–772.

Wingler, Hans M., *Das Bauhaus 1919–1933 Weimar Dessau Berlin und die Nachfolge in Chicago seit 1937* (Bramsche, 1968)

Wirth, Louis, 'Urbanism as a way of life', *American Journal of Sociology,* Vol. 44 (1938), 1–24

Secondary Literature

Abelson, Elaine, *When Ladies go a Thieving: Middle class shoplifters in the Victorian department store* (Oxford, 1989)

Abercrombie, Patrick, 'Some notes on German garden villages', in *The Town Planning Review*, Vol. 1 No. 3 (Oct. 1910), 244–50

Abrams, Lynn, 'Prostitutes in imperial Germany 1870–1918: Working girls or social outcasts?', in R.J. Evans (ed.), *The German Underworld: Deviants and outcasts in German history* (London, 1988)

—— 'From control to commercialization: The triumph of mass entertainment in Germany 1900–25', in *German History*, Vol. 8, No. 3 (1990), 278–93

—— *Workers' Culture in Imperial Germany: Leisure and recreation in the Rhineland and Westphalia* (London, 1992)

—— 'Concubinage, cohabitation and the law: Class and gender relations in nineteenth-century Germany', in *Gender & History*, Vol. 5 No. 1 (Spring 1993), 81–100

Albers, Gerd, 'Changes in German town planning: A review of the last sixty years', in *Town Planning Review*, Vol. 57 No. 1 (1986), 17–33

Albrecht, Paul, *Freiheit der Liebe* ('Der Freie Arbeiter' Osterreich, Berlin, 1926)

Allen, John, Michael Pryke, 'Money cultures after Georg Simmel: mobility, movement, and identity', in *Environment and Planning D: Society and Space*, Vol. 17 (1999), 51–68

Altenloh, Emilie, *Zur Soziologie des Kino: die Kinounternehmung und die sozialen Schichten ihrer Besucher* (Jena, 1914)

Ambrosius, Gerold, William H. Hubbard, *A Social and Economic History of Twentieth-Century Europe* (Cambridge, Mass. and London, 1989)

Anderson, Bonnie S., Judith Zinsser (eds.), *A History of Their Own: Women in Europe from prehistory to the present*, Vol. 2 (London, 1989)

Anderson, Susan C., 'Otto Weininger's masculine Utopia', in *German Studies Review*, Vol. 19 No.3 (Oct. 1996), 433–53

Andreas-Salomé, *Lou: Die Erotik: vier Aufsätze* (orig. 1910, reprint and edited with a postscript by Ernst Pfeiffer, Frankfurt am Main, 1985)

Ankum, Katharina von, 'Gendered urban spaces in Irmgard Keun's *Das Kunstseidene Mädchen*', in Katharina von Ankum (ed.), *Women in the Metropolis: Gender and modernity in Weimar culture* (Berkeley, Los Angeles and London, 1997)

Apple, Rina D., 'Constructing Mothers: Scientific motherhood in the nineteenth and twentieth centuries', in *Social History of Medicine*, Vol. 8 No. 2 (1995), 161–78

Arndt, Karl, 'Tradition und Unvergleichbarkeit zu Aspekten der Stadtplanung im Nationalsozialistischen Deutschland', in Wilhelm Rausch (ed.), *Die Städte Mitteleuropas im 20. Jahrhundert* (Linz, 1984)

Aschaffenburg, Prof. G., *Das Verbrechen und seine Bekämpfung* (Heidelberg, 1903)

Bade, Klaus J., *Vom Auswanderungsland zum Einwanderungsland: Deutschland 1880–1980* (Berlin, 1983)

Bairoch, Paul, *Cities and Economic Development: From the dawn of history to the present*, translated by Christopher Bairoch (Chicago, London, 1988)

Bajohr, Stefan, 'Illegitimacy and the working class: illegitimate mothers in Brunswick, 1900–1933', in R.J. Evans (ed.), *The German Working Class, 1888–1933: The politics of everyday life* (London, 1982)

Barker, Theo, Anthony Sutcliffe (eds.), *Megalopolis: The giant city in history* (Basingstoke, 1993)

Baron, Lawrence, 'Noise and degeneration: Theodor Lessing's crusade for quiet', in *Journal of Contemporary History*, Vol. 17 (1982), 165–78

Bauer, Reinhard, Günther Gerstenberg, Wolfgang Peschel (eds.), *Im Dunst aus Bier, Rauch und Volk, Arbeit und Leben in München von 1840 bis 1945. Ein Lesebuch* (Munich, 1989)

Bauman, Zygmunt, *Modernity and the Holocaust* (Ithaca, N.Y., 1989)

Benevolo, Leonardo, *The European City* (Oxford, 1993)

Benson, John, Gareth Shaw (eds.), *The Evolution of Retail Systems, c.1800–1914* (Leicester, 1992)

Berger, Renate, 'Moments can change your life: Creative crises in the lives of dancers in the 1920s', in Marsha Meskimmon, Shearer West (eds.), *Visions of the 'Neue Frau': Women and the visual arts in Weimar Germany* (Aldershot, 1995)

Berghaus, Günter, '"Girlkultur": Feminism, Americanism and popular entertainment in Weimar', in *Journal of Design History*, Vol. 1 Nos. 3/4 (1988), 193–219

Bergmann, Klaus (ed.), *Schwarze Reportagen; aus das Leben den untersten Schichten vor 1914: Huren, Vagabanden, Lumpen* (Reinbek, 1984)

Bessel, Richard, 'Eastern Germany as a structural problem in the Weimar Republik', in *Social History*, Vol. 3 (1978), 199–218

—— 'Transport', in Colin Chant (ed.), *Science, Technology and Everyday Life 1870–1950* (London, 1989)

Bleek, Stephan, *Quartierbildung in der Urbanisierung: das Münchener Westend, 1890–1933* (Munich, 1991)

Bock, Gisela, 'Antinatalism, maternity and paternity in National Socialist racism', in David Crew (ed.), *Nazism and German Society 1933–1945* (London, 1994)

Bolle, Willi, *Physiognomik der Modernen Metropole* (Europäischekulturstudien Band 6, Cologne, Weimar, Vienna, 1994)

Bollerey, Franziska, Kristina Hartmann, 'A patriarchal utopia: The garden city and housing reform in Germany at the turn of the century', in Anthony Sutcliffe (ed.), *The Rise of Modern Urban Planning 1800–1914* (London, 1980)

Bongers, Hans, *Deutscher Luftverkehr. Entwicklung, Politik, Wirtschaft, Organization. Veruch einer Analyse der Lufthansa* (Bad Godesberg, 1967)

Bosl, Karl, 'Die Mitteleuropäische Stadt des 19. Jahrhunderts im Wandel von Wirtschaft, Gesellschaft, Staat, Kultur', in Wilhelm Rausch (ed.), *Die Städte Mitteleuropas im 19. Jahrhundert* (Linz/Donau, 1983)

Böttcher, Dr, 'Technik und Kultur', in *Verhandlungen des Ersten Deutschen Soziologentages 19–22 Oktober 1910 in Frankfurt a. Main* (Tübingen, 1911), 84–5

Boyne, Roy, Ali Rattansi (eds.), *Postmodernism and Society* (Basingstoke and London, 1990)

Brady, Robert, *The Rationalisation Movement in German Industry: A study in the evolution of economic planning* (Berkeley, 1933)

Brandt, Dr Jürgen, 'Die Beseitigung verwahrlöster Wohnviertel in Deutschland', in *XIII International Housing and Town Planning Congress, Berlin 1931*, Part 1, (Berlin, 1931)

Breckman, Warren G., 'Disciplining consumption: The debate about luxury in Wilhelmine Germany, 1890–1914', in *Journal of Social History*, Vol. 24 No. 3 (1990–1), 485–505

Bredpohl, Wilhelm, *Der Aufbau des Ruhrvolkes im Zuge der Ost-West-Wanderung: Beiträge zur deutschen Sozialgeschichte des 19. und 20. Jahrhunderts* (Soziale Forschung und Praxis, Band 7, Recklinghausen, 1948)

Bridenthal, Renate, 'Something old, something new: Women between the two world wars', in *idem*, Claudia Koonz, Susan Stuard (eds.), *Becoming Visible: Women in European history* (Boston, 1987)

——, Claudia Koonz, 'Beyond *Kinder, Küche, Kirche*: Weimar women in politics and work', in Renate Bridenthal, Atina Grossmann, Marion Kaplan (eds.), *When Biology Became Destiny: Women in Weimar and Nazi Germany* (New York, 1984)

Brockhaus, Gudrun, *Schauder und Idylle: Faschismus als Erlebnisangebot* (Munich, 1997)

Brockmann, Stephen, 'Weimar sexual cynicism', in Thomas W. Kniesche, Stephen Brockmann (eds.), *Dancing on the Volcano: Essays on the culture of the Weimar Republic* (Columbia, S.C., 1994)

Bruch, Rüdiger vom (ed.), *Weder Kommunismus noch Kapitalismus: Bürgerliche Sozialreform in Deutschland vom Vormärz bis zur Ära Adenauer* (Munich, 1985)

Brüggemeier, Franz-Josef, *Leben vor Ort Ruhrbergleute und Ruhrbergbau 1889–1919* (Munich, 1983)

Bullock, Nicholas, 'Housing in Frankfurt 1925 to 1931 and the New Wohnkultur', *The Architectural Review*, Vol. 168 No. 976 (1978), 335–42

——, James Read, *The Movement for Housing Reform in Germany and France 1840–1914* (Cambridge, 1985)

——, 'First the kitchen – Then the facade', in *Journal of Design History*, Vol. 1 Nos. 3/4 (1988), 177–92

Burgdörfer, Friedrich, *Volk ohne Jugend. Geburtenschicksal und Überalterung des Deutschen Volkskörpers: Ein Problem der Volkswirtschaft und Sozialpolitik der nationalen Zukunft* (Berlin-Grunewald, 1934)

Büsch, Otto, *Geschichte der Berliner Kommunalwirtschaft in der Weimarer Epoche* (Berlin, 1960)

Buschan, Georg, *Geschlecht und Verbrechen: Die Grossstadt Hamburg* (Grossstadt Dokumente Vol. XLVIII, Berlin and Leipzig, 1915)

Buse, Dieter K., 'Urban and National Identity: Bremen, 1860–1920', in *Journal of Social History*, Vol. 26 (1993), 521–37

Cahn, Ernst, 'Ein Arbeiterwohnungsviertel in einer süddeutschen Provinzstadt (Bayreuth)', in *Archiv für Soziale Gesetzgebung und Statistik*, 17 (Berlin, 1902), 440–77

Campebll, Joan, *Joy in Work: German work: the national debate 1800–1945* (Princeton, 1989)

Carter, Erica, *How German is She? Postwar West German reconstruction and the consuming woman* (Ann Arbor, Michigan, 1997)

Chapman, Jay, 'Two aspects of the city: Cavalcanti and Ruttmann', in Lewis Jacobs (ed.), *The Documentary Tradition: From Nanook to Woodstock* (New York, 1971)

Chevalier, Louis, *Labouring Classes and Dangerous Classes in Paris During the First Half of the Nineteenth Century* (London, 1973)

Cimbal, Walter, 'Das psychologische Beratungsamt', in W. Jackstein (ed.), *Deutschlands Städtebau: Altona*, (Berlin-Hallensee, 1922)

Cooper, Emmanuel, *The Sexual Perspective: homosexuality and art in the last 100 years in the West* (London, 1994)

Coyner, Sandra, 'Class patterns of family income and expenditure during the Weimar Republic: German white collar employees as harbingers of modern society' (Ph.D. thesis, Rutgers University, New Brunswick, N.J., 1975)

——, 'Class consciousness and consumption: The new middle class during the Weimar Republic', in *Journal of Social History*, Vol. 3 (1977), 310–31

Crew, David, 'Definitions of modernity: social mobility in a German town 1880–1901', in *Journal of Social History*, Vol. 6 (1973), 51–72

——, *Town in the Ruhr: A social history of Bochum* (New York, 1979)

——, 'German Socialism, the state and family policy 1918–1933', *Continuity and Change*, Vol. 1 No. 2 (1986), 235–63

——, *Germans on Welfare: from Weimar to Hitler* (New York, 1998)

Croon, Helmuth, 'Aufgaben Deutscher Städte im Ersten Drittel des 20. Jahrhunderts', in Wilhelm Rausch (ed.), *Die Städte Mitteleuropas* im 20. Jahrhundert (Linz, 1984)

Cross, Gary, *Time and Money: The making of consumer culture* (London, 1993)

Crossick, Geoffrey, Serge Jaumain (eds.), *Cathedrals of Consumption: The European department store 1850–1939* (Aldershot and Vermont, 1999)

Czarnowski, Gabriele, *Das kontrollierte Paar: Ehe- und Sexualpolitik im Nationalsozialismus* (Weinheim, 1991)

Daniel, Ute, *The War from Within: German working-class women in the First World War* (Oxford, New York, 1997)

Danner, Lothar, *Betrachtungen zur Geschichte der Ordnungspolizei 1918–1933* (Hamburg, 1958)

Daunton, Martin, *A House-owning Democracy in Britain* (London, 1987)

Davenport-Hines, R.P.T., *Sex, Death and Punishment: Attitudes to sex and sexuality in Britain since the Renaissance* (London, 1990)

Davidson, Arnold I., 'Sex and the emergence of sexuality', in *Critical Inquiry* (Autumn 1987)

Davies, Andrew, *Leisure, Gender and Poverty* (Milton Keynes, 1992)

Davis, Celia, 'The health visitor as mother's friend: a woman's place in public health, 1900–14', in *Social History of Medicine,* Vol. 8 No. 1 (April 1988), 39–59

Dawson, William Harbutt, *Municipal Life and Government in Germany* (London and New York, 1914)

Denby, Elisabeth, *Europe Re-housed* (London, 1938)

Detlefs, Gerald, *Frauen zwischen Bordell und Abschiebung: Öffentliche Mädchen' und Prostitutions überwachung in der Hamburger Vorstadt St. Pauli 1833–1876* (Regensburg, 1997)

Diederiks, H.A., 'Foreword: Patterns of urban growth since 1500, mainly in Western Europe', in H. Schmal (ed.), *Patterns of Urban Growth since 1500, mainly in Western Europe* (London, 1981)

Diefendorf, Jeffrey, *In the Wake of War: The reconstruction of German cities after World War II* (New York and Oxford, 1993)

Dittrich, Manfred, *Die Entstehung der Angestelltenschaft in Deutschland von den Anfängen bis zum Jahre 1933: ein sozialistischer Versuch* (Leipzig, 1939)

Doan, Laura, 'Passing fashions: Reading female masculinities in the 1920s', in *Feminist Studies,* Vol. 24 No. 3 (1986), 663–700

Doane, Mary Ann, 'The Erotic Barter: *Pandora's Box* (1929)', in Eric Rentschler (ed.), *The Films of G.W. Pabst: An existential cinema* (New Brunswick and London, 1990)

Döblin, Alfred, *Berlin Alexanderplatz: The story of Franz Biberkopf* (1932), trans. Eugene Jolas (New York, 1992)

Docherty, Thomas (ed.), *Postmodernism: A reader* (New York, London, Toronto, Sydney, Tokyo and Singapore, 1993)

Doyle, Barry, 'H.G. Wells's *Time Machine,* then and now', in *London Magazine,* Vol. 38 Nos. 1/2 (April/May 1998), 73–7

Dröge, Franz, Rudolf Krämer-Badoni, *Die Kneipe: zur Soziologie einer kulturform oder '2 Halbe auf mich'* (Frankfurt am Main, 1987)

Dücker, Elizabeth von, '"Bauarbeiten, bei denen beinahe kaum ein Stein auf dem anderen belassen werden kann". Zur Elbuferplanung Konstanty Gutschows', in Stadtteilarchiv Ottensen (ed.), *'Ohne uns hätten sie das gar nicht machen können': Nazi-Zeit und Nachkrieg in Altona und Ottensen* (Hamburg, 1985)

Dülffer, Jost, 'NS-Herrschaftssystem und Stadtgestaltung: Das Gesetz zur

Neugestaltung deutscher Städte vom 4.Oktober 1937', *German Studies Review*, Vol. 12 No. 1 (1989), 69–89

Dülffer, Jost, Jochen Thies, Josef Henke, *Hitlers Städte. Baupolitik im Dritten Reich. Eine Dokumentation* (Cologne, 1978)

Durkheim, Emile, 'Suicide et natalité: étude de statistique morale', in *Revue philosophique de la France et de l'Étranger*, Vol. 26 (1888), 446–63 (translated as 'Suicide and fertility: a study in moral statistics', *European Journal of Population*, Vol. 8 (1992), 175–97)

Eckermann, Erik, *Vom Dampfwagen zum Auto: Motorisierung des Verkehrs* (Reinbek, 1989)

Eggenkämper, Barbara, 'Die Vision vom "aktenlosen Büro": Von der Lochkarte zum Computer', in Burkhart Lauterbach (ed.), *Großstadtmensch: Die Welt der Angestellten* (Frankfurt am Main, 1995)

Ehmer, Josef, 'Wohnen ohne eigene Wohnung: Zur sozialen Stellung von Untermietern und Bettgehern', in Lutz Niethammer (ed.), *Wohnen im Wandel: Beiträge zur Geschichte des Alltags in der bürgerlichen Gesellschaft* (Wuppertal, 1979)

Elsaesser, Thomas, 'Lulu and the meter man: Pabst's Pandora's Box (1929)', in Eric Rentschler (ed.), *German Film and Literature: Adaptations and transformations* (New York and London, 1986)

Emsley, Clive, *Crime and Society in England 1750–1900* (London, 1987)

——, '"Mother, what did policemen do when there weren't any Motors?" The law, the police and the regulation of traffic in England, 1900–1939', in *Historical Journal*, Vol. 36 (1993), 357–81

Engeli, Christian, 'Siedlungsstruktur und Verwaltungsgrenzen der Stadt im Verstädterungsprozeß', in *Die alte Stadt: Zeitschrift für Stadtgeschichte, Stadtsoziologie und Denkmalpflege*, Vol. 4 (1977), 287–307

——, 'Stadterweiterungen in Deutschland im 19.Jahrhundert' in Wilhelm Rausch (ed.), *Die Städte Mitteleuropas im 19.Jahrhundert* (Linz/Donau 1983)

Enzensberger, Hans Magnus, 'A theory of tourism', in *New German Critique*, No. 68 (Spring/Summer 1996), 117–35

Evans, Richard J., 'Prostitution, state and society in imperial Germany', in *Past and Present*, No. 70 (1976), 106–29

——, '"Red Wednesday" in Hamburg: Social Democrats, police and lumpen proletariat in the suffrage disturbances of 17 January 1906', in *Social History*, Vol. 4 (1979), 1–31.

——, *Kneipengespräche im Kaiserreich: die Stimmungsberichte der Hamburger Politischen Polizei 1892–1914* (Reinbek, 1989)

——, *Rituals of Retribution: Capital punishment in Germany, 1600–1987* (Oxford, 1996)

——, *In Defence of History* (London, 1997)

Ewen, Stuart, *Captains of Consciousness: Advertising and the social roots of consumer culture* (New York, 1976)

Fehl, Gerhard, 'The Niddatal Project', in *Built Environment,* Vol. 9, Nos. 3/4 (1983), 185–97

Fehrenbach, Heide, '*Die Sünderin* or who killed the German male: Early postwar German cinema and the betrayal of the fatherland', in Sandra Frieden, Richard W. McCormick, Vibeke R. Petersen, Laurie Melissa Vogelsang (eds.), *Gender and German Cinema,* Vol. 2 (London, 1993)

Feldman, Gerald D., 'The Weimar Republic: A problem of modernization?', *Archiv für Sozialgeschichte,* XXVI (1986), 1–26

Fischer, Gerhard, *Berliner Sportstätten: Geschichte und Geschichten* (Berlin, 1992)

Fischler, Raphael, 'Health, safety, and the general welfare: Markets, politics and social science in early land-use regulation and community design', in *Journal of Urban History,* Vol. 24 No. 6 (Sept. 1998), 675–719

Fisher, Peter S., *Fantasy and Politics: Visions of the future in the Weimar Republic* (Madison, Wisconsin, 1991)

Flavell, M. Kay, 'Über alles die Liebe: Food, sex, and money in the work of George Grosz', in *Journal of European Studies* Vol. XIII (1983), 268–88

Flemming, Jens, Klaus Saul, Peter-Christian Witt (eds.), *Familienleben im Schatten der Krise: Dokumente und Analysen zur Sozialgeschichte der Weimarer Republik 1918–1933* (Düsseldorf, 1988)

Flora, Peter *et al., State, Economy and Society in Western Europe, 1815–1975: a data handbook in two volumes* (London, 1983–7)

Folguera, Pilar, 'City space and the daily life of women in Madrid in the 1920s', in *Oral History,* Vol. 13 No. 2 (1985), 49–56

Foucault, Michel, *The Archaeology of Knowledge* (trans. A. M. Sheridan Smith, London, 1972)

——, *The History of Sexuality,* Vol. 1: *An introduction* (London, 1979)

Fout, John C., 'Sexual politics in Wilhelmine Germany: The male gender crisis, moral purity, and homophobia', in *Journal of the History of Sexuality,* Vol. 2 No. 3 (1992), 388–421

Frame, Lynne, 'Gretchen, girl garçonne? Weimar science and popular culture in search of the ideal new woman', in Katharina von Ankum (ed.), *Women in the Metropolis: Gender and modernity in Weimar culture* (Berkeley, Los Angeles and London, 1997)

Frecot, Janos, 'Von der Weltstadt zur Kiefernheide, oder: Die Flucht aus der Bürgerlichkeit', in Akademie der Künste, *Berlin um 1900: Ausstellung der Berlinischen Galerie in Verbindung mit der Akademie der Künste zu den Berliner Festwoche 1984* (9 Sept.–28 Oct., Berlin, 1984)

Frevert, Ute, 'Vom Klavier zur Schreibmaschine – Weiblicher Arbeitsmarkt und Rollenzuweisungen am Beispiel der weiblichen Angestellte in der Weimarer Republik', in Annette Kuhn, Gerhard Schneider (eds.), *Frauen in der Geschichte 1: Frauenrechte und die gesellschaftliche Arbeit der Frauen im Wandel. Fachwissenschaftliche und Fachdidaktische Studien zur Geschichte der Frauen* (Düsseldorf, 1979)

——, 'Professional medicine and the working classes in imperial Germany', in *Journal of Contemporary History*, Vol. 20 No. 4 (1985), 637–58

——, *Women in German History: From bourgeois emancipation to sexual liberation*, trans. Stuart McKinnon-Evans in association with Terry Bond and Barbara Norden (Oxford, 1989)

——, '"Wo du hingehst . . . " – Aufbrüche im Verhältnis der Geschlechter. Rollentausch anno 1908', in August Nitschke, Gerhard A. Ritter, Detlev J.K. Peukert, Rüdiger vom Bruch (eds.), *Jahrhundertwende: Der Aufbruch in der Moderne 1880–1930*, Vol. 2 (Reinbek, 1990)

Friedrich, Thomas, *Berlin between the Wars* (New York, 1991)

Frisby, David, *Fragments of Modernity: theories of modernity in the work of Simmel, Kracauer and Benjamin* (Cambridge, 1985)

——, *Simmel and since: Essays on Georg Simmel's theory* (London, 1992)

——, *The Alienated Mind: The sociology of knowledge in Germany 1918–1933* (London, 1992)

Fritzsche, Peter, *A Nation of Fliers: German aviation and the popular imagination* (Cambridge, Mass., 1992)

——, 'Machine dreams: Airmindedness and the reinvention of Germany', in *American Historical Review*, Vol. 98 (1993), 685–709

——, 'Landscape of danger, landscape of design: Crisis and modernism in Weimar Germany', in Thomas W. Kniesche, Stephen Brockmann (eds.), *Dancing on the Volcano: Essays on the culture of the Weimar Republic* (Columbia, S.C., 1994)

——, 'Vagabond in the fugitive city: Hans Ostwald, imperial Berlin and the Grossstadt-Dokumente', in *Journal of Contemporary History*, Vol. 29 (1994), 385–402

——, *Reading Berlin 1900* (Cambridge, Mass. and London, 1996)

——, 'Talk of the town: The murder of Lucie Berlin', Paper for the Symposium 'The Criminal and his Scientists' Panel 6, European University Institute/ Centro Studi CISL, Florence, 15–18 October 1998

Fromm, Erich, *To Have or To Be?* (London, 1978)

Fuchs, Konrad, 'Jüdische Unternehmer in deutschen Groß- und Einzelhandel dargestellt an ausgewählten Beispielen', in Werner E. Mosse, Hans Pohl (eds.), *Jüdische Unternehmer in Deutschland im 19. und 20. Jahrhundert* (Stuttgart, 1992)

Führer, Karl-Christian, 'Auf dem Weg zum Massenkultur: Kino in der Weimarer Republik', *Historische Zeitschrift* 262 (1996), 739–81

——, 'A medium of modernity? Broadcasting in Weimar Germany, 1923–1932', in *Journal of Modern History*, Vol. 69 (December 1997), 722–53

Garlay, Inge, 'Stadtplanung Linz – Hitler's Heimatstadt, 1938–1943', in Wilhelm Rausch (ed.), *Die Städte Mitteleuropas im 20. Jahrhundert* (Linz, 1984)

Gassert, Philip, *Amerika im Dritten Reich: Ideologie, Propaganda und Volksmeinung 1933–1945* (Stuttgart, 1997)

Gay, Peter, *Weimar Culture: the Outsider as Insider* (London, 1969)

Gee, Malcolm, Tim Kirk, Jill Steward (eds.), *The City in Central Europe: Culture and society from 1800 to the present* (Aldershot and Vermont, 1999)

Gellately, Robert, *The Politics of Economic Despair: Shopkeepers and German politics 1890–1914* (London and Beverley Hills, 1974)

Gersch, Wolfgang, Werner Hecht (eds.), *Bertolt Brecht, Kuhle Wampe, Protokoll des Films und Materialien* (Frankfurt am Main, 1969)

Ginzburg, Carlo, 'Morelli, Freud and Sherlock Holmes: Clues and scientific method', in *History Workshop* (Spring 1980), 5–36

Glaser, Hermann 'Wohnbilder – Seelenbilder', in Michael Andritzky, Gert Selle (eds.), *Lernbereich Wohnen* (Reinbek, 1987)

Glass, D. V., *Numbering the People: The nineteenth-century population controversy and the development of census and vital statistics in Britain* (Farnborough, 1973)

Glass, Hildegard, 'Responses to the urban challenge in German utopian literature 1871–1914' (Ph.D. thesis, University of Texas, Austin, 1992)

Gleber, Anke, 'Female flanerie and the symphony of the city', in Katharina von Ankum (ed.), *Women in the Metropolis: Gender and modernity in Weimar culture* (Berkeley, Los Angeles and London, 1997)

Goergen, Jeanpaul, *Walter Ruttmann: Eine Dokumentation* (Berlin, n.d.)

Grossmann, Atina, 'Girlkultur or thoroughly rationalized female: A new woman in Weimar Germany?', in Judith Friedlander (ed.), *Women in Culture and Politics: A century of change* (Bloomington, 1986)

——, 'Eine "neue Frau" im Deutschland der Weimarer Republik?', in Helmut Gold (ed.), *Fräulein vom Amt* (Munich 1993)

Grüttner, Michael, 'Sozial Hygiene und Soziale Kontrolle. Die Sanierung der Hamburger Gängeviertel 1892–1936', in Arno Herzig, Dieter Lange-wiesche, Arnold Sywottek (eds.), *Arbeiter in Hamburg: Unterschichtung, Arbeiter und Arbeiterbewegung seit dem ausgehenden 18. Jahrhundert* (Hamburg, 1983)

——, *Arbeitswelt an der Wasserkante: Sozialgeschichte der Hamburger Hafenarbeiter 1886–1914* (Göttingen, 1984)

——, 'Alkoholkonsum in der Arbeiterschaft 1871–1939', in Toni Pierenkemper (ed.), *Haushalt und Verbrauch in Historischer Perspektive: zum Wandel des privaten Verbrauchs in Deutschland im 19. und 20. Jahrhundert* (St Katharinen, 1987)

Habermas, Jürgen, *The Theory of Communicative Action Vol. 2: Lifeworld and system: A critique of fundamental reason* (trans. Thomas McCarthy, Cambridge, 1987)

Hake, Sabine, 'Urban spectacle in Walter Ruttmann's *Berlin: Symphony of the big city*', in Thomas W. Kniesche, Stephen Brockmann (eds.), *Dancing on the Volcano: Essays on the culture of the Weimar Republic* (Columbia, S.C., 1994)

——, 'In the mirror of fashion', in Katharina von Ankum (ed.), *Women in the*

Metropolis: Gender and modernity in Weimar culture (Berkeley, Los Angeles and London, 1997)

Hall, Peter, *Cities of Tomorrow* (Oxford, 1988)

——, *Cities in Civilisation* (London, 1998)

Hartmann, Kristina, *Deutsche Gärtenstadtbewegung: Kulturpolitik und Gesellschaftsreform* (Munich, 1976)

—— 'Städtebau um 1900: Romantische Visionen oder pragmatische Aspekte', in C. Mecksoper, H. Siebenmorgen (eds.), *Die alte Stadt: Denkmal oder Lebensraum* (Göttingen, 1985)

Harvey, David, *The Urban Experience* (Oxford, 1985)

——, *The Condition of Post-Modernity: an enquiry into the origins of cultural change* (Oxford, 1989)

Harvey, Elizabeth, 'Weimar culture', in Mary Fulbrook (ed.), *Germany 1815–1970* (London, 1997)

Haxthausen, Charles W., Heidrun Suhr (eds.), *Berlin: Culture and metropolis* (Minneapolis and Oxford, 1990)

Hays, Samuel P., 'From the history of the city to the history of the urbanized society', in *Journal of Urban History*, Vol. 19, No. 4 (Aug. 1993), 3–25

Hein, Peter Ullrich, *Die Brücke ins Geisterreich: Künstlerische Avantgarde zwischen Kulturkritik und Faschismus* (Reinbek, 1992)

Heine, Werner, '"Futura" without a future: Kurt Schwitters' typography for Hanover Town Council, 1929–1934', in *Journal of Design History*, Vol. 7 No. 2 (1994), 127–41

Hellpach, Willy, *Mensch und Volk der Grossstadt* (Stuttgart, 1939)

Hengartner, Thomas, *Forschungsfeld Stadt: Zur Geschichte der volkskundlichen Erforschung städtischer Lebensformen* (Berlin and Hamburg, 1999)

Henning, Karl Anton Mathias, 'Die Selbstmorde in Köln in den Jahren 1891 bis 1918', *Sonderdruck aus der Kölner Statistik* Jg. 3/4, No. 2 (Cologne, 1920/21), 325–33

Hennock, E.P., 'Social policy under the empire – Myths and evidence', in *German History*, Vol. 16, No. 1 (1998), 58–74

Hepp, Carola, *Avantgarde: Moderne Kunst, Kulturkritik und Reformbewegungen nach der Jahrhundertwende* (Munich, 1987)

Herf, Jeffrey, *Reactionary Modernism: Technology, culture and politics in Weimar and the Third Reich* (Cambridge and New York, 1984)

Hermand, Jost, 'Unity within diversity? The history of the concept "Neue Sachlichkeit"', in Keith Bullivant (ed.), *Culture and Society in the Weimar Republic* (Manchester, 1977)

Hermann, Armin, '"Auf eine höhere Stufe des Daseins erheben" – Naturwissenschaft und Technik, "Die Weltenergien unserer Tage"' in August Nitschke, Gerhard A. Ritter, Detlev J. K. Peukert, Rüdiger vom Bruch (eds.), *Jahrhundertwende: Der Aufbruch in der Moderne 1880–1930*, Vol. 1 (Reinbek, 1990)

Hietala, Marjatta, *Services and Urbanization at the Turn of the Century: The diffusion of innovations* (Helsinski, 1987)

Hilpert, Thilo, *Die funktionelle Stadt: Le Corbusiers Stadtvision, Bedingungen, Motiven, Hintergründe* (Braunschweig, 1978)

Hobhouse, L. T., *The Metaphysical Theory of the State* (London, 1918)

Hochman, Elaine S., *Architects of Fortune: Mies van der Rohe and the Third Reich* (New York, 1990)

Hohenberg, Paul M., Lynn Hollen Lees, *The Making of Urban Europe 1000–1950* (Cambridge, Mass. and London, 1985)

Honhart, Michael, 'Company housing as urban planning in Germany 1870–1940', in *Central European History*, Vol. 23 No. 1 (March 1990), 3–21

Howard, Nick P., 'The social and political consequences of the Allied food blockade of Germany, 1918–19', in *German History*, Vol. 11 No. 2 (June 1993), 161–88

Hubbard, William, 'Social mobility and social structure in Graz 1857–1910', in *Journal of Social History*, Vol. 17 (1983), 453–62

Huber, Brigitte, '"Nach 8 Stunden frisch und vergnügt": Angestellte und Werbung', in Burkhart Lauterbach (ed.), *Großstadtmensch: Die Welt der Angestellten* (Frankfurt am Main, 1995)

Huerkamp, Claudia, 'The history of smallpox vaccination in Germany: A first step in the medicalization of the general public', in *Journal of Contemporary History*, Vol. 20 (1985), 617–35

Hughes, H. Stuart, *Oswald Spengler* (New Brunswick and London, 1992)

Hughes, Robert, *The Shock of the New: Art and the century of change* (rev. edn London, 1980)

Hüter, Karl Heinz, *Das Bauhaus in Weimar: Studie zur gesellschaftspolitischer Geschichte einer deutschen Kunstschule mit 104 Dokumenten* (Berlin, 1976)

Isherwood, Christopher, *The Berlin Stories* (orig. edn, 1935, New York, 1954)

——, *Christopher and his Kind 1929–1939* (Hampshire, 1977)

——, *Goodbye to Berlin* (London, 1989)

Jackson Jnr, James H., 'Overcrowding and family life: Working class families and the housing crisis in late nineteenth century Duisburg', in R.J. Evans, W.R. Lees (eds.), *The German Family: Essays in the social history of the family in nineteenth and twentieth century Germany* (1981)

——, 'Migration in Duisburg 1847–1890: Occupational and familial contexts', in *Journal of Urban History*, Vol. 8 No. 3 (May 1982), 235–70

——, *Migration and Urbanization in the Ruhr Valley 1821–1914* (Atlantic Highlands, N.J., 1997)

Jalla, D., 'Belonging somewhere in the city: Social space and its perceptions: the "barrière" of Turin in the early 20th century', in *Oral History*, Vol. 13 No. 2 (1985), 19–34

James, Kathleen, 'From Messel to Mendelsohn: German department store architecture in defence of urban and economic change', in Geoffrey

Crossick, Serge Jaumain (eds.), *Cathedrals of Consumption: The European department store 1850–1939* (Aldershot and Vermont, 1999)

Jay, Martin, 'The extraterritorial life of Siegfried Kracauer', in *Salmagandi, A Quarterly of the Humanities and Social Sciences,* Nos. 31–32 (Fall 1975–Winter 1976), 49–106

Jefferies, Matthew, 'Back to the future? The "Heimatschutz" movement in Wilhelmine Germany', in *History,* Vol. 72 No. 251 (Oct. 1992), 411–20

Jelavich, Peter, 'Modernity, civic identity, and metropolitan entertainment: vaudeville, cabaret, and revue in Berlin, 1900–1933', in Charles W. Haxthausen, Heidrun Suhr (eds.), *Berlin: Culture and metropolis* (Minneapolis and Oxford, 1990)

——, '"Girls and Crisis": The political aesthetics of the kickline in Weimar Berlin', in Michael Rath (ed.), *Rediscovering History: Culture, politics, and the Psyche* (Stanford, California, 1994)

Joedicke, Jürgen, Christine Plath, *Die Weissenhofsiedlung* (Stuttgart, 1977)

Johnson, Eric A., *Urbanization and Crime: Germany, 1871–1914* (Cambridge, 1995)

Jones, James W., *'We of the Third Sex': Literary representations of homosexuality in Wilhelmine Germany* (New York, 1990)

Jordan, Peter, 'Die Entwicklung der Fremdenverkehrsströme in Mitteleuropa (1910–1990) als Ausdruck politischer und wirtschaftlicher Veränderungen', in *Mitteilungen der Österreichischen Geographischen Gesellschaft,* 132 (Vienna, 1990), 144–71

Jordanova, Ludmilla, 'Fritz Lang's metropolis: Science, machines and gender', in *Radical Science,* 17 (1985), 5–21

Kaes, Anton, 'The cold gaze: Notes on mobilization and modernity', in *New German Critique,* 59 (Spring/Summer 1993), 105–17

——, 'Leaving home: Film, migration, and the urban experience', in *New German Critique,* 74 (1998), 179–92

——, Martin Jay, Edward Dimenberg (eds.), *The Weimar Republik Sourcebook* (Berkeley, 1994)

Kahn, Fritz, *Das Leben des Menschen: Eine volkstümliche Anatomie, Biologie, Physiologie und Entwicklungsgeschichte des Menschen,* Band IV (Stuttgart, 1929)

Kamphoefner, Walter Dean, 'Soziale und demographische Strukturen der Zuwanderung in deutscher Großstädte des späten 19. Jahrhunderts', in Hans-Jürgen Teuteberg (ed.), *Urbanisierung im 19. und 20. Jahrhundert* (Cologne, 1983)

Kaplan, Temma, 'Women and communal strikes in the crisis of 1917–1922', in Bridenthal Renate, Claudia Koonz, Susan Stuard (eds.), *Becoming Visible: Women in European history* (Boston, 1987)

Katznelson, Ira, 'The centrality of the city in social theory', in Irit Rogoff (ed.), *The Divided Heritage: Themes and problems in German modernism* (Cambridge and New York, 1991)

Kaufmann, Doris, *Frauen zwischen Aufbruch und Reaktion: protestant Frauenbewegung in der ersten Hälfte des 20. Jahrhunderts* (Munich, 1988)

Kaufmann, Heinz, *Die Soziale Gliederung der Altonaer Bevölkerung und ihre Auswirkungen auf das Wohlfahrtsamt* (Altona, 1928)

Kavka, Misha, 'The alluring abyss of nothingness: Misogyny and (male) hysteria in Otto Weininger', in *New German Critique*, No. 66 (Fall 1995), 123–45

Kearns, Gerry, 'Zivilis or Hygaenia: urban health and the epidemiologic transition', in Richard Lawton (ed.), *The Rise and Fall of Great Cities: Aspects of urbanization in the western world* (London and New York, 1989)

Kelly, Alfred (ed.), *The German Worker: Working class autobiographies from the age of industrialization* (Berkeley, 1987)

Kenny, Michael and David I. Kertzer (eds.), *Urban Life in Mediterranean Europe* (Illinois, 1983)

Kern, Stephen, *The Culture of Time and Space 1880–1918* (London, 1983)

Klages, Ludwig, *Prinzipien der Charakterologie* (Leipzig, 1910)

Kleßmann, Christoph, 'Integration und Subkultur nationaler Minderheiten: das Beispiel der "Ruhrpolen" 1870–1939', in Klaus J. Bade (ed.), *Auswanderer, Wanderarbeiter, Gastarbeiter: Bevolkerung, Arbeitsmarkt und Wanderung in Deutschland seit der Mitte des 19. Jahrhunderts*, Vol. 2 (Ostfildern, 1984)

Klönne, Arno, *Hitlerjugend: Die Jugend und ihre Organisationen im Dritten Reich* (Hannover and Frankfurt am Main, 1956)

Klotz, Arnold, 'Stadtplanung und Städtebau in Innsbruck in den Jahren 1938–1945', in Wilhelm Rausch (ed.), *Die Städte Mitteleuropas im 20. Jahrhundert* (Linz, 1984)

Knodel, John, *The Decline of Fertility in Germany, 1871–1939* (Princeton, 1979)

Koch, Gertrud, 'Between two Worlds: von Sternberg's the Blue Angel (1930)', in Eric Rentschler (ed.), *German Film and Literature: Adaptations and transformations* (New York and London, 1986)

Kokula, Ilse, 'Lesbisch Leben von Weimar bis zur Nachkriegszeit', in Michael Bolle (ed.), *Eldorado: homosexuelle Frauen und Männer in Berlin 1850–1950. Geschichte, Alltag und Kultur* (Berlin, 1984)

Köllmann, Wolfgang, 'The population of Barmen before and during the period of industrialization', in D. V. Glass, D. Eversley (eds.), *Population in History: Essays in historical demography* (Chicago, 1965)

——, 'The process of urbanization in Germany at the height of the industrialization period', *Journal of Contemporary History*, Vol. 4 No.3 (July 1969), 59–76

Kölner, Verkehrs-Verein, *Köln am Rhein* (Cologne, n.d. *c.*1916)

Koonz, Claudia, 'Eugenics, gender, and ethics in Nazi Germany: The debate about involuntary sterilization, 1933–1936', in Thomas Childers, Jane Caplan (eds.), *Reevaluating the Third Reich* (New York, 1993)

Korff, Gottfried, 'Mentalität und Kommunikation in der Großstadt: Berliner

Notizen zur "inneren Urbanisierung"', in Theodor Kohlmann, Hermann Bausinger (eds.), *Großstadt: Aspekte empirischer Kulturforschung* (Berlin, 1985)

Kornbluh, Andrea Tuttle, 'City sex: Views of American women and urban culture, 1869–1990', *Urban History Yearbook 1991* (Leicester, 1991), 60–83

Koshar, Rudy, 'Against the "frightful leveller": Historic preservation and German cities 1890–1914', in *Journal of Urban History*, Vol. 19 No. 3 (May 1993), 7–29

Kosta, Barbara, 'Unruly daughters and modernity: Irmagard Keun's *Gilgi – eine von uns*', in *The German Quarterly*, Vol. 68 No. 3 (Summer 1995), 271–86

Krabbe, Wolfgang R., 'Eingemeindungsprobleme vor dem Ersten Weltkrieg: Motive, Widerstände und Verfahrensweise', in *Die alte Stadt: Zeitschrift für Stadtgeschichte, Stadtsoziologie und Denkmalpflege*, 7 (1980), 368–87

——, *Die deutsche Stadt im 19. und 20. Jahrhundert* (Göttingen, 1989)

Kracauer, Siegfried, 'Cross-section films', in Lewis Jacobs (ed.), *The Documentary Tradition: From Nanook to Woodstock* (New York, 1971a)

——, *Die Angestellten* (Frankfurt am Main, 1971b)

——, 'Die Wartenden' (1922), and 'Das Ornament der Masse' (1927), both in *Das Ornament der Masse* (Frankfurt a. Main, 1977)

Krafft, Sybille, *Zucht und Unzucht: Prostitution und Sittenpolizei im München der Jahrhundertwende* (Munich, 1996)

Künkel, Fritz, *Charakter Leiden und Heilung* (Leipzig, 1934)

Labanyi, Peter, 'Images of Fascism: Visualization and aestheticization in the Third Reich', in Michael Laffan (ed.), *The Burden of German History* (London, 1988)

Labisch, Alfons, 'Doctors, workers and the scientific cosmology of the industrial world: The social construction of "Health" and the "Homo hygienicus"', in *Journal of Contemporary History*, Vol. 20 (1985), 599–615

——, 'Experimentelle Hygiene, Bakteriologie, soziale Hygiene: Konzeptionen, Interventionen, soziale Träger – eine idealtypische Übersicht', in Jürgen Reulecke, Adelheid Gräfin zu Castell Rüdenhausen (eds.), *Stadt und Gesundheit: Zum Wandel von 'Volksgesundheit' und kommunaler Gesundheitspolitik im 19. und frühen 20. Jahrhundert* (Stuttgart, 1991)

Lacey, Kate, *Feminine Frequencies: Gender, German Radio, and the public sphere, 1923–1945* (Ann Arbor, Michigan, 1996)

Ladd, Brian, *Urban Planning and Civic Order in Germany, 1860–1914* (Cambridge, Mass., 1990)

——, *The Ghosts of Berlin: Confronting German history in the urban landscape* (Chicago, 1997)

Ladwig-Winters, Simone, *Wertheim: Geschichte eines Warenhaus* (Berlin, 1997)

Laforgúe de, Leo, *Symphonie der Weltstadt: Berlin* (orig. edn, 1939, as video re-release Berlin-West, 1950)

Lampard, Eric E., 'Historical contours of contemporary urban society: a comparative view', in *Journal of Contemporary History*, Vol. 4, No. 3 (July 1969), 3–25

——, 'The urbanizing world', in H.J. Dyos, M. Wolff (eds.), *The Victorian City: Images and reality* (London, 1973)

——, 'The nature of urbanization', in Derek Fraser, Anthony Sutcliffe (eds.), *The Pursuit of Urban History* (London, 1983)

Landauer, Gustav, *Aufruf zum Sozialismus* (Berlin, 1920)

Landes, David, *The Unbound Prometheus* (Cambridge, 1969)

Langewiesche, Dieter, 'Wanderungsbewegungen in der Hochindustrialisierungsperiode: Regionale, interstädtische und innerstädtische Mobilität in Deutschland 1880–1914', in *Vierteljahresschrift für Sozial- und Wirtschaftsgeschichte*, Vol. 63 (1977)

——, 'Mobilität in deutschen Mittel- und Großstädten. Aspekte der Binnenwanderung im 19. und 20. Jahrhundert', in Werner Conze, Ulrich Engelhardt (eds.), *Arbeiter im Industrialisierungsprozeß: Herkunft, Lage und Verhalten* (Stuttgart, 1979)

Lash, Scott, 'Postmodernism as humanism? Urban space and social theory', in Bryan S. Turner (ed.), *Theories of Modernity and Postmodernity* (London, Newbury Park and New Delhi, 1990)

Latten, Willy, 'Die niederrheinische Kleinstadt', in *Kölner Vierteljahreshefte für Soziologie: Zeitschrift des Forschungsinstituts für Sozialwissenschaften in Köln*, 8 Jg. Heft 1 (Leipzig, 1929), 312–24

Lauterbach, Burkhart (ed.), *Großstadtmensch: Die Welt der Angestellten* (Frankfurt am Main, 1995)

Laux, Hans-Dieter, 'Dimensionen und Determinanten der Bevölkerungsentwicklung Preussischer Städte in der Periode der Hochindustrialisierung', in Wilhelm Rausch (ed.), *Die Städte Mitteleuropas im 19. Jahrhundert* (Linz/Donau, 1983)

Lavin, Maud, 'Photomontage, mass culture and modernity', in *idem et al.*, (eds.), *Montage and Modern Life, 1919–1942* (Cambridge, Mass., 1992)

Lawton, Richard, 'Introduction: aspects of the development and role of great cities in the Western World in the nineteenth and twentieth centuries', in *idem, The Rise and Fall of Great Cities: Aspects of urbanization in the western world* (London and New York, 1989)

Lee, Joseph, 'Aspects of urbanization and economic development in Germany 1815–1914', in P. Abrams, E. A. Wrigley (eds.), *Towns in Societies: Essays in economic history and historical sociology* (Cambridge, 1978)

Lees, Andrew, 'Debates about the big city in Germany 1890–1914', *Societas*, 5 (1975), 31–47

——, 'Critics of urban society in Germany 1854–1914', *Journal of the History of Ideas*, Vol. 40 (1979), 61–83

——, *Cities Perceived: Urban society in European and American thought 1820–1940* (Manchester, 1985)

——, 'Berlin and modern urbanity in German discourse 1845–1945', in *Journal of Urban History*, Vol. 17 No. 2 (Feb. 1991), 153–80

Lees, Andrew, Lynn Hollen Lees (eds.), *The Urbanization of European Society in the Nineteenth Century* (Lexington, Mass., 1976)

Lehnert, Detlef, 'Mietskasernen – Realität und Gartenstadt-Träume, zur Wohnsituation Jugendlicher in Großstädten der 20er Jahre', in Deutscher Werkbund e.V. und Württemburgischer Kunstverein Stuttgart (eds.), *Schock und Schöpfung: Jugendästhetik im 20. Jahrhundert* (Stuttgart, 1986)

Leinert, Martin, *Sozialgeschichte der Großstadt* (Hamburg, 1925)

Lenger, Friedrich, 'Urbanisierungs- und Stadtgeschichte – Geschichte der Stadt, Verstädterungsgeschichte oder Geschichte in der Stadt?', in *Archiv für Sozialgeschichte*, XXVI (1986), 429–79

Lengerle, Christiane von, 'Homosexuelle Frauen: Tribanden, Freundinnen, Urninden', in Michael Bolle (ed.), *Eldorado: homosexuelle Frauen und Männer in Berlin 1850–1950. Geschichte, Alltag und Kultur* (Berlin, 1984)

Lenz, Rudolf, *Karstadt: ein deutscher Warenhauskonzern 1920–1950* (Stuttgart, 1995)

Lessing, Theodor, 'Ueber Psychologie des Lärms', in *Zeitschrift für Psychotherapie und Medizinische Psychologie* (1909), 77–87

Levin, Thomas Y., 'Introduction', in *idem* (ed.), *Siegfried Kracauer, The Mass Ornament. Weimar Essays* (Cambridge, Mass., London, 1995)

Lewis, Beth Irwin, 'Lustmord: Inside the windows of the metropolis', in Charles W. Haxthausen and Heidrun Suhr (eds.), *Berlin: Culture and metropolis* ((Minneapolis and Oxford, 1990); also repr. in Katharina von Ankum (ed.), *Women in the Metropolis: Gender and modernity in Weimar culture* (Berkeley, Los Angeles and London, 1997)

Liang, Hsi-Huey, 'Lower-class immigrants in Wilhelmine Berlin', in *Central European History*, Vol. 3 (1970), 94–111

Lichtenberger, Elisabeth, 'Die Städtebildung in Europa in der Ersten Hälfte des 20. Jahrhunderts', in Wilhelm Rausch (ed.), *Die Städte Mitteleuropas im 20. Jahrhundert* (Linz, 1984)

Lieberman, Ben, 'Testing Peukert's paradigm: The "Crisis of classical modernity" in the "New Frankfurt", 1925–1930', in *German Studies Review*, Vol. XVII No. 2 (May 1994), 287–303

——, 'Luxury or public investment? Productivity and planning for Weimar recovery', in *Central European History*, Vol. 26 No. 2 (1993), 195–213

Lindner, Rolf, *Die Entstehung der Stadtkultur: Soziologie aus der Erfahrung der Reportage* (Frankfurt am Main, 1990)

——, 'The imaginary city', in Bundesministerium für Wissenschaft und Verkehr und Internationales Forschungszentrum Kulturwissenschaften (ed.), *The Contemporary Study of Culture* (Vienna, 1999)

Lloyd, Jill, *German Expressionism: Primitivism and modernity* (New Haven, London, 1991a)

——, 'The painted city as nature and artifice', in Irit Rogoff (ed.), *The Divided*

Heritage: Themes and problems in German modernism (Cambridge and New York, 1991b)

Lüdtke, Alf, *'Geimeinwohl', Polizei und 'Festungspraxis' staatliche Gewaltsamkeit und innere Verwaltung in Preussen, 1815–1850* (Göttingen, 1982)

Lukacs, John, *Budapest 1900: A Historical Portrait of a City and its Culture* (London, 1988)

Lüken-Isberner, Folckert, 'Das Programm zur (Alt-) Stadtsanierung im Nationalsozialismus', in *idem*, Arbeitsgruppe Stadtbaugeschichte (ed.), *Stadt und Raum 1933–1949, Beiträge zur planungs- und stadtbaugeschichtlichen Forschung II* (Gesamthochschule Kassel, Kassel, 1991)

Lungstrum, Janet, 'Metropolis and technosexual woman of German modernity', in Katharina von Ankum (ed.), *Women in the Metropolis: Gender and modernity in Weimar culture* (Berkeley, Los Angeles and London, 1997)

Lüsebrink, Karin, *Büro via Fabrik: Entstehung und Allokationsprinzipien weiblicher Büroarbeit 1850 bis 1933* (Berlin, 1993)

Lütgens, Annelie, 'The conspiracy of women: Images of city life in the work of Jeanne Mammen', in Katharina von Ankum (ed.), *Women in the Metropolis: Gender and modernity in Weimar culture* (Berkeley, Los Angeles and London, 1997)

Lutz, Richard, 'Der Öffentliche Nahverkehr in Altona und die Städtische Verkehrspolitik 1918–1933', in Arnold Sywottek (ed.), *Das andere Altona: Beiträge zur Alltagsgeschichte* (Hamburg, 1984)

Masse, Kaspar, *Grenzenloses Vergnügen: der Aufstieg der Massenkultur 1850–1970* (Frankfurt am Main, 1997)

Maier, Charles, 'Between Taylorism and technocracy: European ideologies and the vision of industrial productivity in the 1920s', *Journal of Contemporary History*, Vol. 5 No. 2 (1970), 27–61

Makela, Maria, 'The Misogynist machine: Images of technology in the work of Hanna Hoch', in Katharina von Ankum (ed.), *Women in the Metropolis: Gender and modernity in Weimar culture* (Berkeley, Los Angeles and London, 1997)

Mannheim, Hermann, *Comparative Criminolgy: A text book*, Vol. 1 (London, 1965)

Marcuse, Max, *Die geschlechtliche Aufklärung der Jugend: Vortrag gehalten am 5. April 1905 zu Berlin im Bund für Mütterschutz* (Leipzig, 1905)

Marschalck, Peter, *Bevölkerungsgeschichte Deutschlands im 19. und 20. Jahrhundert* (Frankfurt am Main, 1984)

Marsh, Jan, *Back to the Land: The pastoral impulse in England, from 1880 to 1914* (London, 1982)

Masterman, Charles Frederick Gurney (ed.), *The Heart of Empire: Discussions of problems of modern city life in England* (London, 1901)

Matthews, Jill, '"They had such a lot of fun": the Women's League of Health and Beauty', in *History Workshop* 30 (Autumn 1990), 22–54

Matzerath, Horst, 'Städtewachstum und Eingemeindungen im 19.Jahrhundert', in Jürgen Reulecke (ed.), *Die deutsche Stadt im Industriezeitalter: Beiträge zur Modernen deutschen Stadtgeschichte* (Wuppertal, 1978)

——, 'The influence of industrialization on urban growth in Prussia (1815–1914)', in H. Schmal (ed.), *Patterns of European Urbanization since 1500* (London, 1981)

——, 'Berlin, 1890–1940', in Anthony Sutcliffe (ed.), *Metropolis 1890–1940* (London, 1984)

——, *Urbanisierung in Preussen 1815–1914* (Stuttgart, 1985)

Mayne, Alan, 'Representing the slum', in *Urban History Yearbook* 1990 (Leicester, 1990), 66–84

——, *The Imagined Slum* (Leicester, London and New York, 1993)

McCannell, Dean, *The Tourist: A new theory of the leisure class* (New York, 1976)

McCormick, Richard, 'From Caligari to Dietrich: Sexual, social and cinematic discourse in Weimar film', in *Signs* (Spring 1993), 640–68

McElligott, Anthony P., 'Das "Abruzzenviertel": Arbeiter in Altona 1918–1933', in Arno Herzig, Dieter Langewiesche, Arnold Sywottek (eds.), *Arbeiter in Hamburg: Unterschichtung, Arbeiter und Arbeiterbewegung seit dem ausgehenden 18.Jahrhundert* (Hamburg, 1983)

——, 'Workers' culture and workers' politics on Weimar's new housing estates: a response to Adelheid von Saldern', *Social History*, Vol. 17, No. 3 (Jan. 1992), 101–13

——, 'Per Fahrrad, Bus und Bahn: Angestellten Unterwegs', in Burkhart Lauterbach (ed.), *Großstadtmenschen: Die Welt der Angestellten* (Frankfurt am Main, 1995)

——, *Contested City: Municipal politics and the rise of Nazism in Altona 1917–1937* (Ann Arbor, Michigan, 1998)

——, 'Walter Ruttmann's *Berlin: Symphony of a city:* traffic-mindedness and the city in interwar Germany', in Malcom Gee, Tim Kirk, Jill Steward (eds.), *The City in Central Europe since 1800* (Aldershot and Vermont, 1999)

McKay, John P., *Tramways and Trolleys: The rise of urban mass transport in Europe* (Princeton, NJ, 1976)

Meller, Helen, 'Cities and evolution: Patrick Geddes as an international prophet of town planning before 1914', in Anthony Sutcliffe (ed.), *The Rise of Modern Urban Planning 1800–1914* (London, 1980)

——, 'Planning theory and women's role in the city', in *Urban History Yearbook 1990* (Leicester, 1990), 84–98

——, *Towns, Plans and Society in Modern Britain* (Cambridge, 1997)

Meskimmon, Marsha and Shearer West (eds.), *Visions of the 'Neue Frau': women and the visual arts in Weimar Germany* (Aldershot, 1995)

Miller, Michael B., *The Bon Marché: Bourgeois culture and the department store, 1869–1920* (London, Boston and Sydney, 1981)

Miller Lane, Barbara, *Architecture and Politics in Germany 1918–1945* (second edn, Cambridge, Mass., 1985)

——, 'Architects in Power: Politics and ideology in the work of Ernst May and Albert Speer', *Journal of Interdisciplinary History*, Vol. XVII, No. 1 (Summer 1986), 283–310

Mitchell, Brian, *European Historical Statistics 1750–1970* (abr. edn, London, 1978)

Mitterauer, Michael, *Ledige Mütter: zur Geschichte illegitimer Gebürten in Europa* (Munich, 1983)

——, Reinhard Sieder, *Vom Patriarchat zur Partnerschaft: zum Strukturwandel der Familie* (Munich, 1980)

Monaco, Paul, *Cinema and Society: France and Germany during the twenties* (New York, 1976)

Morgenroth, Wilhelm, 'Die Gemeindestatistik in Deutschland', in Paul Flaskämper, Adolf Blind (eds.), *Beiträge zur Deutschen Statistik: Festgabe für Franz Zizek* (Leipzig, 1936)

Morris, R.J., R. Rodger (eds.), *The Victorian City: A reader in urban history 1820–1914* (Marlow, 1993)

Mort, Frank, *Cultures of Consumption: Commerce, masculinities and social space* (London, 1996)

Mort, Frank, Peter Thompson, 'Retailing, commercial culture and masculinity in 1950s Britain: the case of Montague Burton, the "Tailor of Taste"', in *History Workshop: A journal of socialist and feminist historians*, 38 (Autumn, 1994), 106–27

Mosse, W.E., *Jews in the German Economy: the German–Jewish economic elite, 1870–1935* (Oxford, 1987)

——, *The German–Jewish economic elite, 1820–1935: A socio-cultural profile* (Oxford, 1989)

Mougenot, Catherine, 'Promoting the single family house in Belgium', *International Journal of Urban and Regional Research*, Vol. 12, No. 4 (1988)

Müller, Martin L., 'Körperkultur in Frankfurt am Main während des Kaiserreichs und der Weimarer Republik', *Archiv für Sozialgeschichte*, XXXIII (1993), 107–36

Müller, Michael, 'Sozialgeschichtliche Aspekte des Wohnens', in Michael Andritzky, Gert Selle (eds.), *Lernbereich Wohnen* (Reinbek, 1987)

Mullin, John Robert, 'City planning in Frankfurt, Germany 1925–1932: A study in practical utopianism', *Journal of Urban History*, 4 (1977), 3–28

——, 'Ideology, planning theory and the German city in the interwar years', Part 2 in *Town Planning Review*, Vol. 53 No. 3 (July 1982), 257–72

Mumford, Lewis, *The Culture of Cities* (London, 1938)

——, *The City in History: Its origins, its transformations, and its prospects* (London, 1961)

Myers, Tracy, 'History and realism: Representations of women in G.W. Pabst's *The Joyless Street*', in Sandra Frieden, Richard W. McCormick, Vibeke R. Petersen, Laurie Melissa Vogelsang (eds.), *Gender and German Cinema*, Vol. 2 (London, 1993)

Neefe, M., 'Gebiet, Lage und natürliche Verhältnisse der Städte', in *Statistisches Jahrbuch Deutscher Städte*, Jg. 2 (1892), 1–9

Nenno, Nancy, 'Femininity, the primitive, and modern urban space: Josephine Baker in Berlin', in Katharina von Ankum (ed.), *Women in the Metropolis: Gender and modernity in Weimar culture* (Berkeley, Los Angeles and London, 1997)

Nerdinger, Winfried (ed.), *Bauhaus Moderne im Nationalsozialismus: zwischen Anbiederung und Verfolgung* (Munich, 1993)

Neuman, R.P., 'Industrialization and sexual behavior: Some aspects of working-class life in imperial Germany', in R.J. Bezucha (ed.), *Modern European Social History* (Lexington, Mass., 1972)

Neumann, Dietrich, 'The urban vision in *Metropolis*', in Thomas W. Kniesche, Stephen Brockmann (eds.), *Dancing on the Volcano: Essays on the culture of the Weimar Republic* (Columbia, S.C., 1994)

Neundörfer, Ludwig, *Die Angestellten: Neuer Versuch einer Standortbestimmung* (Stuttgart, 1961)

Newman, Allen R., 'The influence of family and friends on German internal migration, 1880–85', in *Journal of Social History*, Vol. 13 (1979), 277–88

Nicolson, Harold, 'Berlin revisited', in *British Zone Review*, Vol. 2 No. 17 (20 Nov. 1948)

Niederich, Nikolaus, '"Über Berg und Tal": Skizzen zur Stuttgarter Stadt- und Straßenbahnentwicklung', in Horst Matzerath (ed.), *Stadt und Verkehr im Industrizeitalter* (Cologne, Weimar and Vienna, 1996)

Niethammer, Lutz, Franz-Josef Brüggemeier, 'Wie wohnten Arbeiter im Kaiserreich?', *Archiv für Sozialgeschichte*, XVI (1976), 61–134

Noakes, Jeremy and Geoffrey Pridham, *Documents on Nazism, 1919–1945* (New York, 1974)

Nolan, Mary, 'Housework made easy: The Taylorized housewife in Weimar Germany', *Feminist Studies*, Vol. 16 No. 3 (1990), 549–77

——, 'Imagining America, modernizing Germany', in Thomas W. Kniesche, Stephen Brockmann (eds.), *Dancing on the Volcano: Essays on the culture of the Weimar Republic* (Columbia, S.C., 1994)

——, *Visions of Modernity: American business and the modernization of Germany* (New York, 1994)

Nolte, Paul, '1900: Das Ende des 19. und der Beginn des 20. Jahrhunderts in sozialgeschichtlicher Perspektive', in *Geschichte in Wissenschaft und Unterricht* 5/6/96 (1996), 281–300

O'Connell, Sean, *The Car in British Society: Class, gender and motoring 1896–1939* (Manchester, 1998)

Offen, Karen, 'The theory and practice of feminism: Nineteenth-century

Europe', in Renate Bridenthal, Claudia Koonz, Susan Stuard (eds.), *Becoming Visible: Women in European history* (Boston, 1987)

Ostwald, Hans, *Männliche Prostitution im kaiserlichen Berlin* (Leipzig, 1906, reprint Berlin, 1992)

——, *Sittengeschichte der Inflation: Ein Kulturdokument aus dem Jahren des Marksturzes* (Berlin, 1931)

Overy, Richard, 'Heralds of modernity: Cars and planes from invention to necessity', in Mikulas Teich, Roy Porter (eds.), *Fin de Siècle and its Legacy* (Cambridge and New York, 1990)

Pahl, R.E., 'Contexts: Pursuing the urban of "Urban sociology"', in Derek Fraser, Anthony Sutcliffe (eds.), *The Pursuit of Urban History* (London, 1983)

Park, Robert E., Ernest W. Burgess, Roderick D. McKenzie, *The City* (Chicago, 1925)

Partsch, Cornelius, 'Hannibal ante Portas: Jazz in Weimar', in Thomas W. Kniesche, Stephen Brockmann (eds.), *Dancing on the Volcano: Essays on the culture of the Weimar Republic* (Columbia, S.C., 1994)

Paul, Christa, *Zwangsprostitution: staatlich errichtete Bordelle im Nationalsozialismus* (Berlin, 1994)

Peach, Mark, '"Der Architekt Denkt, Die Hausfrau Lenkt": German modern architecture and the modern woman', in *German Studies Review*, Vol. 18 No. 3 (Oct. 1985), 441–63

Petersen, Klaus, 'The Harmful Publications (Young Persons) Act of 1926: Literary censorship and the politics of morality in the Weimar Republic', in *German Studies Review*, Vol. 15 No. 3 (1992), 505–23

Petro, Patrice, *Joyless Streets: Women and melodramatic representation in Weimar Germany* (Princeton, N.J., 1989)

Petro, Patrice, 'Perceptions of difference: Women as spectator and spectacle' in Katharina von Ankum (ed.), *Women in the Metropolis: Gender and modernity in Weimar culture* (Berkeley, Los Angeles and London, 1997)

Petrow, Stefan, *Policing Morals* (Oxford, 1994)

Peukert, Detlev J. K., *Grenzen der Sozialdisziplinierung: Aufstieg und Krise der deutschen Jugendfürsorge von 1878 bis 1932* (Cologne, 1986)

——, 'The Weimar Republic: Old and new perspectives', in *German History*, Vol. 6, No. 2 (1988), 133–44

——, *The Weimar Republic: The crisis of classical modernity*, translated by Richard Deveson (Harmondsworth, 1991)

——, 'Das Mädchen mit dem wahrhafte Bubikopf', in Peter Alter (ed.), *Im Banne der Metropolen: Berlin und London in den 20er Jahren* (Göttingen, 1993)

Philippovich, Eugen von, 'Wiener Wohnungsverhältnisse', in *Archiv für Sozialgesetzgebung und Statistik*, 7 (Berlin, 1894), 215–77

Pick, Daniel, *Faces of Degeneration: a European disorder, c.1848–c.1918* (Cambridge, 1989)

Pine, Lisa, 'Hashude: The imprisonment of "Asocial" families in the Third Reich', *German History*, Vol. 13, No. 2 (1995), 182–97

Pirker, Theo, *Büro und Maschine: Zur Geschichte und Soziologie der Mechanisierung der Büroarbeit, der Mechanisierung des Büros und der Büroautomation* (Basel, 1962)

Pollock, James, *The Government of Greater Germany* (New York, 1940)

Poor, Harold, 'Anti-urbanism in the Weimar Republic', *Societas*, Vol. 6 No. 3 (Summer 1976), 177–92

Pore, Renate, *A Conflict of Interest: Women in German Social Democracy, 1919–1933* (Westport Conn. and London, 1981)

Pounds, Norman J. G., *An Economic Geography of Europe* (Cambridge, 1990)

Prinz, Michael, 'Die Arbeitswelt in der Weimarer Republik zwischen Weltkrieg und Wirtschaftskrise: Die Ausgangssituation im Deutsche Reich', in August Nitschke, Gerhard A. Ritter, Detlev J.K. Peukert, Rüdiger vom Bruch (eds.), *Jahrhundertwende: Der Aufbruch in der Moderne 188–1930* (Reinbek, 1990)

Prumm, Karl, 'Dynamik der Großstadt: Berlin-Bilder im Film der Zwanziger Jahre', in Gerhard Brunn, Jürgen Reulecke (eds.), *Berlin . . . Blicke auf die deutsche Metropole* (Essen, 1989)

Radkau, Joachim, 'Die wilhelminische Ära als "nervöses Zeitalter", oder: die Nerven als Netzwerk zwischen Tempo- und Körpergeschichte', in *Geschichte und Gesellschaft*, Vol. 20 (1994), 211–41

Ras, Marion de, '"Wenn der Körper restlos rhythmisch ist und hemmungslos innerviert . . . " Mädchenästhetik im Wandervogel', in Deutscher Werkbund e.V. und Württemburgischer Kunstverein Stuttgart (eds.), *Schock und Schöpfung: Jugendästhetik im 20. Jahrhundert* (Stuttgart, 1986)

Reagin, Nancy R., '"A true woman can take care of herself": The debate over prostitution in Hanover, 1906', in *Central European History*, Vol. 24 No. 4 (1991), 347–80

Reichhardt, Hans J., Wolfgang Schäche, *Von Berlin nach Germania, über die Zerstörungen der 'Reichshauptstadt' durch Albert Speers Neugestaltungsplanungen* (Berlin, 1998)

Reinhardt, Dirk, *Von der Reklame zum Marketing* (Berlin, 1993)

Reulecke, Jürgen, 'Sozio-ökonomische Bedingungen und Folgen der Verstädterung in Deutschland', in *Die alte Stadt: Zeitschrift für Stadtgeschichte, Stadtsoziologie und Denkmalpflege*, 4 (1977), 269–87

——, 'The Ruhr: Centralization versus decentralization in a region of cities', in Anthony Sutcliffe (ed.), *Metropolis 1890–1940* (London, 1984)

——, *Geschichte der Urbanisierung in Deutschland* (Frankfurt am Main, 1985)

Reulecke, Jürgen, Adelheid Gräfin zu Castell Rüdenhausen (eds.), *Stadt und Gesundheit: Zum Wandel von 'Volksgesundheit' und kommunaler Gesundheitspolitik im 19. und frühen 20. Jahrhundert* (Stuttgart, 1991)

Reuter, Thomas, '"Wir sind Nackt und nennen uns Du": Von Lichtfreunden und Sonnenmenschen', in Deutscher Werkbund e.V. und

Württemburgischer Kunstverein Stuttgart (eds.), *Schock und Schöpfung: Jugendästhetik im 20. Jahrhundert* (Stuttgart, 1986)

Rexroth, Susanne, Jan Wolter, 'Neukölln: sozial, politisch, wirtschaftlich betrachtet', in Neuköllner Kultur Verein e.V., *Vom Ilsenhof zum Highdeck: Modelle Sozialen Wohnens in Neukölln* (Berlin, 1987)

Ribhegge, Wilhelm, 'Die Systemfunktion der Gemeinden: Zur deutschen Kommunalgeschichte seit 1918', in *Aus Politik und Zeitgeschichte: Beilage zur Wochenzeitung Das Parlament* B47 (1973)

Richter, Lina, *Family Life in Germany under the Blockade* (London, 1919)

Rickels, Laurence, 'War neurosis and Weimar cinema', in Thomas W. Kniesche, Stephen Brockmann (eds.), *Dancing on the Volcano: Essays on the culture of the Weimar Republic* (Columbia, S.C., 1994)

Riechenberg, Martin, *Der Büro und Kassendienst* (1929)

Ritter, Gerhard A., *Social Welfare in Germany and Britain: Origins and development* (trans. Ian Traynor, Leamington Spa and New York, 1986)

Roberts, James, *Drink, Temperance and the Working Class in Nineteenth-century Germany* (Boston, Mass. and London, 1984)

Roberts, Robert, *The Classic Slum: Salford life in the first quarter of the century* (Harmondsworth, 1973)

Rodriguez-Lores, Juan, 'Stadthygiene und Städtebau: Am Beispiel der Debatten im Deutschen Verein für öffentliche Gesundheitspflege 1869–1911', in Jürgen Reulecke, Adelheid Gräfin zu Castell Rüdenhausen (eds.), *Stadt und Gesundheit: Zum Wandel von 'Volksgesundheit' und kommunaler Gesundheitspolitik im 19. und frühen 20. Jahrhundert* (Stuttgart, 1991)

Röse, C., 'Die Grossstadt als Grab der Bevölkerung', in *Aerztliche Rundschau*, XV (1905), 275–61

Rosenhaft, Eve, 'Working-class life and working-class politics: Communists, Nazis and the battle for the streets, Berlin 1928–1932', in Richard Bessel, Edgar J. Feuchtwanger (eds.), *Social Change and Political Development in Weimar Germany* (London, 1981)

——, 'Organising the "Lumpenproletariat": Cliques and Communists in Berlin during the Weimar Republic', in Richard J. Evans (ed.), *The German Working Class 1888–1933: The politics of everyday life* (London, 1982)

——, 'Women in modern Germany', in Gordon Martel (ed.), *Modern Germany Reconsidered 1870–1945* (London, 1992)

——, 'Brecht's Germany: 1898–1933', in Peter Thomson, Glendyr Sacks (eds.), *The Cambridge Companion to Brecht* (Cambridge, 1994)

——, 'Lesewut Kinosucht Radiotismus: zur (geschlechter-) politischen Relevanz neuer Massenmedien in den 1920er Jahren', in Alf Lüdtke, Inge Marßolek, Adelheid von Saldern (eds.), *Amerikanisierung: Traum und Alptraum im Deutschland des 20. Jahrhunderts* (Stuttgart, 1996)

Roßbach, Erich Carl, *Betrachtungen zur wirtschaftlichen Lage der technischen Privatangestellten in Deutschland* (Karlsruhe i. Br., 1916)

Roters, Eberhard, *et.al.*, *Berlin 1910–1933* (New York, 1982)

Rudder Bernhard de, *Biologie der Großstadt* (Dresden, Leipzig, 1940)

Rumpf, Hans, *Das war der Bombenkrieg: Deutsche Städte im Feuersturm, Ein Dokumentarbericht* (Oldenburg, Hamburg, 1961)

Rutsky, R.L., 'The mediation of technology and gender: Metropolis, Nazism, modernism', in *New German Critique*, 60 (1993), 8–32

Sachße, Christoph, *Mütterlichkeit als Beruf* (Frankfurt am Main, 1986)

——, Florian Tennstedt, *Geschichte der Armenfürsorge in Deutschland, Band 2: Fürsorge und Wohlfahrtspflege 1871 bis 1929* (Stuttgart, 1988)

Sackett, R. E., 'Antimodernism in the popular entertainment of Modern Munich: Attitude, institution, language', in *New German Critique*, 57 (Fall 1992), 123–55

Saldern, Adelheid von, 'Neues Wohnen, Wohnverhältnisse und Wohnverhalten in Großanlagen der 20er Jahre', in Axel Schildt, Arnold Sywottek (eds.), *Massenwohnung und Eigenheim: Wohnungsbau und Wohnen in der Großstadt seit dem Ersten Weltkrieg* (Frankfurt am Main and New York, 1988)

——, 'The workers' movement and cultural patterns on urban housing estates and in rural settlements in Germany and Austria during the 1920s', *Social History*, Vol. 15 No. 3 (Oct. 1990), 333–54

——, '"Daheim an meinem Herd . . . " Die Kultur des Wohnens', in August Nitschke, Gerhard A. Ritter, Detlev J. K. Peukert, Rüdiger vom Bruch (eds.), *Jahrhundertwende: Der Aufbruch in der Moderne 1880–1930*, Vol. 2 (Reinbek, 1990)

—— (ed.), *Wochenend und Schöner Schein: Freizeit und Modernes Leben in den Zwanziger Jahren: das Beispiel Hannover* (Berlin, 1991)

—— 'Cultural conflicts, popular mass culture, and the question of Nazi success: The Eilenriede motorcycle racers, 1924–39', in *German Studies Review*, vol. XV No. 2 (May 1992), 317–38

——, *Häuserleben: zur Geschichte städtischen Arbeiterwohnens vom Kaiserreich bis Heute* (Bonn, 1995)

Sandford, John, 'Chaos and control in the Weimar film', in *German Life and Letters*, Vol. 48, No. 3 (July 1995), 311–23

Schäche, Wolfgang, *Architektur und Städtebau in Berlin zwischen 1939 und 1945: Planen und Bauen unter der Aegide der Stadtverwaltung* (Berlin, 1991)

Schäfer, Hans Dieter, *Berlin im Zweiten Weltkrieg: der Untergang der Reichshauptstadt in Augenzeugenberichten* (Munich, 1985)

——, 'Berlin – Modernität und Zivilisationslosigkeit', in Derek Glass, Dietmar Rösler, John J. White (eds.), *Berlin: Literary images of a city: Eine Großstadt im Spiegel der Literatur* (Berlin, 1989)

Schäfers, Bernhard, 'Phasen der Stadtbildung und Verstädterung', in *Das alte Stadt: Zeitschrift für Stadtgeschichte, Stadtsoziologie und Denkmalpflege*, 4 (1977), 243–68

Schär, Christian, *Der Schläger und seine Tänze in Deutschland der 20er Jahre:*

Sozialmusikalische Aspekte zum Wandel in der Musik- und Tanzkultur während der Weimarer Republik (Zurich, 1991)

Scharfe, Martin, 'Die Nervosität des Automobilisten', in Richard van Dülmen (ed.), *Körper-Geschichten* (Frankfurt am Main, 1988)

——, '"Ungebundene Circulation der Individuen": Aspekte des Automobilfahrens in der Frühzeit', in *Zeitschrift für Volkskunde*, Vol. 86 (1990), 216–43

Scheffauer, Herman, 'The City Without Night: Berlin 'Twixt Dusk and Dawn', *The Pall Mall Magazine*, Vol. 53 No. 251, 1914 (March), 280–1

Schildt, Axel, '"Gesunde Jugend" – "gesunde Stadt", zur Förderung von Erholung und Freizeit der großstädtischen Jugend in der 1920er Jahren am Beispiel von Hamburg', in Jürgen Reulecke and Adelheid Gräfin zu Castell Rüdenhausen (eds.), *Stadt und Gesundheit: Zum Wandel von 'Volksgesundheit' und kommunaler Gesundheitspolitik im 19. und frühen 20. Jahrhundert* (Stuttgart, 1991)

Schlierkamp, Petra, 'Die Garçonne', in Michael Bolle (ed.), *Eldorado: homosexuelle Frauen und Männer in Berlin 1850–1950. Geschichte, Alltag und Kultur* (Berlin, 1984)

Schlör, Joachim, *Nights in the Big City: Paris, Berlin, London 1840–1930*, trans. Pierre Gottfried Imhof and Dafydd Rees Roberts (London, 1998)

Schlüpmann, Heide, 'The brothel as an Arcadian space? Diary of a lost girl (1929)', in Eric Rentschler (ed.), *The Films of G.W. Pabst: An existential cinema* (New Brunswick and London, 1990)

Schoenbaum, David, *Hitler's Social Revolution* (New York, 1967)

Schoppmann, Claudia, *Days of Masquerade: Life stories of lesbians during the Third Reich* (New York, 1996)

——, 'National Socialist policies towards female homosexuality', in Lynn Abrams, Elizabeth Harvey (eds.), *Gender Relations in German History* (London, 1996)

Schorske, Carl E., *Fin-de-Siècle Vienna: Politics and culture* (New York, 1980)

Schulze, Gustav, 'Die Heimat als Jungbrunnen für Körper und Geist', in *Gewerkschaftsbund der Angestellten Jugendbund*, Führerschriften 1 (Berlin, 1921), 2–6

Schulze-Gävernitz, G. von, 'Die Maschine in der kapitalistischen Wirtschaftsordnung', in *Archiv für Sozialwissenschaft und Sozialpolitik*, 63 (Tübingen, 1930), 225–73

Schütz, Erhard, 'Beyond glittering reflections of asphalt: Changing images of Berlin in Weimar literary journalism', in Thomas W. Kniesche, Stephen Brockmann (eds.), *Dancing on the Volcano: Essays on the culture of the Weimar Republic* (Columbia, S.C., 1994)

Schwartz, Michael, '"Proletarier" und "Lumpen": Sozialistische Ursprünge eugenischen Denkens', in *Vierteljahreshefte für Zeitgeschichte*, Vol. 4 Nr 4 (1994), 537–70

——, *Sozialistische Eugenik: eugenische Sozialtechnologien in Debatten und Politik der deutsche Sozialdemokratie 1890–1933* (Bonn, 1995)

Schwarz, Angela, *Die Reise ins Dritten Reich: kritische Augenzeugen im Nationalsozialistischen Deutschland (1933–39)* (Göttingen and Zurich, 1993)

Sennett, Richard (ed.), *Classic Essays on the Culture of Cities* (New York, 1969)

Shand, James D., 'The Reichsautobahn: Symbol for the Third Reich', in *Journal of Contemporary History,* Vol. 19 (1984), 189–200

Shapiro, Theda, 'The metropolis in the visual arts: Paris, Berlin, New York, 1890–1940', in Anthony Sutcliffe (ed.), *Metropolis 1890–1940* (London, 1984)

Shaw, Albert, *Municipal Government in Continental Europe* (London, 1895)

Shaw, Gareth, 'Large-scale retailing in Germany and the development of new retail organisations', in John Benson, Gareth Shaw (eds.), *The Evolution of Retail Systems, c.1800–1914* (Leicester, 1992)

Sheehan, James, 'Liberalism and the city in nineteenth century Germany', *Past and Present,* No. 51 (1971), 116–37

Sieder, Reinhard, 'Housing policy, social welfare and family life in "Red Vienna" 1914–34', in *Oral History,* Vol. 13 No. 2 (1985), 35–48

——, '"Vata, derf i aufstehn?": Childhood experiences in Viennese working-class families around 1900', in *Continuity and Change,* Vol. 1 No. 1 (1986), 53–88

Sieferle, Rolf Peter, *Die konservative Revolution: Fünf biographische Skizzen (Paul Leusch, Werner Sombart, Oswald Spengler, Ernst Jünger, Hans Freyer)* (Frankfurt am Main, 1995)

——, Clemens Wischermann,'Die Stadt als Rassengrab', in Manfred Smuda (ed.), *Die Grossstadt als 'Text'* (Munich, 1992)

Sigsworth, Eric, *Montague Burton: The tailor of taste* (Manchester, 1990)

Silverman, Dan P., 'A pledge unredeemed: The housing crisis in Weimar Germany', in *Central European History,* Vol. 3 (1970), 112–39

Smart, Barry, 'Modernity, postmodernity and the present', in Bryan S. Turner (ed.), *Theories of Modernity and Postmodernity* (London, Newbury Park and New Delhi, 1990)

Sofsky, Wolfgang, 'Schreckbild Stadt: Stationen der modernen Stadtkritik', in *Die alte Stadt: Zeitschrift für Stadtgeschichte, Stadtsoziologie und Denkmalpflege,* 13 (1986), 1–21

Sombart, Werner, 'Der Begriff der Stadt und das Wesen der Städtebildung', in *Archiv für Sozialwissenschaft und Sozialpolitik,* 25 (Tübingen, 1907), 1–9

——, 'Technik und Kultur', in *Verhandlungen des Ersten Deutschen Soziologentages 19–22 Oktober 1910 in Frankfurt a. Main* (Tübingen, 1911), 63–83

Spencer, Elaine Govka, 'Policing popular amusements in German cities: The case of Prussia's Rhine Province 1815–1914', in *Journal of Urban History,* Vol. 16 No. 4 (August 1990), 366–85

Spiekermann, Uwe, 'Theft and thieves in German department stores, 1895–1930: a discourse on morality, crime and gender', in Geoffrey Crossick, Serge Jaumain (eds.), *Cathedrals of Consumption: The European department store 1850–1939* (Aldershot and Vermont, 1999)

Spree, Reinhard, *Soziale Ungleichheit vor Krankheit und Tod* (Göttingen, 1981)

Stark, Gary D., 'Pornography, society, and the law in imperial Germany', in *Central European History*, Vol. 14 (1981), 200–29

Steinmetz, George, *Regulating the Social: The welfare state and local politics in imperial Germany* (Princeton, N.J., 1993)

Stekel, Wilhelm, *Sadism and Masochism: The psychology of hatred and cruelty* (London, 1935)

Steward, Jill, '"Gruss aus Wien": urban tourism in Austria-Hungary before the First World War', in Malcolm Gee, Tim Kirk, Jill Steward (eds.), *The City in Central Europe since 1800* (Aldershot and Vermont, 1999)

Stirk, Peter (ed.), *Mitteleuropa: History and prospects: 1815–1990* (Edinburgh, 1994)

Stoob, Heinz, 'Zur Städtebildung in Mitteleuropa im industriellen Zeitalter', in Helmut Jäger (ed.), *Probleme des Städtewesens im Industriellen Zeitalter* (Cologne and Vienna, 1978)

Strohmeyer, Klaus (ed.), *Berlin in Bewegung: Literarischer Spaziergang,* 2 vols. (Reinbek, 1987)

Südekum, Albert, *Grossstädtisches Wohnungselend* (Grossstadt-Dokumente, Vol. XLV, Berlin, 1905)

Sultano, Gloria, *Wie geistiges Kokain: Mode untern Hakenkreuz* (Vienna, 1995)

Sulzenbacher, Hannes, '"Homosexual" men in Vienna, 1938', in Tim Kirk, Anthony McElligott (eds.), *Opposing Fascism: Community, authority and resistance in Europe* (Cambridge, 1999)

Sutcliffe, Anthony (ed.), *The Rise of Modern Urban Planning 1800–1914* (London, 1980)

—— (ed.), *Towards the Planned City: Germany, Britain, the United States and France, 1780–1914* (Oxford, 1981)

——, 'Urban planning in Europe and North America before 1914: International aspects of a prophetic movement', in Hans-Jürgen Teuteberg (ed.), *Urbanisierung im 19. und 20. Jahrhundert* (Cologne, 1983)

——, 'The metropolis in the cinema', in *idem* (ed.), *Metropolis 1890–1940* (London, 1984)

Sywottek, Arnold, 'Zwei Wege in die Konsumgesellschaft', in *idem,* Axel Schildt (eds.), *Modernisierung im Wiederaufbau: die westdeutsche Gesellschaft der 50er Jahre* (Bonn, 1998)

Tafuri, Manfredo, *The Sphere and the Labyrinth* (Cambridge, Mass., 1990)

Tarn, J. N., 'Housing reform and the emergence of town planning in Britain before 1914', in Anthony Sutcliffe (ed.), *The Rise of Modern Urban Planning 1800–1914* (London, 1980)

Tatar, Maria, *Lustmord Sexual Murder in Weimar Germany* (Princeton, N.J., 1995)

Tenfelde, Klaus, 'Großstadtjugend in Deutschland vor 1914: Eine historisch-demographische Annäherung', in *Vierteljahresschrift für Sozial- und Wirtschaftgeschichte*, Vol. 69, Nr 2 (1982), 182–218

Terhalle, Fritz, *Finanzwirtschaft* (Jena, 1930)

Teuteberg, Hans-Jürgen, Clemens Wischermann, *Wohnalltag in Deutschland 1850–1914: Bilder, Daten, Dokumente* (Münster, 1985)

Theilhaber, Felix A., *Das sterile Berlin* (Berlin, 1913)

Theweleit, Klaus, *Male Fantasies*, 2 vols (Cambridge/Oxford, 1987, 1989): Vol. 1: 'Women, floods, bodies, history'

Thies, Jochen, 'Nationalsozialistische Städteplanung: "Die Führerstädte"', in *Die alte Stadt: Zeitschrift für Stadtgeschichte, Stadtsoziologie und Denkmalpflege*, 5 (1978), 23–38

Thilen, Johannes, *Denkschrift über zunahme des Alkoholismus und Ausbau der Spezialfürsorge für Alkoholkranke und Gefährdete* (n.p. 1928)

Tietze, Christoph, 'German population movements and some comparisons with those of other countries', in *The Eugenics Review*, Vol. XXI (April 1929–Jan. 1930), 265–7

Timm, Christoph, *Gustav Oelsner und das Neue Altona: Kommunale Architektur und Stadtplanuung in der Weimarer Republik* (Hamburg, 1984)

——., 'Der Preussische Generalsiedlungsplan für Gross-Hamburg von 1923', in *Zeitschrift des Vereins für Hamburgische Geschichte*, 71 (1985), 75–125

Toepfer, Karl, 'Nudity and modernity in German dance 1910–1930', in *Journal of the History of Sexuality*, Vol. 3 No. 1 (1992), 58–108

——, *Empire of Ecstasy: Nudity and movement in German body culture, 1910–1935* (Berkeley, 1997)

Tower, Beeke Sell, '"Ultramodern and ultraprimitive": Shifting meanings in the imagery of Americanism in the art of Weimar Germany', in Thomas W. Kniesche, Stephen Brockman (eds.), *Dancing on the Volcano: Essays on the culture of the Weimar Republic* (Columbia, S.C., 1994)

Triebel, Arnim, 'Soziale Unterschiede beim Konsum im Ersten Weltkrieg und danach – Bruch mit der Vergangenheit?', in Toni Pierenkemper (ed.), *Haushalt und Verbrauch in Historischer Perspektive: zum Wandel des privaten Verbrauchs in Deutschland im 19. und 20.Jahrhundert* (St Katharinen, 1987)

——, 'Variations in patterns of consumption in Germany in the period of the First World War' in Richard Wall, Jay Winter (eds.), *The Upheaval of War: Family, work and welfare in Europe, 1914–1918* (Cambridge, New York, New Rochelle, Melbourne and Sydney, 1988)

——, 'Vergleichbar machen, ohne Gleichzumachen. Äquivalenzskalen in der historischen Konsumforschung', in Toni Pierenkemper (ed.), *Zur Oekonomik des privaten Haushalts: Haushaltsrechnungen als Quelle historischer Wirtschafts- und Sozialforschung* (Frankfurt am Main, 1991)

Tucholsky, Kurt, *Deutschland, Deutschland über alles* (1929), trans. Anne
    Halley with an afterword and notes by Harry Zahn (Amherst, Mass., 1972)
Turner, Bryan S. (ed.), *Theories of Modernity and Postmodernity* (London,
    Newbury Park and New Delhi, 1990)
Urrichio, William Charles, 'Ruttmann's "Berlin" and the city film to 1930',
    (Ph.D. thesis, New York University, New York, 1982)
Usborne, Cornelia, 'The Christian churches and the regulation of sexuality
    in Weimar Germany', in Jim Obelkevich, Lyndal Roper, Raphael Samuel
    (eds.), *Disciplines of Faith: Studies in religion, politics and patriarchy*
    (London, 1987)
——, *The Politics of the Body in Weimar Germany* (London, 1992)
——, 'The New Woman and generational conflict: perceptions of young
    women's sexual mores in the Weimar Republic', in Mark Roseman (ed.),
    *Generations in Conflict: Youth revolt and generation formation in Germany
    1770–1968* (Cambridge, 1995)
Vogel, Katharina, 'Zum Selbstverständnis lesbischer Frauen in der Weimarer
    Republik. Eine Analyse der Zeitschrift "Die Freundin" 1924–1933', in
    Michael Bolle (ed.), *Eldorado: homosexuelle Frauen und Männer in Berlin
    1850–1950: Geschichte, Alltag und Kultur* (Berlin, 1984)
Vogt, Jochen, 'The Weimar Republic as the "Heritage of our Time"', in
    Thomas W. Kniesche, Stephen Brockman (eds.), *Dancing on the Volcano:
    Essays on the culture of the Weimar Republic* (Columbia, S.C., 1994)
de Vries, Jan, *European Urbanization 1500–1800* (London, 1984)
Walkowitz, Judith, *City of Dreadful Delight: narratives of sexual danger in
    late-Victorian London* (London, 1992)
Waller, Philip J., *Town, City and Nation: England 1850–1914* (Oxford, 1983)
Walser, Karin, 'Prostitutionsverdact und Geschlechterforschung: Das Beispiel
    der Dienstmädchen um 1900', *Geschichte und Gesellschaft*, Vol. 11 (1985),
    99–111
——, 'Frauenarbeit und Weiblichkeitsbilder – Phantasien über Dienstmädchen
    von 1900', in Ruth-Ellen B. Joeres, Annette Kuhn (eds.), *Frauen in der
    Geschichte VI: Frauenbilder und Frauenwirklichkeiten. Interdisziplinä*re
    Studien zur Frauengeschichte in Deutschland im 18. und 19. Jahrhundert
    (Düsseldorf, 1985)
Walther, Andreas, *Neuere Wege zur Grossstadtsanierung* (Stuttgart, 1936)
Walvin, James, *Beside the Sea* (London, 1978)
Warner, Jr., Sam Bass, 'The management of multiple urban images', in Derek
    Fraser, Anthony Sutcliffe (eds.), *The Pursuit of Urban History* (London,
    1983)
Weber, L.W., 'Grossstadt und Nerven', in *Deutsche Rundschau*, vol. CLXXVII
    (Dec. 1918), 391–407
Weber, Matthias M., *Ernst Rudin: Eine kritische Biographie* (Berlin, 1993)
Weindling, Paul, *Health, Race and German Politics between National
    Unification and Nazism 1870–1945* (Cambridge, 1989)

——, 'Degeneration und öffentliches Gesundheitswesen 1900–1930', in Jürgen Reulecke, Adelheid Gräfin zu Castell Rüdenhausen (eds.), *Stadt und Gesundheit. Zum Wandel von "Volksgesundheit" und kommunaler Gesundheitspolitik im 19. und frühen 20. Jahrhundert* (Stuttgart, 1991)

Weingart, Peter, Jürgen Kroll, Kurt Bayertz, *Rasse, Blut und Gene: Geschichte der Eugenik und Rassenhygiene in Deutschland* (Frankfurt am Main, 1988)

Weininger, Otto, *Geschlecht und Charakter: eine prinzipieller Untersuchung* (orig. edn, 1903, reprint Munich, 1980)

Weinstein, Deena, Michael A. Weinstein, 'Simmel and the theory of postmodern society', in Bryan S. Turner (ed.), *Theories of Modernity and Postmodernity* (London, Newbury Park and New Delhi, 1990)

Weisstein, G., 'Sind die Städte wirklich Menschenverzehrer?', in *Deutsche Städte-Zeitung* (1905), 153–4

Welch, David, 'Cinema and society in imperial Germany 1905–1918', in *German History,* Vol. 8 No. 1 (1990), 28–45

Wenz-Gahler, Ingrid, 'Die Küche', and 'Wohnen mit Kindern', in Michael Andritzky, Gert Selle (eds.), *Lernbereich Wohnen* (Reinbek, 1987)

Werner, Paul, *Die Skandal Chronik des Deutschen Films, Band 1: von 1900 bis 1945* (Frankfurt am Main, 1990)

Werth, Hans, 'Öffentliches Kinematographen-Recht' (Diss. Jur. Fakultät, Friedrich-Alexanders-Universität zu Erlangen, 1910)

Westphal, Uwe, *Werbung im Dritten Reich* (Berlin, 1989)

——, *Die Berliner Konfektion und Mode 1836–1939: Zerstörung einer Tradition* (2nd edn Berlin, 1992)

White, Iain Boyd, 'Berlin 1870–1945: An introduction framed by architecture', in Irit Rogoff (ed.), *The Divided Heritage: Themes and problems in German modernism* (Cambridge and New York, 1991)

White, Jerry, 'Campbell Bunk: a lumpen community in London between the wars' in *History Workshop Journal,* Vol. 8 (Autumn 1979), 1–49

White, John J., 'Sexual mecca, Nazi metropolis, city of doom: The pattern of English, Irish and American reactions to the Berlin of the inter-war years', in Derek Glass, Dietmar Rösler, John J. White (eds.), *Berlin. Literary Images of a City: Eine Großstadt im Spiegel der Literatur* (Berlin, 1989)

Wildt, Michael, 'Plurality of taste: Food and consumption in West Germany during the 1950s', in *History Workshop Journal,* Vol. 39 (Spring 1995), 23–41

Will, Wilfried van der, 'The body and the body politic as symptom and metaphor in the transition of German culture to National Socialism', in Brandon Taylor, Wilfried van der Will (eds.), *The Nazification of Art: Art, design, music, architecture and film in the Third Reich* (Winchester, 1990)

Willett, John, *The New Sobriety: Art and politics in the Weimar period 1917–1933* (London, 1978)

Williams, John Alexander, '"The chords of the German soul are tuned to nature": The movement to preserve the natural Heimat from the Kaiserreich to the Third Reich', in *Central European History,* Vol. 29 No. 3 (1994), 339–86

Williams, Rosalind, *Dream Worlds: Mass consumption in late 19th century France* (Berkeley, 1983)

Wilson, Elizabeth, *The Sphinx in the City: Urban life, the control of disorder, and women* (Berkeley, Los Angeles and Oxford, 1991)

Winter, James, *London's Teeming Streets, 1830–1914* (London, 1993)

Wischermann, Clemens, *Wohnen in Hamburg vor dem Ersten Weltkrieg* (Münster, 1983)

——, *Die Zeit der Metropolen: Urbanisierung und Großstadtentwicklung* (Frankfurt am Main, 1996)

Wohl, Anthony S., *The Eternal Slum: Housing and social policy in Victorian London* (London, 1977)

Wolff, Helmut, 'Sport und Leibesübungen', in Hugo Lindemann, Otto Most, Oskar Mulert (eds.), *Kommunales Jahrbuch* (Jena, 1931), 235–8

Wuttke, Robert (ed.), *Die Deutsche Städte: geschildert nach den Ergebnissen der ersten deutschen Stadtausstellung zu Dresden 1903* (Leipzig, 1904)

Zahlen, Gerwin, 'Metropole als Metapher', in Gotthard Fuchs, Bernhard Moltmann, Walter Prigge (eds.), *Mythos Metropole* (Frankfurt am Main, 1995)

Zehr, Howard, *Crime and the Development of Modern Society: Patterns of criminality in nineteenth century Germany and France* (London, 1976)

Zeller, Susanne, *Volksmutter – mit staatlicher Anerkennung: Frauen im Wohlfahrtswesen der Zwanziger Jahre* (Düsseldorf, 1987)

Zimmermann, Susanne, 'Making a living from disgrace: the politics of prostitution, female poverty and urban gender codes in Budapest and Vienna, 1869–1920', in Malcom Gee, Tim Kirk, Jill Steward (eds.), *The City in Central Europe since 1800* (Aldershot and Vermont, 1999)

Index

CPSIA information can be obtained
at www.ICGtesting.com
Printed in the USA
LVOW13s2119291217
561207LV00002B/54/P

9 780415 121156